C000022784

Dare To Dream Bigger

The 'Inside Work' Handbook For Entrepreneurs And Passionate World-Changers

Clare Josa

Dedication

To Mum

You were more of a role model than you ever realised; without your courage, I might never have dared to dream bigger.
Thank you.

© Clare Josa, 2016

Published by Beyond Alchemy Publishing, UK. For bulk orders, contact hello@beyond-alchemy.com

Book's Website: www.DareToDreamBiggerHandbook.com

A CIP catalogue record for this title is available from the British Library.

Hardback ISBN 978-1-908854-79-7 (UK)

Paperback ISBN 978-1-908854-82-7 (Rest Of World)

eBook ISBN 978-1-908854-80-3

Audio Book ISBN 978-1-908854-83-4 (MP3s)

The right of Clare Josa to be identified as the Author of the Work has been asserted by her, in accordance with the Copyright, Designs and Patent Act 1988.

All rights reserved. No part of this publication may be reproduced, stored in a retrieval system, or transmitted, in any form or by any means, without the prior written permission of the Author.

Cover design by Jo Smith Creatives and Richard Playall

Printed and bound in Great Britain by Clays Ltd, St Ives plc

Limit of liability:

The advice in this book is intended for educational purposes only, and is only for personal use. It is not intended to substitute for professional advice, based on your personal circumstances. Just as the Author and Publisher would not claim the credit for the successes you create, as a result of reading this book, so they do not accept responsibility or liability for the effects of your actions. If you are in doubt as to the suitability of the concepts in this book for your individual situation, always consult your chosen professional, first.

Every effort has been made to ensure all information in this book is correct. Any unintended errors will be corrected in the next edition.

Know What You Want

Clear Out The Blocks

Take Inspired Action

Pulling It All Together

BEFORE WE START

My Promise To You

---

*You have all the answers you need, inside of you, and
I want to show you how to find them.*

A re you hungry to make a bigger difference in the world, feeling that you have an important message to share, but you secretly suspect you're getting in your own way?

You can feel your heart calling you to expand and grow, but your head is telling you all the reasons why you can't or you're not good enough?

And maybe you've been trying hard, doing all the 'right' things, following the expert advice, but just not getting the results? Or maybe you just feel too busy to take the step back and lay the foundations?

It's so easy to subconsciously self-sabotage our dreams; to convince ourselves we feel safe and snug in our comfort zones. But when that quiet, persistent voice inside is asking you to step up and Dare To Dream Bigger, that's when we need to press pause on the 'outside world' actions and do some 'inner work', to clear out the hidden blocks, fears, excuses, limiting beliefs and out-of-date habits that would otherwise derail us, no matter how hard we try.

The world needs you and your unique message now, more than ever, so it's time to Dare To Dream Bigger. You've been given your dream for a reason. The world needs your unique voice, your unique talents, your unique expertise, now, more than ever. And the only thing that will ever block you is you. But that's brilliant news, because it means you can do something about it. And I want to show you how.

This is your Handbook for that 'inside work' and it's going to guide you, step by step, through how to lay the foundations for Daring To Dream Bigger, stepping up to the next level. You'll get total clarity about what you want to create, you'll learn how to clear out the 'inside blocks' that would otherwise get in your way, and how to spot and then take the inspired actions that create breakthroughs, rather than overwhelm.

I'm going to share with you the exact same tools and techniques I have spent 14 years refining, so you can shortcut your learning curve, gain life-changing insights and step up to make the next level of difference you're here to make, even if that currently feels hard or scary.

The practical, inspirational strategies in this Handbook are broken down into bite-sized chunks that you can play with and easily apply, no matter how hectic life is. This book is designed to be a complete resource, on its own, but I want you to feel fully supported. So for any areas that resonate with you, where you want to dive in more deeply, there are 'deep-dive' audios and videos waiting for you, online, over at the Readers' Club, as well as Google-proof discussions in our private forum, so you can get answers to your questions, with accountability and motivation from others sharing this journey.

I'm on a mission to change the way we change the world, because it's not so much about what you do, as who you allow yourself to *become*. I believe that is what Gandhi meant when he said, "Be the change."

And I promise that the Dare To Dream Bigger Handbook will make a profound difference for you, if you let it. I've made it as easy as possible for you. In return, I ask for three things from you:

1. Curiosity
Because every great journey and exploration begins with curiosity.

2. Courage
Because courage will fuel you on this transformational process – and you only need a little – it doesn't have to be scary. Without it, these secrets and strategies risk getting stuck as 'nice ideas' on a dusty bookshelf. Courage will inspire you and give you strength to take action to release those hidden blocks - and to expand to become who you really are. And that's where the fun starts!

3. Commitment
Because I can't do this for you. But I will make it as simple as possible for you, and even kick your butt at key points. A little commitment will reap lifelong dividends for you, through this work.

Are you in?

How To Join The Readers' Club

www.DareToDreamBiggerHandbook.com/club

Go to www.DareToDreamBiggerHandbook.com/club and choose your login details to register. It will take you straight to the Readers' Club home page. It's brimming with bonus videos, audios, workbooks (with each exercise in, so you can jot your answers down there, instead of in a notebook, if that's what you prefer), expert interviews, deep-dive techniques and even a Google-proof forum, so you can share the journey with like-minded World-Changers.

I haven't included the links to individual websites in this Handbook, because the internet changes too quickly. So, instead, everything is kept up-to-date in your members' area. That way you'll avoid the frustration of future '404 page not found' errors.

How To Get The Most From This Handbook

Don't try to swallow the elephant in one go. Allow the process to take its time. You'll instinctively know when it's time to pause, and when it's time to plough on through. Work through the Handbook in order, the first time you do it, and be aware that any sections you might find yourself resisting often hold the biggest rewards. Don't beat yourself up – enjoy the journey – and make one change at a time. You'll get best results from this Handbook if you do four things:

1. Actually use the stuff I'm sharing with you.

Although some of the sections are designed to create life- and attitude-shifts, as you're reading them, many of them require you to play with concepts or techniques and try them on for size. If you don't do that, you'll be massively missing out. The exercises are clearly marked and most have downloadable worksheets and audios, over at the Readers' Club. But I know what it's like to be busy, so it's all designed to be broken down into bite-sized chunks that you can practise in less time than it takes a kettle to boil - or your Americano to filter.

Don't let these concepts stagnate as 'nice ideas' in your head. They're here to take you to the next level - but that requires a teeny bit of effort on your part. The book, on its own, can't do that for you.

2. Little and often, rather than 'blitz and burn'.

We're going to be reprogramming your neural pathways, releasing decades of out-of-date habits, and shifting hidden 'stuckness', masquerading as legitimate excuses.

Whilst full-steam-ahead can be great fun, there will be times when you need to pause and integrate. I could guess where these points might be, from my experience of 14 years of mentoring, but I'm not living in your head, so you'll need to be the judge of this. If you need some time out, take it, but make a commitment in your diary for when you'll come back to the next step.

I strongly suggest that you treat yourself to proper chunks of time to work through the seven key Steps of this book. Turn off your email, stop multi-tasking, find somewhere quiet, and flick your phone onto silent. These small time investments will pay back richly, over the coming years. And if you find yourself struggling to make time for this, get it in your schedule, perhaps block out a few half-days. Treat this next step towards your future as a non-negotiable appointment.

3. Go And Join The Readers' Club - Now!

www.DareToDreamBiggerHandbook.com/club

This Handbook is intended to be a full and complete resource for you, but there may be times when you want to explore concepts from another angle or deep-dive on certain topics, and that's where the Readers' Club comes in. You will find bonus videos, downloadable workbooks for each step's exercises, audios and even guided meditations, as well the chance to get answers to your questions and support others in the private forum. There are deep-dive resources, for when you need a bit more encouragement. The Readers' Club is great for accountability and idea-bouncing. The Readers' Club bonuses are my gift to you and your future.

4. Scribble Away!

I'm going to suggest something that would have horrified my dear friend Toby, who once nearly passed out when he saw me with a book and a pencil and the intention for the two to meet. I want you to scribble notes and ideas all over this book. Use highlighter pens. Use sticky labels - whatever it takes to make this a living, breathing, life-changing, world-changing course for you. I'm hoping this Handbook will be something you'll come back to, over and over, whenever you're ready to step up to the next level, because the insights and techniques I'm sharing with you are designed to work more deeply, each time you read and apply them.

Making notes shifts you from the autopilot 'what-was-in-those-last-three-pages?' part of your brain to the learning part that processes, integrates and creates change, even while you're reading.

And to help you get over any secret fears you might have about daring to write in a book (it was a near-death-sentence-punishable offence at my school), I'm going to be running a competition on a regular basis, via my Facebook page. Post a photo of yourself with this Handbook - with notes and highlights (relevant and polite, please!) and sticky notes or whatever works for you - on my Facebook page, and I'll randomly select winners to get one of my online courses, as my gift. You can find me at www.Facebook.com/cjosa

What to expect

I'm not usually big on 'expectations', because they tend to squeeze our experience of life into an uncomfortably small box, even before you get there. But I want to share with you some of what might happen, as we go through the Dare To Dream Bigger Handbook process together.

- There will be times when your heart will sing 'Hallelujah!' (or your favourite equivalent) as you resonate with what I'm saying. And there may be times when you'll want to lob rotten tomatoes at me. Both are perfect and part of the journey. All I ask is that you genuinely try things on for size, before you write off any of the ideas.
- There will be concepts or techniques that you may find yourself resisting - or even rejecting. I know from personal experience how strong this reaction can be. But I also know that this is where your hidden gems lie. Get to the other side of the resistance and you'll have created breakthroughs you'll love.
- Be gentle on yourself. You're going to be working at many levels, during our time together here. Some of the changes you're going to make are going to be deep-acting and will take time and space to unfold. Allow yourself that time. Allow this process to flow, rather than pushing it. And I suggest you do all of this with a smile on your face – it will make it more fun.

- I strongly encourage you to keep notes - or a journal - for this next stage of your journey. Sometimes it's only when we look back that we truly notice how far we have come. And that feels so good. I don't want you to miss out on that.

If at any stage you have any questions, or you want to share successes and lightbulb moments, please pop by the Readers' Club. There's bound to be a discussion thread that will help and, if there isn't one, you can start it.

Do You Have To Be Running A Business, To Benefit From This?

No! The strategies, tools and techniques for the 'inside work' in this Handbook apply equally well to high-performing entrepreneurs, as to part time yoga teachers, departmental managers, dentists, acupuncturists, admin assistants, CEOs, freelancers, coaches, creatives, widget designers, nutritionists, stay-at-home parents, landscape gardeners and anyone else who wants to make a positive difference in the world.

At points during the book I talk about how to apply the insights to a business, but if that's not you, please just tweak the concepts so that they work for you, in your unique situation. Whatever it is we want to create in life, we all suffer from the same fears, blocks, and hidden excuses. And we all get excited by connecting with our purpose and passion. That's what this Handbook is here to help with.

A Warning To The Grammar Police

I'm going to be doing something in this book that might annoy you, if you're anything like me and wish you could punctuate hashtags. I'm using capital letters for our key concepts, to turn them into 'proper nouns', because I believe they are so important that they deserve that status.

You might have spotted a few of them already. Concepts like Big Why, Big Vision and Big Message and Dream Audience are going to keep this trend going, to remind you how vital they are to you Daring To Dream Bigger. Apologies in advance for any adverse reactions that this gratuitous use of additional capital letters causes.

And, in case you hadn't noticed, I'm a Brit, so we'll be using British English spelling. I hope that's ok with you!

And now it's time for an overview of the journey we're going to take together.

What Are We Going To Be Covering?

I'm borderline-allergic to 'processes' and 'sausage machines' and 'blueprints' and 'cookie-cutter swipe files'.

Why? Because, like your favourite shirt, there is no one-size-fits all solution for making a bigger difference in the world. What works for someone else did just that - it worked for someone else. It *may* help you, or it may not. There is no one-size-fits-all answer for changing your life – or the world. No one can tell you what will work for you. We are all wonderfully unique.

That's why I resisted talking to you about the '7 Cs of business breakthroughs'. It risks sounding just like one of those cookie-cutter formulae, doesn't it? But here's how what we're going to be doing together is different:

I'm not giving you templates and cheat sheets and instructions. Instead, I'm sharing with you a framework of strategies and questions you can ask yourself, so you can easily figure out what will work for you, with your individual experience, fears, hopes, dreams and mission.

The framework covers seven critical factors for making a bigger difference in the world. They come from studying, analysing, reverse-engineering ('modelling', in the NLP[1] world) and refining what works - and what doesn't - and why. They all begin with a C, so they quickly got nicknamed 'The 7 Cs'.

When you work through the 7 Cs in order, you're pretty much guaranteed your projects will succeed, because you will have total clarity about what you want to create, you'll have cleared out your hidden blocks and secret self-sabotage patterns, and you'll know how to take inspired action, rather than drowning in overwhelm.

The 7 Cs are stages on the journey, and instead of bossing you around and telling you what to do or think at each step, I'm going to be empowering you to find the answers that are already waiting for you, inside you. I'm going to be (hopefully!) inspiring you to find your own solutions, in ways that fit beautifully for your Big Vision, your Dream Audience, the difference you are here to make. That way, because it has come from inside *you*, and not from me, you know it will be the perfect fit

---

[1] NLP is Neurolinguistic Programming – a branch of practical, modern psychology that deals with how our thoughts create our experience of life, and how you can change your thoughts, to change your life. It's like the user manual for your brain.

for you.

The middle stage of the 7 Cs is all about finding those hidden blocks that might get in the way of your dreams; that's the bit that most people aren't talking about. And instead of trying to squeeze those silent saboteurs into the dusty corner cupboard in your brain, we're going to get them out and celebrate them - and turn them into your biggest assets. The techniques we'll be covering could become lifelong friends and the shifts they create will inspire your journey for decades to come.

Your Whistle-Stop Tour Of The 7 Cs:

We're actually going to add in an extra C (apologies to my inner mathematician, who wants to point out that this takes us up to 8), to help you get the most from the Dare To Dream Bigger Handbook. If we were on a Mastermind retreat together, you'd do 'Step 0' before even arriving on the retreat. So I'm including it here, because it's the most important place to start.

Step 0 – Clear Out And Declutter

When you want to create change, you need to create space for it. You don't want to amplify chaos. So Step Zero is looking for the quick wins to give you more time, headspace and physical-world calmness, to make the rest of the 7 Cs easier and more fun.

Know What You Want

Step 1 - Clarity

So many of us miss this out. We get inspired and excited by an interesting idea and dive straight into taking action, without first pausing to get totally clear about what we want, why, who we want to serve and how we're going to fix their burning problems, in a way that no one else does.

The absence of clarity is the biggest cause of procrastination, inexplicable out-of-character addictions to cutesy cat videos on social media, overwhelm and half-baked results.

I know that 'doing your homework' before you get active isn't trendy, but I promise you, once you have experienced the deliciousness of total clarity and alignment with your Big Vision, your Big Why and your Big Message, you'll change your mind on that one.

Clearing Out Your Blocks

Step 2 - Confidence

This is the biggie. The difference between hugely successful people and those who wish they had been successful is a little bit of luck and planning, but a lot of confidence. In this section we'll be dealing with everything from limiting beliefs, to hidden fears and excuses, to subconscious self-sabotaging behaviour, to self-esteem and even who you really are. You'll discover how to turn these round, to fast-track your way towards making a bigger difference in the world.

Step 3 - Credibility

I have lost count of how many brilliant world-changers I have met, hiding in the proverbial corner, desperately wanting to get their message heard, but also secretly scared that anyone might notice they're there.

So we're going to deep-dive on how to get comfortable with being visible (wave goodbye to Imposter Syndrome and feeling like a fraud), and you're going to create a practical action plan to become the go-to expert in your field.

Take Inspired Action

Step 4 - Connection

Once you've got clarity about what you're doing, for whom, and why, and you're starting to convince yourself and the world that you're a credible expert, then it's time to get connected.

In this section we'll get connected with yourself - your inner wisdom; your Dream Audience, so you can magnetise your Tribe and your Dream Team, who are the vital support team and the partners who help you get your Big Message out there.

Step 5 - Creativity

This is where we unleash those inspired actions. We're going to explore how to easily connect with your creativity, no matter what is going on. You'll also learn insider secrets from my former career as Head Of Market Research for a major international brand, so you can use that creative genius (yes, you have it), to create products and services that your dream customers will rave about. In fact, they'll feel like you've been mind-reading their biggest problems and they'll love you for it.

Step 6 - Commitment

Without this, those brilliant ideas will never make it to reality. Commitment to complete projects is vital. In this section you'll discover how to build the habit, so that commitment becomes easier, even if you're secretly suffering from 'Shiny Object Syndrome'.

Step 7 - Celebration

We so often miss this out. But if you're having a tough day, cultivating the habit of celebrating your successes, no matter how small, will keep you going. We rarely take time out to notice the progress we're making, yet weaving a few minutes of gratitude into your daily life can be transformational, turning your Inner Critic into your Biggest Cheerleader.

You can use the 7 Cs wherever you are in your journey, whether you're just starting out, whether you're moving from, say, hobby to business, or business to a legacy and a revolution.

Why Other People's Stuff Isn't Working For You

I have spent a long way into 5-figures on business programmes over the past 15 years. I'm sure it makes my accountant cry, especially given that most of them didn't really work.

What *did* work was the short-term boost on inspiration and energy that comes from hanging out with others who are also excited about growing their businesses. But in most cases, the 'how to' and the 'strategies' didn't get me anything like the results that were promised. Is that because I'm a rubbish business woman? No. Or at least I hope not. And I have seen this in nearly every programme I have paid for - hardly anyone else gets the promised breakthroughs, either. The 'acceptable response' is to take full responsibility for it being *your* fault, not the expert's 'sausage machine'. After all, it worked for the guru - and the two or three high-octane success stories.

It's not that these biz gurus are rip-off fraudsters. I believe that vast majority of them genuinely care and believe that their programmes work – for them and those they have worked with, personally. But having watched this happen to people over and over, for years, I have seen three main reasons why other people's stuff isn't working for you:

1. They will have cleared out their hidden blocks, to achieve what they have...

... but few of them mention that in their 'sausage machine' processes, usually because they didn't realise how important that step was, or they had support from their Mentor on that bit. In fact, their success is most likely down to this one step, rather than the process they now use.

2. Being a Master and expert doesn't automatically make you a great teacher.

There's a real skill in being able to have enough self-awareness to reverse-engineer the key points of what you did and then translate them into actions that someone earlier on in the journey will understand. I know, because it's a major part of becoming an NLP Trainer, and it's not an easy skill to learn.

3. Their 'sausage machine' works for their business model and their audience.

It might not work for yours. For example, some of the Big Names are currently recommending 'squeezing' all new customers through 'high-contact' sales funnels (read that as at least daily emails), and 'ditching' them if they don't buy. Your target audience might freak out if you do that - and it could close down your business.

This biggest of these is the first: clearing out your blocks. There's nothing wrong with the fact that the how-to for the block-clearing isn't part of the experts' public processes – it's not their Inner Genius (see Step 1). Their intention is to teach you their business growth strategy, not to become your Analyst. But it's easy to underplay the importance of the block-clearing work, to make space for success. Without first clearing out your hidden self-sabotage patterns, their processes are less likely to work for you.

So if you have ever felt like a failure or judged yourself for trying out other people's strategies and finding they didn't work for you, please let it go. There's nothing wrong with you. There's nothing to fix. It's just that vital pieces of that puzzle were missing. And in this Handbook, we're going to find them, together. We're going to do the 'inside work' that makes the vital difference.

What On Earth Is 'Inside Work'?

I was at an event recently when someone asked me why I talk about doing the 'inside work' or 'inner work', in order to create change in the 'outside world'.

I explained how it's about 'getting out of your own way', so you don't self-sabotage, so you don't turn down opportunities that you later regret, and so you don't play small, when your heart is calling you to play big.

But even then, they still thought I was a bit crazy, and couldn't see the need. So we ran the event and, sure enough, none of the business owners was blocked on the 'what' - the strategy - the things to do to take their businesses to the next level. That was easy enough to figure out, or to find on Google. Each of them was stuck on inside blocks, which included:

- Causing them not to take the actions they knew they needed to do
- Making them say no to easily-available ways to get their word to reach a wider audience
- Stopping them from really standing in their customers' shoes, and seeing what their clients wanted, instead of what they thought their clients should want
- Creating sales pages that somehow didn't 'feel' right, but no amount of tinkering was improving
- Over-giving, so that they were exhausted and struggling to fill the fridge; they aren't earning enough money
- Only contacting their customers when they were desperate to raise funds, unintentionally turning their mailing list into a 'pitch & burn' spam-fest
- Not building relationships from a place of expertise and trust, instead trying to be too much of a 'friend', and being surprised when their long-nurtured customers went elsewhere to buy
- Hiding their light and inner genius behind the veneer of things they were good at, which felt safe, rather than what they are truly great at
- Not wanting to send out messages to their email subscribers because they were secretly scared people would feel 'bothered' by them, rather than seeing that these people had registered because they were hungry for the help this person could offer
- Playing safe with entry-level products and services, because they were scared that no one would want to buy their premium products
- Jumping from one exciting, shiny new idea to another, never

allowing any of them to take root and grow

- Confusing their customers with mixed messaging for different target audiences with widely differing needs and interests
- Dumbing down the transformation they could create, because they were scared to let people down and secretly believed they weren't good enough
- Not sharing the case studies and testimonials that they had, in abundance, which would have easily convinced people to buy from them
- Having lots of amazing ideas, but not turning them into reality - I call these mañana-day dreams
- Having drafts for maybe 15 brilliant projects lying around, but secretly knowing they'll never happen
- Finding they were too busy with the day-to-day stuff, to be able to take time out to focus on their Big Vision
- Getting to the end of the year and realising how few of their business goals were implemented
- Telling themselves that's ok, because they were too busy, or too tired, or whatever else, but deep down not feeling happy about it

These are just SOME of the warning signs that your inner blocks, out-of-date habits, limiting beliefs, fears and excuses are getting in the way. But these symptoms are just at the tip of the iceberg, easily visible, above the water, when you know how to spot them. What lie below the surface are the deeper blocks, which have a much bigger impact on your behaviour and success.

When you move from behavioural blocks and surface beliefs, then you enter the realm of 'who am I'. Blocks and misalignment at this deeper level will affect every thought, feeling and choice you make on the 'outside'. Fortunately, it's also easy to spot this level of blocks. Here are warning signs you'll notice in your inner dialogue - or conversations with others:

- Who am I, to be doing this?
- I'm not good enough
- I'm not ready
- I don't know what my purpose is
- I don't know where to start to step up to the next level
- I can't decide which idea to pick

- I feel like I'm an imposter; someone is going to catch me out if I let myself be seen
- Everyone else is better than me
- Stuff works for others, but not for me
- I'm too busy to take time for 'navel-gazing'
- I'm scared I'll fail and look like an idiot, so I'd rather not try

The more blocks you clear out on the inside, the fewer blocks you will encounter on the outside, and life will start to flow, instead of being hard work.

The world has moved wonderfully far since I started doing this work, in 2002. Back then, if I talked to people about clearing out their limiting beliefs, most of them would give me the 'crazy-lady' stare and glaze over – or run. Nowadays, even mainstream neuroscientists accept that we have 'inside blocks' act as filters in your brain, as hard-wired habits in your neural pathways and your beliefs act as filters in your brain (more on that in Step 2); we see what we expect to see. And those brain-filters influence which thoughts we feed, which habits we develop, which emotions we feel and even our physical health.

Your success in life is less about what you do, and more about who you allow yourself to become.

And the key part of that 'becoming' is releasing the out-of-date, hidden blocks. This is why action without block-removing or connecting with your Big Vision so rarely leads to success. Changing the world is an 'inside job'. And the Dare To Dream Bigger Handbook makes that 'inside change' as easy – and fun – as possible for you. All you need is to be open-minded and to *use* the stuff I'm sharing with you in here – and to make the most of the bonuses in the Readers' Club.

Why Bother With All This 'Navel-Gazing'?

I surveyed a group of 100 successful entrepreneurs and asked them what the one most critical quality was in their success; and here is what they told me:

action alignment allowing
authenticity balance
commitment confidence
connection consistency
courage curiosity dedication desire determination
discipline faith
empowering
fearlessness flow focus fulfilment guidance
hard work heart honesty
inspiration intuition kindness
mindset passion patience
perseverance play
self-belief

We're going to be covering the 'how-to' for all of these qualities, in this Handbook. Yes, you can scrub the 'navel-gazing' and just dive in and take action, but then you'll be missing out on the improving the vast majority of qualities that these entrepreneurs valued the most – and credited as being responsible for their success.

Because changing the world is an 'inside job'.

Your hidden blocks risk getting in the way, at the most unhelpful moments. If you don't deal with them, you'll keep getting the results you've been having so far, which I'm guessing are no longer enough for you, or you wouldn't be reading this Handbook.

Alternatively, you can put in a little time and effort (it doesn't take much) to get the next level of clarity, to reconnect with your energy and passion, clearing out the subconscious blocks, fears, excuses and limiting beliefs, so you can take the inspired actions that create breakthroughs. I hope you agree that all of that is worth a teeny bit of 'navel-gazing'?

The 3-Lettered Word That Changes The World

If you've been hanging around with me a while, you'll know I regularly bang on about your limiting beliefs, hidden blocks, excuses and secret fears getting in the way of the difference you want to make in the world. And, if you've tried it on for size, you'll know that the stuff I teach works. You might even think it rocks. It has helped many thousands of passionate world-changers, just like you, to create breakthroughs in their lives, and the lives of others.

But here's the thing: the work I share is wasted, for possibly 95% of the people who use it. Why? It's not because it doesn't get results – it does – with knobs on. It's because most people never actually make the commitment to take inspired action on their dreams.

They might be scared, or confused, or feeling too busy. They might think that 'visualising the desired outcome' is enough. But until you make that unshakable decision to turn your dreams into reality, it's like driving with the accelerator pedal and brake both down at the same time.

Here is what I find really sad: there is a step I can't take for you; a block I can't 'fix'. And it's the one that stops most people from ever, ever, ever creating their dreams.

It's that 3-lettered word that changes the world:

Yes.

That's all it takes - a commitment; the decision to take action.

When it comes to the difference you're here to make in the world, there must be part of you that is hungry for it, or you wouldn't be reading this Handbook, surely? Do you want to risk it being a mañana-day dream, until your 80th birthday and beyond? I can't *make* you say, "Yes!" to taking massive action your dreams. Only you can do that. But without that 'yes', your dreams stay stuck as nice ideas.

Gary Vaynerchuk did a great video on regret (you can find it in the Readers' Club). He said that when you talk to 90 year olds about their life, one of the first things they say is, "I wish…" They look back at all the things they wish they had done. And he concludes (and I agree with him) that regret can poison your experience of life.

So he encourages you to seize every opportunity to turn your dreams into reality and (for his target audience) to grow your entrepreneurial business and legacy.

And he reminds us that those currently in their 90s didn't have the opportunities that we have. They didn't have computers or email or print-on-demand. They didn't have websites to handle their marketing. They didn't have social media, to get their message out there.

But we do.

> *So here's the thing: I don't want you to ditch your limiting beliefs, unless you're ready to say 'yes!' to you dreams.*

Ditching your limiting beliefs and hidden, subconscious blocks is a Big Deal – to be celebrated – because it will shift you from "I can't..." to "I can..." But that's not enough. Sorry. I know that block-busting was hard work and I AM genuinely proud of you for doing it, but it's simply not enough. Since 2002, I have worked with thousands of entrepreneurs and passionate world-changers, and there is one critical element that made the difference between those who, a decade on, are still stuck in desk jobs or relationships that they hate, and those who have been making the difference they dream of.

It's that 3-lettered word again: saying 'yes' and meaning it.

Someone shared a social media quote with me, which inspired me to write about this for you:

"You have to get up every morning and tell yourself, 'I can do this'."

No. "I can", on its own, changes nothing, other than giving you a warm, glowy feeling inside. After a while, that glowy feeling disappears and you wind up with even more inner pain – an inner conflict – because your mind is telling you that you *can*, but your heart is asking you why you *aren't*.

Changing the world isn't about what you think or believe; it's about who you allow yourself to become. And then it's about taking inspired action from the 'place' of *being* that version of 'you'.

And this is the difference that makes the difference – the one leap I can't push you through – the one block I can't release for you, no matter how much I want to.

Once the 'yes' is out of the way, once that decision has been made, then the miracles can line up for you; the people you have been needing will show up to help; you'll find the energy to take the actions you need to take.

But if they haven't made that commitment yet - if their 'yes' is still a 'maybe', then there's very little I can do to help, other than sticky plasters to ease the immediate pain.

Variations of this quote are attributed to Goethe, loosely translated from Faust:

Whatever you can do or dream you can, begin it;
Boldness has genius, power, and magic in it.
Until one is committed there is hesitancy, the chance
to draw back.
Begin it and the work will be completed.

I can give you every step of the 'how to', once you have made the commitment. But I can't make the commitment for you.

Sure, I can apply leverage, and in the sales world, that's surprisingly common, but to me it feels like bullying and scarcity-tactics.

It's how the some of the super-biz-gurus get you parting with thousands, almost without realising it. Then they keep you hyped up, so you don't get buyer's remorse. And if it doesn't work, it's because it's *your* fault, not theirs, and they make their guarantee terms so tricky that only a red-blooded pedant would be able to jump through those hoops.

I could use the fear-based marketing tactics; I could prey on your emotions; I could use fake scarcity; I could use the scarily-common sleazy sales tactics.

But I won't.

Why? Because I don't want to do that. It's not authentic and, frankly, it feels like bad karma.

I don't want you to spend even one more day, just dreaming about the next stage of your dream. **I want you to be taking massive, positive, inspired action.** Without that, there's not a huge amount of point in clearing out your blocks, because the happiness and relief that creates will soon be eclipsed by the icky feeling of not living your Path.

Sure, I can help you to crank up the passion and excitement with techniques from Step 1, but even then, the only person who can make the decision to take action, to say yes to your dreams, is you.

Without that decision – and it *is* just a choice – to take inspired action, there's little point in me teaching you how to connect with your Big Vision and clear out your blocks. I risk making it worse for you.

Just imagine if your favourite author on the planet had let their secret fears get in the way of saying 'yes' to their dream of writing that book you loved. Just imagine if your favourite actor or life-change expert or world-changer had kept quiet and got themselves a 'nice little day-job', instead. Imagine if they had let their excuses, fears, hidden blocks and limiting beliefs get in the way. Think how much you would have missed out on.

Somewhere out there are people who are lying awake at night, wishing for the solution you offer, even if they don't know it yet. The world needs you to say 'yes'.

When Gandhi told us to 'be the change', he wasn't talking about sitting around *thinking* about making a difference in the world. He was encouraging us to live and breathe that change, through every thought and action; to get out there and make a difference.

If you really want to do something, you'll find a way. If you don't, you'll find an excuse. ~ Jim Rohn

We often use convenient excuses to put off the things (like doing the 'inside work'!) that are most likely to sky rocket us towards our dreams, as though we're silently scared of that success.

What Would It Take For You To Say 'Yes'?

What would need to happen, for you to step up and take that next step towards 'yes', fulfilling the next stage of your dream, and making a bigger difference in the world?

Need some motivation and butt-kicking? Raynold Alorse gave an inspirational TEDx talk on harnessing the power of decisions. You can find it in the Readers' Club. In his talk, he reminds us how it is not the ideas that lead to results, but our decisions. Making a firm and resolute decision has the power to change your life.

Today's choices create your tomorrows.

Even a non-decision is still a decision. It is a choice - conscious or otherwise - NOT to take action. Procrastination is a decision. Distraction is a decision. And both of them prevent you from making the commitment towards your future.

How Do You Break Through This Self-Imposed Glass Ceiling?

If you could momentarily press 'pause' on the 'how?' and the 'money' and the rest of your fears (the answers tend to come once we commit - and I'll be helping you with those worries soon), could you say 'yes'?

You could choose to say 'yes'. Right here, right now. No fancy 'processes' or 'interventions' required. In fact, just imagine how it might feel, to have said 'yes' to your dreams? Forget about the detail for a moment. Just go with the feeling – imagining that it is all possible, and that somehow you found a way. Allow that feeling to gently spread to fill each and every cell in your body. Want that feeling? You can connect with it each day of your journey.

It's a choice. Pure and simple. Make a decision and the how-to follows. And, yes, you can make it now. Shall we? I'm here – virtual-hand-holding – walking by your side, TOTALLY believing in you, your mission, your dreams and your ability to make a difference in the world.

Is It Time To Say 'Yes'?

Ok – let's do it. I'm here. You're not alone. You can do this.
One, two, three, step up!

Yes!

Woo hoo! Now how does that feel?

I'm so proud of you – and excited for you. The 'future you' is already doing a happy dance! Time for a celebratory cuppa!

So shall we deal with the number one dream-trashing excuse?

The Excuse That Is Most Likely To Derail You?

It's our favourite excuse for not taking action on our dreams. We tell ourselves we don't have enough time.

It becomes a self-fulfilling mantra.

As you tell yourself, "I don't have enough time," your unconscious mind takes it as an instruction and fires off the chemical reactions in your body that support your Truth of not having enough time.

Your stress responses will kick in. Your cortisol levels rise. Your breathing becomes more rapid and moves to your upper chest and your brain sends extra oxygen to the primal part of your brain, responsible for survival, rather than to the pre-frontal cortex which, until that 'time statement', was happily planning the next steps in your Big Vision journey (or remembering to buy milk at the shops on the way home).

If we keep feeding that thought of not having enough time, it becomes harder to concentrate, as your mind-chatter volume and speed increase and, before you know it, job done! You didn't have enough time.

I don't want that to get in the way of you Daring To Dream Bigger. And I want us to handle it, before we get started in this book, so that you can't use it as an excuse when we get to the deep-dive stuff.

So before we even get started, I'm going to share with you the most important things you need to know about finding the time to work through and implement everything we're going to be doing here.

"I don't have enough time," is a belief, not a fact. And whether you believe you have enough time, or you believe you don't, you're right.

I often find myself juggling so much that my time stories get in the way. And yet, when that unexpected phone call comes in, I can make time for it. When that 'you-have-to-watch-this!' video shows up in your news feed, you find time to watch it. When we consciously choose how to spend our time – like the most valuable currency in existence – and we have said that 'yes' about taking action on our dreams, the time will appear and the distractions will melt away.

If you were to look at what typically steals your time during the day, I'm guessing there are things you could ditch or delegate, to find the time you crave. It takes a choice and self-discipline. And I know you can do it.

Our biggest time thieves are the stress-stories we tell ourselves about not having enough time. And if those time-poor stories are going crazy (as they sometimes still do with me), I use my favourite time-creating mantra:

Right here, right now, I have all the time I need. And I am grateful for the time I have.

Saying this - and meaning it - resets your nervous system so that the stress hormones calm down, your brain starts to listen to the wisdom of the pre-frontal cortex again, you're able to concentrate again, and life feels calmer and happier. As a Meditation Teacher, I also throw in some mindful breathing, for good measure (sit quietly, with your eyes closed, and notice the physical sensations, as you breathe in and out, from your belly. Simple. Profoundly effective. Free.)

Most of us have secret time-stealers that waste hours of our time each day, and I invite you to look for and ditch a few of your worst offenders, while you're going through this Handbook. You're heading out on the next stage of what I hope will be an exciting and transformational journey, but it will take a little time (not huge amounts; it's all broken down into bite-sized chunks).

Exercise: How To Find The Time?

There's a worksheet for this over in the Readers' Club. It's important to deal with your time-objections before we start, so that you make sure that 'time' doesn't get in the way of the changes you want to make.

- How might you find the time to do the exercises in this book?
- How might you remind yourself to take the actions to cultivate the new habits you're going to want to create?
- What has worked for you in the past?
- And how might you motivate yourself to keep to that commitment?
- Are there any time-thieves you want to ditch?
- What support do you need, to create the time you need?

If you're stuck for ideas - or want to share some of your favourites - we've got a special discussion thread for this over at the Readers' Club forum.

There are also some time-creating bonus resources for you in the Readers' Club, including a video on how to spot your secret time thieves, a podcast on practical strategies for ditching overwhelm and a short video on my personal secrets for getting stuff done, a video on how to 'magically' make more time, especially when you're feeling super-stressed, and even a deep-dive online course for you on Time Secrets For Busy Entrepreneurs. Here's where to find them:

www.DareToDreamBiggerHandbook.com/club

What Do You Want From This Handbook?

I'd love to know: what is it you want from working through this Handbook? Shall we find out?

Have you ever had a 'desired outcome' for reading a book before? I know it's not something we normally do. But I really want you to get the most you can from the next 300 pages, and this exercise doesn't take long.

You wouldn't get in your car and set out on a journey without knowing where you're heading and actually expect to get there, would you? To be able to plot a route, you need to know where you are and where you want to be instead. And that's what we're going to do with this next exercise.

There's a worksheet for you to download for this in the Readers' Club, as well as an MP3 of the questions, so it feels like we're sitting in a room working together on this, in a mentoring session.

We'll be doing exercises like this at key points in this Handbook. The more of them you do, the better results you'll get. So please don't just skim over them. Take a few minutes to actually do them. It's the key to finding the answers that are waiting there for you, deep inside.

Exercise: What Do You Want From This Handbook?

I invite you to pause for a moment and answer these questions. I really do recommend writing them down, because it helps you to focus in a way that just 'thinking around the questions' won't. And it gives you a record to come back to at the end of this Handbook, so you can see how far you have travelled.

There's an audio to guide you through this exercise and a downloadable workbook, for you to write down your answers, in the Readers' Club.

- What are you currently loving about your business or career or world-changing mission?
- Which bits do you avoid, put off or dread?
- Where are you feeling stuck?
- Where do you wish you could have more success?
- How do you feel about your business / career / mission, right now?
- If you could wave a magic wand, what would you change?
- How might it feel, if you do that? Pause and really *feel* this!
- What will happen if I *don't* make those changes?
- What scares me most about making those changes?
- Where do you want your business (and life) to be in 6 months? 12 months? 5 years? Note: it doesn't matter too much at this stage - we'll be diving in to this in stage 1.
- I want this book to help me to...

If you'd like to share any of your answers or insights from these questions, there's a special discussion thread, over at the Readers' Club.

And now it's time to lay the foundations for the rest of the work in this Handbook, with Step 0.

Clear Out And Declutter

Clear out before you grow. Don't amplify chaos.

Clearing out and decluttering might not sound like an exciting place to start, if you want to change the world, but I promise you: you don't want to amplify chaos. And I'm talking chaos both inside and out.

When you're about to make shifts so that you can grow to the next level, it's important to take a step back and clear out anything that you don't want to take with you. If your life and living space are already full, then there's no room to expand; there's no space for anything new or better.

As within, so without. If your outside world is chaotic and stressful, then chances are that your 'inside world' will be, too. And 'outside world' clutter and overwhelm tends to trigger our 'inside world' clutter and overwhelm, feeding painful emotions, fears and hidden blocks.

The good news is that clearing out our 'outside world' can help to declutter and free up our 'inside world'.

I remember years ago, back in the days of analogue television with TV aerials, that we needed booster boxes to be able to get enough signal to see a decent picture. Now, as a reformed engineer, I know from my control theory lectures that if you put the booster box next to the television, it amplifies the TV signal. That's great. But it also amplifies all of the noise and interference between the aerial and the TV, in that tatty old weather-beaten cable. So you amplify the picture, but you also amplify the hissing and the flickering.

If you put the booster box nearer to the aerial, it boosts the TV signal, but not the interference. So you get a much clearer picture and better sound quality. The background noise that was getting in the way of you enjoying that programme is reduced.

If you grow and expand, but you keep the systems, the processes, the physical environment stresses and the to-do list that you currently have, you'll end up growing that chaos, losing sight of your Big Vision, hidden by the background noise. When you deal with it and clear out the chaos and stress, before you expand, you'll reduce your resistance and also grow something that's manageable. You get to grow the bits you love and ditch the bits you don't. Fear of overwhelm is one of the biggest blocks that keeps us stuck; that's why we're dealing with decluttering first.

Is Your Desk A Mess?

The easiest place to start is perhaps your environment; your physical surroundings. You don't need to be a Feng Shui expert to know that if you're living in clutter and disorganisation and dirt, it's hard to think clearly or to feel relaxed. So one of the things that I strongly invite you to do this week is to apply an incredibly simple method to clearing out your environment – and to do one small space at a time. You might start with a drawer in your bedside table or your desk or workspace, for example.

Applying this method to the physical 'stuff' in your life reduces your stress levels, helping you to feel calmer and to think more clearly. It removes the distractions, but at an engineer-approved woo-woo level, it also releases blocked energy.

You see, the clutter we collect brings with it memories, emotions and often 'to do' list items. That vase Aunty Sheila gave you for your wedding – the one you never use but which sits on the mantelpiece anyway and isn't really to your taste – requires looking after – cleaning, caring for it, making sure the occasional rogue elbow doesn't smash it. But it also brings emotions. It might be gratitude, but so often the stuff we hold on to without really wanting to brings us the emotions of guilt and fear.

"I can't get rid of that because so-and-so gave it to me, and they'd be really upset if they knew I didn't like it."
"I can't get rid of that because I spent a fortune on it!"
"I can't get rid of that because I might need it one day."

Over the years, we risk surrounding ourselves with objects that we don't really like, or don't need, which take up space and time in our lives – at the very least, collecting dust, which the Feng Shui world considered to be 'blocked chi' or stagnant energy. It takes our energy, even if we don't realise it. And it means we don't have space for things we would really love, which would lift our spirits and energise us. If your home or office is a Temple to chaos and clutter, and it's full of to-do list things that are shouting at you, then you're not going to be able to focus on your dreams.

Have nothing in your house that you do not know to be useful, or believe to be beautiful. ~ William Morris

Decluttering creates the space for growth and more of the life experiences we want, helping to let go of the past. And that letting go isn't just about 'things'; it's also about out-of-date inner blocks. Letting go of the guilt about Aunty Sheila's vase, for example, will also unravel and release all of the behavioural and thought habits you have held on to that are associated with that variation of guilt.

Exercise: It's Time For A Clear-Out

So here's my 3-step pain-free process for letting go and clearing out the non-essential, non-loved stuff in your life, without needing Therapy:

Step 1: Pick up one item and really focus on it. Hold it. Feel it. See it. Notice the physical reaction in your body, because it will tell you the truth, whatever stories your mind tells you. Notice your emotions about it. Notice your thoughts.

Step 2: Ask yourself: does this lift my spirits, or does it drag me down? If it lifts your spirits, ask yourself: do I really need this, or is it time to pass it on to someone else who might love it more?
If it drags you down, it goes! Even if it's useful, you don't want stuff around you that makes you feel bad or zaps your energy levels.

Step 3: For the things you keep, as you choose where they will go, make sure they are clean and properly repaired, and that where they are going is also clean. Thank them for what they do for you.
For the stuff that's going, give each item a heartfelt thank you for the role it has played in your life, then imagine you are cutting the invisible ties you had to it – any guilt, obligation or fear – with a massive pair of scissors. Watch as the two ends of that tie melt away, filled with 'thank yous' and finally letting go.

Allow yourself to feel the relief and lightness, as your world clears of things you no longer love or need, and feels more spacious. Do this one small space at a time – perhaps a section of a cupboard each day for a week – and you'll be amazed by the positive impact it will have. You might want to turn it into a fun experience by playing some of your favourite music, as you're doing it.

Travel lightly through life; carry only what you love.

If physical-world clutter is a really big issue for you, then Marie Kondo's book on "The Life-Changing Magic of Tidying" is an inspiration. You can find details in the Readers' Club.

Put An End To 'To Do' List Nightmares

The next thing to declutter is your 'to do' list.

If it's already full and you're feeling overwhelmed, then the likelihood of you having space in your schedule for the inspired actions your dreams ask of you is low.

This is one of the biggest hidden blocks I see with my clients - and with myself. Your unconscious mind is secretly terrified that if you are more successful, you'll drown in your 'to do' list, have to give up sleeping, and never see your loved-ones again. That's a pretty powerful motivator to subconsciously self-sabotage, isn't it?

Our life is frittered away by detail. Simplify, simplify, simplify! ~ Henry David Thoreau

One of my clients was running this pattern. She was ticking along with one-to-one clients and had a brilliant idea for how she could expand her business to reach a wider audience. She felt really inspired and was taking daily action to move her towards this new goal. But she kept not quite making it. She would 'forget' to return a call that would have given her the publicity her new idea needed. She would be 'too busy' to reply to enquiries for her new service. She would miss deadlines for articles she had planned to send to her newsletter subscribers.

She came to me wanting accountability, so she could use willpower to 'push' her way through these blocks. But willpower costs, big time. It uses up your energy and often an creates internal 'tug of war', where one part of you is all-out going for the goal, so the bit of you that is scared has to crank up the volume, too.

So instead of working with her to help her force her way through her blocks, we looked at what the hidden blocks were.

She had total clarity on what she wanted to create; she had dealt with the usual blocks of not feeling good enough to offer the new service. And she was - mostly - taking the inspired action. So why wasn't it working? Why was she self-sabotaging?

Because she believed that, if she grew her business with this service, she wouldn't have time for her kids any more. And seeing her children was incredibly important to her. Her unconscious mind was putting the brakes on as hard as it could, to protect her from her fear of being a 'bad mother', because her work 'took over'.

So we dealt with the triggers behind this. We looked at what she could simplify, ditch or declutter. She connected with her Inner Genius, so she could prioritise doing the things that she did best, and we identified the tasks that needed to be done by someone who had a love of admin and detail.

Once those foundations were laid, and we had re-routed the neural pathway that was running the auto-pilot connection between 'grow business' and 'be a bad mother' (I'll show you how in stage two, and no, it doesn't hurt!), she felt free to expand her business to include the new service, and her clients loved her for it.

Exercise: What Might Be Getting In Your Way?

I'm curious: does this resonate with you?

- If you were to zoom, say, a year into the future, having grown your business or career or Big Vision to the next level, how would that feel?
- Is there any resistance or worry about being overloaded?
- How does your *body* react? (Hint: it always tells the truth)
- What are you scared you might lose or have to give up?
- Are there any of your business processes or life areas that need streamlining?
- Is there anything on your 'to do' list that doesn't really belong to you? Could you ditch it? Delegate it?

If this is a big issue for you, there's a worksheet waiting for you in the Readers' Club, with a 'spinning plates' exercise, to help you to get your 'to do' list back under control. And remember there are the 'how to make more time' resources there for you, too. There are discussion threads in the forum, where you can share ideas and get answers to your questions.

Decluttering Your Mind's Stories

If your Monkey Mind (that chattering, topic-jumping inner dialogue) is full of stories of everything that's going wrong and all the reasons why you can't succeed, then your chances of success are low. We're going to be looking in detail at how to tame your mind – and your Inner Critic – in Step 2. But for now:

We love telling stories. It's ancient. It goes back thousands of years. People have entertained each other by telling stories since the beginning of the spoken word. And we do it in our heads, too.

When you tell yourself a story about what you can achieve, what your skills are, what your clients might think of you, what stress levels you're running, how much you have to do, it's just a story. But sometimes that story can cause us pain and it can mean we don't take the inspired action our dreams need.

In addition, your mind and body are linked – and your body feels every thought you think; it feels every emotion you feel; and it fires off the same neurotransmitters and chemical reactions as though whatever you are thinking about were actually happening.

If you're telling yourself stories of stress, whether it's something that's happened in the past or a worry about something that might happen in the future, your body reacts as thought you were living that stress, right now. It fires off its stress responses; cortisol and adrenalin flood your system. It activates the primal part of the brain, responsible for fight or flight, as the sympathetic nervous system fires off, meaning you lose the ability to look at long-term consequences of short-term survival-level decisions.

How can you spot which stories you're telling? How about looking at something that's in your to-do list that maybe feels like an "I don't really want to do that" job. Pause for a moment and notice the dialogue that goes on in your head or the kind of images that you're seeing. What are you telling yourself about that?

Is that story actually true? Is it fact based? If you were in a court of law, would the barrister present that story in that way, or is it full of drama? Is it full of emotion? Is the 'story' full of conjecture? Is it full of projecting 'maybes', which you are listening to as 'deep truths'?

When you strip out what's real and what's true, you release the emotion and drama.

Here's the crazy thing: at some level, that story is doing something for you. It's called 'Secondary Gain' by psychologists and we're going to dive into it in Step 2. But to get to the 'positive intention' behind the story-telling, it's important to identify and address the unmet need or fear or limiting belief that fed the story. I'll be showing you how.

Exercise: How To Spot Your Hidden Stories

For now, here's a short exercise you can use, whenever you spot a story that's making you feel bad:

- Which elements are really true? *This strips out most of the drama, emotions and pain.*
- What is it doing for me? *This gives you the Secondary Gain secrets.*
- Do I really want to keep telling myself this story? *Any change needs a decision – a choice.*
- What do I need to believe about myself for that story to come up? *Write those answers down – we'll come back to them in Step 2.*
- Which story would I like to tell myself instead? *This turns the ship around to head towards a brighter future.*

I would love to hear from you via the forum. What is the new story that you want to tell yourself instead?

And now that we've had a bit of a clear out, it's time to figure out what you really want.

Know What You Want

Clarity

Clarity is the process of shining a light on your dreams, so that they can come to life.

Clarity is the most potent way to line up with what feels like miracles and synchronicities, but most people don't really know what they want. And they don't realise that. So they are super-busy, but making little progress, despite huge effort.

When I talk with fellow Mentors about this, we're unanimous: few of our Clients arrive with total clarity about the difference they want to make, or what they want to create. They are building their business or legacy on the initial excitement of a 'rough idea'. Once that excitement fades into the reality of needing to put in the huge effort and commitment that it inevitably takes, then the projects fizzle out.

Clarity connects you with your passion – your driving force – to break through blocks and to keep going, to create breakthroughs. It's the key to feeling motivated and inspired.

If you're feeling overwhelmed, if you're feeling stuck, if you're feeling exhausted, if you're doing too much, then you're likely to be missing this first C.

Imagine setting out on a journey, with only a vague idea of where you're heading. What's the likelihood of getting to where you wanted to go? Near zero. Yet so many of us do this with our life's dreams. We have a rough idea of what we want to create - the difference we want to make - but we're missing that laser-focused clarity that would keep us going, and makes decisions easy, even if the going gets tough.

When I work with entrepreneurs, it's really common to hear people complain that they don't know why they're 'here' - and I don't mean in my office. "I don't know what my soul purpose is. What's my life purpose? What am I *supposed* to be doing?" They're missing that clarity. Yet they're hugely busy doing things that may or may not line up with what they feel they're 'meant' to be doing. Or maybe they're not even getting started, because they feel paralysed by looking for perfection in the definition of their life's purpose. We use that 'busyness' to distract ourselves from the secret pain of not having that clear sense of direction and purpose.

Your sense of purpose is the fuel for life's adventure.

When you have clarity, then it's easy to answer questions like:

"Who am I?"
"Who am I serving?"
"What difference do I make?"
"Why am I unique and worth working with?"
"Why do I want to do this?"
"What's the contribution to the world that only I can make?"

When you've got clarity on these and you set your goals from that level of focused understanding - that deep knowing - your to-do list becomes much easier. Prioritising becomes simple. You can go through your to-do list and check each item against your Big Vision, asking yourself, "does it move me towards whatever it is I'm aiming for?" If yes, great! Do it! If not, then you either need to ditch it or delegate it.

It makes big decisions is easier. You don't have to work as hard. It's amazing how many things you can say no to and still make massive progress. Remember Pareto's rule of thumb, that 20% of your actions bring 80% of your results? Having clarity about what you're doing, why and for whom is a brilliant way of spotting the 20% that will bring greatest results. I call those 'inspired actions' and we'll be getting to those in Step 5.

When we don't have clarity, we distract ourselves from the pain of not being true to who we really are, why we're here, and the difference we're here to make, by being busy 'doing'. We procrastinate. We fill our time with activities that don't produce results, but which leave us exhausted. We distract ourselves. If you're drowning in your to-do list, it's likely to be at least partly because you don't have the clarity that connects you with your passion and energy for your Big Message.

When I talk about clarity, I split it into four main sections.

The first one is: **What's your Big Why.**

Why do you want to make the difference you're here to make – or any difference, if you're not yet clear on that?

The second one is: **What's your Big Vision?**

What's that revolution that you want to start? *How* do you want to express your Big Why?

The third one is: **What's your Big Message?**

If somebody met you and they said, "What do you stand for? *What* is that thing that you're doing that nobody else is?" How would you describe that?

The fourth one is: **Who is your Dream Audience?**

Who is secretly lying awake at night, wishing you would step up to the next level, so that they can find you?

You might find these questions easy to answer, which is great, though it's still worth reading the end of this section to gain more depth of understanding. But if the answers to those questions aren't rolling off the tip of your tongue, then I've got plenty of strategies to help you.

Why Bother? And Why Most People Don't

Surely it's better just to dive in and take action and figure it out as you go along?

'Learning by doing' it used to be called. And, of course, you can try it that way, but surely it makes more sense to get clear about what you want to create - the difference you want to make - before you can go out there and make it? Otherwise your results are unlikely to bring you the sense of fulfilment that we crave.

Action, without clarity, is just 'filling time'.

Clarity about what is motivating you, why you want to make the difference you want to make, and exactly what that difference is, is what will get you started and keep you motivated. It helps you to burn through blocks, to keep going when you're not in the mood, and to magnetise your Dream Audience.

I interviewed William Buist, Founder of the exclusive xTEN Club, as part of writing this Handbook. His main advice comes in Step 4, on Masterminds, but we talked about Clarity, too.

William has helped thousands of entrepreneurs through his Masterminds and other projects and says that the hardest thing to 'sell' to them is 'clarity', because most of us think we already have it. It's not until he asks them his penetrating, insightful questions that they realise they're not really clear on what they want to create, after all.

In these social media, crowd-sourced times, William has seen how many of us turn to our peers for input on our vision, especially if we're doubting ourselves. But that risks leading to us diluting our message and heading up blind alleys. Facebook groups can be an echo chamber, where everyone is stuck on the same kinds of problems. You're unlikely to connect with your life's purpose – your Big Message – by asking for help on social media.

His advice is that, once you have your Big Vision, you need to simplify it. Make it maximum one sentence. And a short one, if you can. Get to the essence of it. Then it's easier to communicate it. And it's easier to use it for your big decisions: "Does this move me towards [Big Vision statement]?"

In this Step, I'm going to share with you the processes I use with my clients, to help them to move from confusion to clarity, but first I want to give you a word or two of warning.

Why 'Fake It Till You Make It' Doesn't Cut It Any More

Back in 2002, when I first started mentoring and running workshops, the popular trend was to 'fake it till you make it' - especially in what now seems to have been the 'fledgling' online world. If you didn't feel confident, fake it so that others think you do. If you didn't really have the skills, fake it and study them as you go along. If you didn't know how to run a business, fake it while you read a few books.

And, for a while, for many people, it worked.

But it also created an industry where customers became scared of 'snake oil merchant's. So the '32 page sales letter' became the rage, to beat your potential customers into a 'yes' through exhaustion or confusion and fake scarcity.

But here's why I don't want you to fake it: if you're faking it, you're doing three things:

1. You're out of synch with who you really are.
We'll discover in a moment why that's such a big problem. But, for now, it'll leave you feeling like a fraud.

2. It perpetuates your Inner Critic's message that you're not good enough.
After all, you have to pretend to be something or someone you're not, in order to succeed, which means you're feeding the subconscious message that the 'real' you is not good enough.

3. You'll come across as inauthentic.
People can sniff pretence a mile off. Their radar is much more finely honed than it was a decade ago. And when you get caught out, the results aren't pretty.

Lying To Yourself Doesn't Work
When you think about something stressful, your body fires off chemical reactions to deal with stress, including cortisol and adrenalin, and it diverts oxygen from non-essential areas of the body, to prepare you to run, if you need to.

When you think about something happy, your body shifts its serotonin and endorphin production up a gear or three, calming down your sympathetic nervous system (the 'fight / flight / freeze' response) and helping you to feel happy and relaxed.

Your body feels every thought you think.

If you're living a lie, you'll be thinking stress-based and fear-based thoughts. You'll be running an inner dialogue of self-doubt. You're likely to be beating yourself up and feeling scared about being 'found out'.

You can't just override that body chemistry and those thought habits with brute force. Ok, so you can, but it's very hard work. And it sets up a fabulous inner conflict, taking up way too much of your energy and headspace.

The likelihood of you performing to the best of your ability under such circumstances is low.

Strangely enough, my research has shown that the much easier option is to do the 'inside work' - the change-work below the surface - and then the surface-level 'pretending' is no longer needed.

Over the course of this book, I want to make that as easy for you as possible. So let's start with looking at why most people are building their business or Big Vision dreams upside down - and why that makes it so easy for our dreams to fall over.

Why Most People Are Building Their Business Upside Down

Nowadays, I joke that I'm 'unemployable'. The freedom of being an entrepreneur and guiding my own decisions makes it hard to imagine going back to an environment where someone else sets the destination.

But, back in my corporate life, I never had any problems with knowing what to do. I had clear objectives set in my annual appraisal and I had my boss checking up on me every week, to find out where my team was up to on what we were delivering. Even when I was managing multi-million pound budgets and we were launching major products abroad, it was still straightforward. Yes, it was hard work, but I always knew what we needed to achieve. I was involved in creating those goals, and my team supported me to get it done.

When I set up my own business, it slowly fell apart. Suddenly I was the boss, the boss's boss, the team, and all of the decision makers rolled into one. Many of the good habits I had when I was employed started to disappear, as I picked up the bad habits of a solopreneur. I was doing everything myself. I didn't have a strong network or mastermind to bounce ideas off. I would constantly chase the next shiny, exciting thing. I wasn't a completer-finisher.

Over the years, as I made mistakes, I learned to build my team around me. I learned how important it is to have a mastermind of people you can connect with, so that when you have a brilliant idea, you can get that sounding board to either give you a sanity check or to help you make it even better.

I hear daily that people are so busy 'doing' and so busy working *in* their business or career, they don't have time to work *on* it. They'll say they are too busy to do planning, for example. Then they feel stressed that they're not achieving their dreams and goals.

They feel too busy to invest in their personal development, but then find it hard to watch their industry overtaking them.

When we meet someone at a party, the first thing we ask, after getting their name, is *what do you do?*

But what we *do* is just the outside-world manifestation of a huge amount of inside-world stuff. And it often has little to do with who we really *are*.

What we do is just the tip of the iceberg. Everything underneath is what lays the foundations for your business - and your life. Below the "what you do" is what you think. Looking at it from the perspective of the NLP Neurological Levels model by Robert Dilts (details in the Readers' Club), our thoughts govern our actions. The stories we tell ourselves, that little Inner Critic, the negative thinking or the positive thinking; these drive which actions we choose and which habits we form.

The next layer down that is what we believe: whether we believe we can do something, whether we believe we can't. The layer below that is what's important to us. What are our values? What are our hidden needs? And the foundation layer is "who am I?" - the really deep, identity-level existential stuff – why am I here?

Most people build their business or career on the tip of the iceberg – on what they *do*.

Most people build the foundations of their dreams on an upside-down pyramid.

That upside down pyramid is precariously balancing on its pinnacle. Unless what you are doing is supported by your self-talk, your empowering beliefs, your values and your sense of identity and purpose, then all it takes is one gentle nudge and your pyramid topples over.

When you turn it up the other way and you start to build your business or career with "Who am I?", "What's my genius?", "What do people love about working with me?", "Who does that make me as a person?", then you create a life that is inspired by what motivates you - your driving passions. You will be lined up with your values, what's important to you, both at work and at home.

In Ancient Sanskrit this is known as your Dharma – that difference in the world that only you are here to make.

The word can also be translated to mean 'duty' – that's how seriously the Ancients took their life purpose. When you let your foundations be your sense of purpose and what's important to you, then your next job is to cultivate beliefs that will support your dreams – clearing out those that were getting in the way. Your beliefs influence your thoughts, both triggering which ones pop up and also those that we choose to feed - the stories we tell ourselves. When you shift what you believe, you'll change the thoughts you think. They're just neural pathways in your brain. They can be changed, and I'm going to share with you the step-by-step how-to, later in this Handbook.

Then come your actions. At the top of the pyramid, where they belong.

That's the *doing* bit that most people are using as their foundation and time-swallowing focus. But when you start at the "Who am I?" level, you'll build much firmer foundations and are much more likely to be successful – and to love what you're doing.

When you're 'doing' without 'direction', it's much harder to reach your goals. But 'what?' (traditional goal-setting) doesn't motivate us anywhere near as much as 'why?'. When you know *why* you want to make your difference in the world, it makes your choices easier. Everything can be weighed up against your Big Why and your Big Vision. You no longer say 'yes' to everything. In fact, as Derek Sivers beautifully puts it:

"No more yes. It's either HELL YEAH! or no."

Wouldn't that make life easier? And what if you could build up the confidence and self-belief to be able to say 'no' more often? Well, we handle this in Steps 2 and 3.

Would you love to be able to make easier decisions; to be able to focus and take inspired actions that actually get results; to feel confident in your message, appeals to you? Then you're in the right place! But first I want to explain why we are *not* going to be doing the kinds of things you may be used to, from past training courses. We're going to be changing the rules.

Why Training Courses In My Corporate Days Rarely Worked

Nearly every training course I was sent on in my corporate days dealt with 'effect' – the symptoms and behaviours my bosses objected to. If I was lucky, it dived in to handle a few thought patterns and occasionally I would stumble across one that mentioned beliefs, in passing. But I never got to work at that level, until I trained to become an NLP Trainer.

When you only deal with the surface level aspects of life - your thoughts and actions - you are dealing with the things that are at 'effect', rather than at a 'causality' level. So the below-the-surface triggers for those thoughts and actions remain in place, continuing to trigger those thoughts and actions, while you have to use willpower and gritted determination to try to change what's going on at the surface. But, when you make changes at the levels of your beliefs, values and identity, the change automatically happens on the surface. Deal with the causes and the problematic effects melt away.

Your power to create change lies in the below-the-surface causes, not the surface-level symptoms.

When you're playing up at the surface, it's all about willpower and forcing and "having to," which takes effort and energy. When you're down at 'cause', it's about creating ease and flow and "magic."

If you're feeling stuck, you're feeling overwhelmed, you're putting in all the effort, and you're just not getting the results, it's because something under the surface is triggering thoughts or actions that are getting in the way.

That's why, in this Handbook, we're going to start with 'sticky plasters' (Band Aids), to ease the pain of the surface-level thoughts and actions, but then we're going to dive in with the below-the-surface stuff that's really running the show.

You can apply these insights and techniques to your home life, your personal development and your business growth, even to managing your team.

So we're going to start with the most important element of your foundations: your Big Why.

What's Your Big Why?

What's secretly motivating you to make the difference you're here to make?

In his fascinating book "Start With Why" (details in the Readers' Club), Simon Sinek says that people buy a 'why', not a 'what'. And my market research days confirm that. People buy on emotion and then justify through facts. Every time. Even if we try to convince ourselves otherwise. We buy the Why - the ultimate benefits – "What does this do for me?" - not the features. This is what motivates our choices in life.

The UK's EU referendum showed this, too. The surprise win for the Leave campaign has been heavily researched and it was concluded that the facts didn't change people's minds, on either side, because that wasn't what they were voting for. They were voting for a vision - for a 'why' - and that's one of the reasons why the expert opinions were so widely ignored.

So if you start to grow your business, career or world-changing mission based on 'what' - the 'to do list' of actions - you'll risk ending up exhausted, but also not exciting people.

*They don't connect with what you **do**; it's who you **are** that counts - and how you express your Big Why.*

When you build your Big Vision on your "Why am I doing this?", you'll find it much easier to connect with your passion and excitement - and motivate and inspire others to connect with it, too.

I remember being told a story about some research done a few years ago about photocopier queues (as you do). A female researcher went to a machine with a long queue and asked to jump the queue. Sometimes people let her, but often they didn't.

They repeated the research, but this time the female researcher gave a reason why she wanted to jump the queue. She used the word 'because'. The reason wasn't exciting or compelling. It was mundane. But the proportion of times she was allowed by those in the queue to jump ahead massively increased.

Why?

Because we buy into 'why'. We need a reason to care.

Often, when we are feeling bored and overwhelmed, it's because we have lost touch with the real reason why we are doing what we're doing. So how might it shift things for you if, instead of thinking about growing a business, you were focus on growing a movement? A revolution? How would that feel for you?

Many years ago, I was interviewed by a major car component manufacturer, because I was applying to be a 'sponsored student', meaning they would employ me each summer and pay a grant towards my University costs of my Engineering degree. These sponsorship places were like solid gold hen's teeth and I really wanted one. But it didn't start well.

Looking back, I knew I wasn't going to get the job when I sat in the interview room and crossed my legs on the chair, pixie style. Big mistake. The joys of being 17 and being authentic, in a world that felt alien.

Things went steadily downhill and reached their climax when the manager asked me what engineers do. Like a typical 17-year-old, I knew pretty much nothing about anything, but thought I knew everything. So I waffled politely while my brain processed the question, trying to coherently explain why I wanted to study engineering (against the advice of my 'A' level physics teacher, who warned I had no natural talent) and what I knew about the profession, which was very little, and then I proudly announced my answer:

"They solve problems," I smiled, certain of a positive response.

The interview panel members looked at each other, some with eyebrows raised to the ceiling. One audibly sighed and drummed his fingers on the table. The Chief Engineer replied, "No. They make money."

Obviously I didn't get the job. Luckily other companies offered me sponsorship and the one I chose gave me a brilliant start on my engineering career, for which I am very grateful. But why was my answer 'wrong'? And why does it matter to you and your dreams now?

Because of the differences in our Big Why answers.

Our 'Big Why' is what keeps us motivated, even when times are hard. It inspires you. It makes you go the extra mile. When you're totally lined up with your Big Why, decisions become easier. You feel energised. People can feel it and will love being around you. You inspire *them*, without even trying.

Looking at it from the perspective of the 7 Cs, they are like a tree, with your Clarity about what you want to create being the roots. Your Big Why is right there at the bottom of the tree, like the tap root, and it's vital to anchor that tree, so it can be healthy and strong, even in a gale.

In that engineering interview, the differences between our Big Whys made us incompatible. I became an engineer because I loved problem solving. I loved figuring out how things work and how to make them so good that customers loved them. I adored the intellectual and practical challenge of streamlining manufacturing processes and learning from the best methods in the world for improving designs and factories.

I needed to be in an environment where my personal Big Whys had space to breathe and grow, otherwise I would have been out of synch with what was important to me. I would have felt squashed and restricted and that flame of passion inside me would have slowly died. There's no way I would have reached my potential or given my employer a decent return on their investment of hiring me.

Of course, making money is essential to any engineering business, but it wasn't my Big Why, so I would have been the proverbial square peg in a round hole, had I worked for a firm that not only didn't value my deeply-unconscious desire to fix problems with my creativity, but whose Chief Engineer rejected it. Ironically, engineers solving problems is what makes the money...

The Problem With Being Out Of Synch With Your Big Why

This one works two ways. Firstly, if you're in a role that doesn't resonate with your Big Why, then you're going to have to work hard to feel energised and motivated. You're likely to be disconnected from your deeper passion and risk ending up 'going through the motions'.

Secondly, your customers, colleagues and loved-ones will feel it. We can all tell when we're being pitched by someone who isn't really excited about what they're selling. For example, if your business is marketing a product that you don't really care about, you're not likely to create marketing materials that excite people and get them past the resistance, inertia and fear of buying.

Also there's a hunger these days - and rightly so - to do business with people who are congruent, who we feel we can trust, who are 'walking their talk' – who are being authentic.

Businesses talk about their Values and their Mission Statement, but these are rarely phrased in a way that excites their staff. If, instead, they talked about their Big Why, and phrased it in a way that their employees could really connect with, emotionally, rather than cognitively, then they could transform their business - and the experience of their staff and customers. It makes it easy for employees to make decisions, based on whether something fits with the business's 'because'. Firms who do this find that staff retention, customer satisfaction and even profits will increase.

People Can Smell Your Intention - Your Big Why

My social media newsfeed is usually full of glossy adverts from über-perfect coaches and business gurus, marketing 'high end' (i.e. very expensive) business or marketing programmes.

Sadly, when you look more deeply, there is often little substance. Some are brilliant, but for others it's all about cheat sheets and templates and 'make 5 figures in the next 30 days, just like I did, telling people how to make 5 figures in the next 30 days'. I see so many coaches, for example, who have been in business for less than six months, marketing themselves as business mentors, and charging scary amounts for their services. It can feel like the blind leading the blind.

The 'guru' may have achieved good results, but may not understand enough about the nuances of how they did it to be able to reverse-engineer their process, or to be able to teach it in a way that others can easily apply it.

I'm a member of many business groups in social media. And in one of them, for experienced entrepreneurs, rather than newbies, one of the members posted a hugely sad business story. She had been taken in by persuasive sales copy and paid well into 4 figures for a course to help her to grow the size of her email subscriber list. But when she got into the course (which had a zero refund policy), she found it was 'smoke and mirrors', rather than useful, actionable, workable strategies. When this lady tried to get a refund (she even had to send a legal letter), she was reminded about the 'no refund' policy and the seller refused to give her back a single penny.

The lady felt devastated at what she described as being 'taken in' by this person's promises and having believed the testimonials. She decided, in the end, to walk away and to consider the course price as an investment in lessons-learned. But she is not alone in experiencing this.

How did it happen? Because the Big Why for the person marketing the course wasn't about deeply helping people; it was about making money and creating their own 'lifestyle business'.

Of course, there's nothing wrong with making money, but to be able to sleep at night, I need to know that I have made money by genuinely serving and making a difference, rather than by convincing people to pay more than they want, for something they don't really need. If you build your dreams around making a difference to YOUR life, rather than other people's, then you're likely to struggle.

People *feel* your motivation. It triggers our Sixth Sense. Your intention sings out loud and clear through the words you use and even your body language – getting woo-woo about it: it's a vibe. They want to feel that they **matter**, that you passionately care about them and the transformation or experience your business creates.

If your motivation - your Big Why - is about making a difference, about serving others, about helping to solve someone's burning problem, then your Dream Audience, colleagues and support team will be magnetised to you, because they can feel that you come from a heart-based place of passionately wanting to make a positive difference in the world. Lining up with your Big Why is the key to your passion and success. And here's how to figure out what yours is.

How To Find Your Big Why

It's really important to uncover WHY you are running your business or making the difference you want to make, before you dive into any of the other sections of this book, because it forms the foundation for the rest of the strategies. Even if you have been running your business for years, it's important to revisit this, because it changes over time.

Your Big Vision is about how you will apply this - what will you use it for - what difference do you want to make in the world. And your Big Message is the next step towards your Big Vision. It's like your medium-term mission and goals.

We start this section with getting really clear about your Big Why, because that is the soil from which the Big Vision and Big Message are grown. Do you know why you're in business or wanting to make this difference in the world? There could be many layers of your Big Why and there's no such thing as a 'wrong' answer, but your body will tell you if you have hit upon your Big Why - it will release tension and start to feel excitement, when you think about it.

Exercise: What's Your Big Why?

Here are some questions for you to explore. There's a worksheet and audio for this over at the Readers' Club. It's really important just to play with this – not to try to force yourself to find the 'perfect' Big Why. Experiment and see what comes up for you. You can't get this 'wrong'.

To begin, I invite you to take three deep sighing breaths, in through your nose, and out through your mouth with an 'ahhh' sound. As you exhale, allow yourself to come back to this moment, releasing any stress or tension, so that your awareness is here, now, with this exercise.

Now ask yourself each of these questions in turn, allowing the answers to bubble up, without critique, analysis or judgement:

- In the context of the difference I want to make in the world, who am I? *Jot down the first keywords that bubble up.*
- Is that who I want to be? If not, *who* do I want to be instead?
- The difference I want to make is important to me, because...
- The difference I want to make is important to the world, because...
- When I get to do the things I love, it makes me feel...
- If I couldn't get to make the difference I want to make, what would I miss out on?
- How would I describe my 'Big Why', at this point in time?

There's no right or wrong. Your Big Why can be something about making a difference in people's lives or it could be something about wanting to expand and grow. You'll know when you find it - or when you're close to it - because you'll feel excited and your body will do whatever it does when excitement hits. You'll feel a burst of energy. You'll no longer be going through the motions.

And if it's not feeling totally clear yet, that's ok! Just go with the best 'feeling' you have for it. It's important not to over-think this and not to let perfectionism get in the way. Your Big Why is about connecting with the sense of excitement and passion you have for the difference you're here to make. Any movement you can make along that scale is great.

If you want more inspiration from seeing the Big Why for others – or if I could tempt you to share your Big Why with fellow readers - there's a special discussion thread over at the Readers' Club forum.

For example, my Big Why is that I want to set you free to be the beautiful being that you really are, free from blocks and fears and subconsciously self-imposed limits – and layers of brown stuff that cover your inner diamond. I want to inspire and empower you to be happy, so that you can do the same for others.

My Big Vision is to inspire and empower passionate World-Changers to get clarity, to clear out their hidden blocks and to take inspired action, because I can see that most of us are paralysed by fear and self-doubt. I have been there myself. And I know that, together, we can spread a wave of positive change and happiness that reaches far wider than any one person could ever reach, on their own.

My Big Message, for this stage of my journey, is that it is time for you to step up and make a bigger difference in the world, and that you *can* Dare To Dream Bigger - and make that difference - and it's easier than you might have been telling yourself. I'm doing this through my work with the Dare To Dream Bigger Tribe, my Mentoring Clients, my Masterminders (those stepping up to the next level in my Mastermind groups), my Dare To Dream Bigger Academy Members and this Dare To Dream Bigger Handbook.

Around that framework, I build my goals and actions.

The Two 4-Lettered Words That Change Everything

In business, if you're feeling financially stuck, there may be bills you can postpone or renegotiate, and there are those you can't. And your annual tax bill is in the 'can't' box.

In the UK, most micro businesses have to pay their annual business tax at the end of January. So you earn and spend all year, but if you didn't predict your tax bill and put cash aside, it leaves you with a big problem. I have seen so many entrepreneurs fly into panic in early January, as they realise they have to raise funds to pay their tax bill in the next few weeks.

You see them running crazy offers, and emergency launches; desperation fills the virtual airwaves.

In the current climate of building a 'lifestyle business', it's not uncommon for an entrepreneur to have spent the year jetting around beach resorts, whilst they grow their empire. It can be hard to manage cash flow and it's easy to forget to put funds aside for your end of year tax bill. You might even end up dipping into your savings, to pay the rent on the luxury home you have chosen to live in, to validate your 'lifestyle'.

It's easy to fall into the trap of not keeping business cash separate from personal cash and, before you realise it, the pot is empty.

The business data goes off to your accountant and you get a shock. I have seen entrepreneurs having a tax liability that runs well into 5 figures, and no cash.

Many in this position do what most of us would consider doing - launching an emergency high-ticket programme. I saw an example of this, a few years ago, with a male entrepreneur. As a gifted salesman, launching a high-ticket programme would normally have been a roaring success. But he sold just a couple of places - nowhere near enough to cover his tax bill, but taking up so much of his time that he couldn't do anything else to raise funds.

When you know about the 4 lettered-words that secretly runs behind every word you write, behind every word you speak, you'll understand why his launch flopped. And it's vital to check your Big Why against this.

We have all had times where we needed to take massive action, to cover an up-coming expense or launch a product or new service - or book. But which of the two 4-lettered words you weave into the process will radically transform your experience of it, and the results you get.

All of our experiences in life are driven by two primary emotions. Those 4-lettered words I promised you:

Fear   *Love*

These underlie all our other emotions. And our emotions are what motivate us. Even the most rational decision has an emotional trigger behind it.

Fear breeds panic and stress and worry and pushing and desperation. It triggers your 'fight / flight / freeze' mechanism and keeps you stuck in short-term, emergency-level fire-fighting and decision-making. It brings you customers who are attracted by those fear-based qualities, who will often be harder to please and less willing to pay.

Love gives you access to your full flow of creativity, inspiration and intuition. It brings you excitement and connects you with your passion. You feel motivated and happy and can produce your best work. It brings you customers you enjoy working with, who value your work and are happy to recommend you.

Going back to the tax-bill scenario, we have two major choices on how to respond:

Option 1:

You feel the pressure. You know you have to make it work, or something terrible will happen. You feel scared that it might fail. Your stress levels rise. Your body triggers its fire-fighting hormone responses, as you feel adrenalin racing. These hormones mean your body signals to the primal part of your brain that you're in a near-constant 'fight or flight' situation, which means you connect solely with the part of your brain that handles short-term sabre-toothed-tiger-fleeing decision making and you lose touch with the pre-frontal cortex, which allows you to see strategic and long-term implications of actions.

Your tone of communicating will change. You'll come across as more tense. You'll be pushing for the sale and using hard-sell tactics. There will be urgency and desperation. Your Dream Audience will smell it; sense it.

Option 2:

You choose not to feel the pressure. You choose to believe, 100%, that you will take the necessary inspired action that means things will work out. You stay calm and in flow and connected with creating whatever it is your Dream Audience is dreaming of.

Your stress levels don't rise and you keep access to the strategic-thinking part of your brain, so you can make those leaps and spot those insights. You'll feel confident and more empowered. You come across as happy and confident in your communications. And your Dream Audience will smell it; sense it.

Try it on for size

Think for a moment of a situation when you acted from fear in your business or career. Allow yourself to sink into that memory (please pick a 3-4 out of 10 - not a block-buster!). Notice which emotions come up for you. Become aware of how your body changes - where your breathing moves to; how your posture shifts; what happens to the muscles in your face and your jaw; how your thoughts change. And ask yourself, "Where in my body do I feel this most?"

Now shake that off.

Think now of a situation when you acted from love in your business.

Allow yourself to sink into that memory (make this one as big as you like!). Notice which emotions come up for you. Become aware of how your body changes - where your breathing moves to; how your posture shifts; what happens to the muscles in your face and your jaw; how your thoughts change. And ask yourself, "Where in my body do I feel this most?"

What did you notice? Any insights? Surprises? Lightbulbs? Which kind of business would you rather run? It's worth taking a moment to jot down some notes on this. What were your experiences of the differences between these memories?

> *Any choice made from a position of freedom creates*
> *more freedom. ~ James Twyman*

In this context, choices made from love create a sense of freedom. Similarly: Choices made from fear create more fear. And experience has taught me that customers gained through fear bring trouble and strife.

I'm not suggesting you have to become a sandal-wearing, lentil-munching, loved-up hippie, to run a good business (though there's nothing wrong with that and I regularly do all of these). But you CAN choose, in each and every moment, whether to feed thoughts that fill you with fear, or thoughts that move you back towards feeling happiness, freedom and love. (I give you the full how-to on this in Step 2).

This isn't about positivity-white-washing. It's about consciously choosing to manage your internal state, as you take inspired action.

It can feel hard to change your thoughts, if you're used to them running wild, but there's good news. You don't have to. The exercise you've just done shows you that your thoughts, emotions and physical sensations are all linked. Change one and you'll affect the others. So if you want to move from a fear-based experience to one that's close to love, focus on your body. Consciously shift your posture, your breathing, your facial expression and the other things that changed to be those from your happy memory. Then move the focus point in your body that was the 'fear' emotion to the place that your body felt the happier memory. Take three deep breaths to anchor it and then get on with your day.

So here's the question I invite you to consider:

> *Is your Big Why coming from a place of love or fear?*
> *And is that what you really want?*

"Live What You Love" And All That **

If you're stuck in a day-job you hate, or running a business that has become a millstone around your neck, then being told to 'follow your passion' or 'live what you love' is going to push your buttons.

Yet it's true that when you follow your passion, the customers and the money come, but only if you have a powerful Big Vision and have cleared out your blocks.

Most of us end up in the career or business we're in out of habit, rather than choice. And sometimes we might feel like there is no way to change what we're doing. So I want to let you in on a secret:

Living what you love is a moment-by-moment choice.
You can always choose to love what you live.

If you don't feel you can change what you're doing, you can always choose how to experience it. You can choose to enjoy it – to give it your all – to do what you do best, and to do it well. You can weave your Big Why into almost any activity, with a little imagination. And then make sure there's an extra dollop of doing things that make your heart sing, outside of your working hours.

Living what you love brings you success and magnetises your Dream Audience because it shifts you from someone who is stuck on the complaining train, en route to the land of victimhood (see Step 2 on 'Secondary Gain') to being someone who is happy and living a life from a place of gratitude and personal power.

I am where I am and it's the best starting point I could
ever have for the next stage of my life's journey.
Where do I want to go from here?

It's never too late to change direction, if what you're doing isn't working for you. Louise Hay didn't open Hay House Publishing until she was 62. Anton Bruckner didn't compose his first symphony until he was 41. Laura Ingolls Wilder, author of the Little House On The Prairie series, didn't publish the first of these until she was in her sixties. One of my friends, Rosa, didn't start to train as a meditation teacher until she was in her eighties. If you're still breathing, then connecting with your Big Why and living what you love – or choosing to love what you live – is still an option for you. And there's another ingredient in this recipe:

A Quiet Word About Your Inner Genius...

I feel passionately about spending as much time as I can in what Gay Hendricks, in his book The Big Leap, describes as your Zone Of Genius. My clients like to think of it as their 'superpower'. It's the stuff you're brilliant at (Inner Critic permitting), where the magic happens, where you love it so much that you lose track of time.

But most of us spend very little of our time in that zone.

If you really want to make a difference in the world, then it's essential that your Big Vision and your Big Message line up with your Zone Of Genius.

I've links to find out more about Gay Hendricks' work, over at the Readers' Club, if this is resonating for you. There's also an insight-packed interview waiting for you. Nancy Marmolejo mentors entrepreneurs and business leaders about how to spot your deepest talents and inner genius. Here is some of what Nancy wants to share with you:

Nancy has a natural gift for being able to see past your fears and self-protection layers, to be able to connect with your innate beauty and inner genius. She intuitively knows which questions to ask, and she loves 'joining the dots', to help you figure out your natural talents and gifts for the world. When you talk with Nancy, her heartfelt passion for seeing the 'real' you and your talents is magnetising.

But Nancy admits she's not sitting in an Ivory Tower on this. Years ago, not long after she established her business, she was having great success with her social media campaigns, and people were asking her how she did it. Her advice helped them to create breakthroughs and, almost without realising, her business direction shifted. She ended up in the realms of teaching tech stuff and social media strategy, losing the connection with her own, inner genius. She was doing a great job and serving her clients well, but it wasn't fulfilling her.

Then life 'conspired' to give her the kick she needed, to make her wake up and realise that she had been heading in the wrong direction. Nancy had the courage to change course and step into her 'real mission'; since then she has flourished and is reaching a much larger audience, having a much bigger impact than she would have had, had she kept on with what she was 'good at', instead of what she is 'great at'.

Nancy describes 'genius' as being our exceptional, natural abilities. It's not an intellectual thing. They're the things we love doing, which make our hearts sing, which we're really good at. When we build our business or career around our talent, we love what we do, and we are living what we love.

So many of us resist connecting with our deepest talents, perhaps because of childhood conditioning or self-esteem issues. We settle for 'mediocre', because we feel scared; and that's understandable. But when you connect with what you are really good at and build on it, your confidence will grow; you will start to trust in your gifts; you will want to use them more.

It might not seem possible to build your income around your talent and genius, and it's an objection that often gets in the way of making a difference in the world. If that is the case for you, then Nancy would encourage you to consciously choose to express your genius in whatever way you can, within your current circumstances. There is always a way, if you allow it!

If your current business is struggling, it could be that you're doing what Nancy did (and I did… Listen to the interview!), and heading in a direction that doesn't ignite your inner passion and excitement, doing things that you're 'good at', when your Soul is yearning for 'genius'.

Once you are ready to take the leap and make following your talent and genius your passion, you still need to be a 'grown up' about it and have a strategy for how you will create something that allows you to put food in the fridge. When you throw away the rule book, you might be surprised at the creative ways you could make this happen.

If you're stuck on figuring out what your inner talent and genius are, please make sure you listen to Nancy's full interview now, before we move with the rest of this Handbook.

What's Your Big Vision?

*How do you want to **matter**? What's your legacy going to be?*

Your Big Vision is about the difference that you are here to make - the movement you want to create - the revolution you want to start. Once you know what's motivating you, your Big Why, then it's much easier to connect with your Big Vision. – your 'How?"

It doesn't have to be perfect - and it doesn't have to be 'stuck in time' - it's not a 'forever' Big Vision. And you can't get it 'wrong' – each iteration moves you closer to being who you really are and the 'Dharma' we talked about on page 45.

Very few people have clarity on this. We might run from it because we feel scared, or inadequate or time-poor or wonder how we would make enough money to pay the bills. The good and the bad news is that we'll be dealing with all of those blocks in this Handbook.

It's Ok To Ask For What You Want – In Fact, It's The Only Way You'll Ever Get It

Have you noticed how easily children let us know what they want and need? Then it's as though we spend their entire education trying to drum that out of them, getting them to hide their desires and put social etiquette ahead of their dreams.

Let's take the example of Olympic athletes. They know what they want. You can see it in their faces as they run. You can see it in their muscles as they jump, throw, swim, sail and ride. They are putting every bit of effort into going for what they want - achieving their dreams. They trust. And they expect to succeed. They have taken the actions needed to get them to where they want to be. They aren't pretending.

And by doing this, they are inspiring us. They are showing us the full extent of what is possible when we focus all of our attention, efforts, thoughts, feelings and emotions on steering our choices in the direction of what we want.

Not what we don't want. But what we want instead. It's ok to ask for what you want, especially when it's a desire or dream that could make a difference to the world.

What are you asking for today? And are you asking loudly enough? Shall we find out? Because that's what your Big Vision is all about.

Exercise: What's Your Big Vision?

As in the Big Why exercise, I suggest you start with 3 deep sighing breaths, to come back to this moment, and then allow the answers to bubble up for you.

1. Who do I help and how? Which pain-points or problems do I solve?
2. What difference do I want to make?
3. What makes me different?
4. Who do I love working with - and why?
5. Which revolution do I want to start?
6. What would I create in the world, if money and time were no object, and I knew I couldn't fail?
7. Where do I want to be in 12 months' time? In 5 years' time?
8. What is important to me, in the context of my Big Vision?
9. What do I believe about my ability to create my Big Vision?
10. What might get in my way?
11. Is there anything I need to start doing or thinking differently, to allow my Big Vision to become a reality?

"Revolution", from question 5, is a word people sometimes object to because it feels too big and too scary. If you focus on growing a business or a career, then you'll grow a business or career. If you focus on growing a movement, on changing the world, on making an experience for people that changes lives, then you will grow a movement that starts a revolution. You need to stand for something, or nobody will remember you.

When you stand for something and you build your foundations on that, there might be a 'Marmite reaction'. For those who aren't in the UK, Marmite is a yeast extract savoury spread that you put on toast, and which people either love or hate. Sounds gross. I'm a Marmite-lover.

If everybody likes you, you're being too 'beige'.

When you stand for something and you've cleared out your blocks, you will magnetise those who want to work with you. That's what I mean by starting a revolution: standing for something and wanting to make a difference that people can connect with and identify with.

When you get your audience falling in love with your message and the revolution you want to inspire, they'll flock to you, like moths to a candle flame, and they'll ignore your competitors.

If that's in a business, it's easy to imagine. If it's in somebody else's business, then who do you want to be in the context of your role? And how do you want to create the change that needs to happen in that business? In any area of life, how do you want to fully express yourself in the gifts that you bring to the world? Let me know about your Big Vision in the Readers' Club discussion forum. And if you'd like a stretch objective of creating a vision board for your Big Vision, there is a 'how-to' guide in there, too.

How Can You Move Towards This, If You're Employed?

You don't have to run a business to make a difference in the world with your Big Vision. For example, one of my clients has a Big Vision of 'expanding and growing myself, whilst raising happy kids'. She uses it as a decision-metric in her management position at work and her 'to do' list at home. You can bring your Big Vision into someone else's business – or your home life – simply by living and breathing it.

But if you are looking to make the leap from being employed to running your own business, then I strongly suggest you work through this Handbook first.

Draw up a clear plan, having cleared out your inner blocks, and then ramp things up. Be ruthless in clearing out distractions and time-thieves, so that you have the time to focus on your dreams, as well as your current commitments. Little and often tends to produce faster results.

It's ok to start small, and build on your successes, rather than allowing your inner perfectionist to stop you from ever taking the first step. I suggest you go through this Handbook and focus on the actions that will make the biggest difference for you. Then, as your dreams grow, re-read it and take the next level of actions. And remember your moral support and idea-bouncing Tribe is waiting for you, in the Readers' Club.

And here's an example of how important clarity about your Big Vision can be, when it comes to creating a movement and inspiring others to join you, moving them from angry to inspired to take massive action:

In late 2014, I heard about a piece of European legislation that was designed to stop big businesses from locating in low-tax EU Member States, in order to benefit from lower sales tax (VAT) rates. The intention, for digital downloads, was that the businesses should levy VAT according to where the customer was based, rather than the business's location. This makes sense, because VAT is a 'consumption tax', so should be charged in the country where the product or service will be 'consumed' or used.

It applied to everything from eBooks to downloaded software to online courses, to digital knitting patterns, to website hosting. But it didn't apply if there was enough 'human intervention' to mean that the service was not 'digitally delivered'. So a live webinar, for example, although delivered over the internet, would fall outside of the rules, but paying to watch the replay would class it as 'digitally-delivered'.

The intention behind the legislation was honourable. It was passed by the governments of all 28 EU Member States. But there was a problem:

Most micro businesses didn't have access to the data required to prove their customer's location, and their shopping cart systems couldn't handle the complex VAT calculations, with VAT potentially needing to be paid at two different rates, to two different countries, in one invoice, if someone purchased, say, a live webinar at the same time as an eBook.

It risked accidentally closing hundreds of thousands of businesses. A group of us got chatting on social media and decided to look for the campaign group to support, as it was only five weeks until the rules became law. But there wasn't one. So we formed EU VAT Action.

It became a living, breathing lesson in the power of intention and the importance of your Big Vision. We ended up representing thousands of micro businesses in meetings at Downing Street and the European Parliament and Commission. Our Big Vision was clear:

Let's fix this mess and make sure nothing like it can happen again, but we don't care about blame. That's someone else's problem.

We wanted to lead a positive campaign, rather than look for heads to roll. And we got feedback, throughout the following year, that our no-blame attitude, along with our calm, data-backed arguments, allowed us to co-create breakthroughs, including the 'light touch' concessions we negotiated with the UK Government, in the final days before the new laws were introduced. When things got tough and we secretly wanted to scream, coming back to the no-blame, forward-looking essence of our Big Vision kept us positive and allowed us to lead and inspire, rather than spreading negativity and anger.

What's Your Big Message?

If you could tell the world just one thing…?

Your Big Message is what you stand for. It's the next stage of turning your Big Vision into reality – an expression of the "What?". It's like a 'super-goal' for the next phase of your journey, which can be broken down into your smaller, step-by-step goals and monthly key action steps.

Exercise: What's Your Big Message?

Here's a simple exercise to help you get a feel for your Big Message. There's a worksheet and audio waiting for you at the Readers' Club.

- If you could tell the world just one thing, right now, what might it be?
- What might the next step 'inspired action' be, on this journey? What might make the biggest difference?
- What would 'success' mean to you, in this context? How might you measure it?

It's really important to be able to simplify your message to just one or two sentences - something that people 'get', which inspires them.

- Pause for a moment; *feel* into what your next Big Message might be.
- What are the main goals I need to create, so that my Big Message turns into reality?
- What are the key things I need to achieve, to do this? In the next six months? In the next year? In the next five years?

Make sure it's something that excites you – to which you're prepared to give a large amount of your energy and time of the coming year(s). If not, it needs cranking up or reworking. Top tip: make sure it is *your* Big Message, and not one that someone else has persuaded you into. It's *your* life, not theirs. Please be true to yourself on this.

If you want inspiration from seeing the Big Message for other readers there's a special discussion thread in the Readers' Club forum.

Who Is Your Dream Audience?

What's secretly motivating you to make the difference you're here to make?

One of the biggest mistakes we can make is to try to please – or serve – everyone. Very few people have clarity on who they are serving – who their dream customer is, and who it isn't. And when I talk to networking or business events about the vital importance of having a tight niche – and 'owning' it – most people object violently. I sometimes feel I'm dragging them, kicking and screaming, towards defining who they would love to work with. When I see this happening, I know it's likely to be because of:

The Oprah Complex

Don't get me wrong, I love Oprah. But it is so frustrating to watch a brilliantly passionate world-changer exhaust themselves, achieving nearly nothing, diluting their message, because they're trying to appeal to as many people as Oprah does.

This is an epidemic - and definitely not just in the self-help world.

For example, when I talk to entrepreneurs about who they serve and they reply, "Oh, everyone!" then there's a subconscious 'Oprah Complex' running. And it's a fear-based mistake. We do it because we feel scared to turn potential customers away. Oprah has the funds, following, support team and platform to serve nearly everyone. If you believe you have the budget, PR team and energy to be nearly-everything to pretty-much everyone, then go ahead and 'do an Oprah'.

But, paradoxically, you're going to grow your business much faster if you choose a narrow niche and dive in deeply. Becoming well-known in your super-tight niche creates credibility and visibility. You will 'own' that niche – people will recognise you, get to know you, and learn to trust what you're saying. And then you can easily expand, because you are already established as a credible expert. As you grow, that expansion continues, until one day Oprah might be phoning you for world-domination advice.

But if you start with a super-wide, unfocused audience, and try to become their expert, then you'll be spreading yourself so thinly that the likelihood of success is near-zero. It's really hard to become a credible authority in a multi-billion person niche.

So I strongly suggest starting with the super-narrow-niche of your absolute Dream Audience. It know it can feel scary and, believe me, I have listened to objections to niching from so many entrepreneurs (and from myself!), over the years, but if you try to appeal to everyone, then you're likely to resonate with no one.

Don't be afraid that the niche will be too small. Of the billions of people on this planet, there really are likely to be enough in your chosen audience to grow a successful business. And once you have picked that 'home' to start in, live it and breathe it. But more on that in a bit.

And, also, please don't feel that because you're defining who you would really love to work with, you're in any way rejecting others. You're actually doing your non-ideal audience a favour. If you'd rather not work with them – or you just feel 'ok' about working with them – then they wouldn't get as much from the interaction as someone you really resonate with, would they? So surely it's fairer on them to let them find someone they're an ideal match for, to work with, instead? Compassionately, but firmly, dissuading unsuitable clients from working with you increases your credibility and gains you respect.

When you know who is in your Dream Audience and they resonate with your Big Message, you'll grow a community, not just customers.

> Lorraine Dallmeier, CEO of the Organic Skincare School Formula Botanica, proves this. She originally feared that a company about how to set up your own organic skincare business might be too small a niche, but a couple of years later, she has students on her courses in 95 countries, studying skincare and launching successful businesses of their own. Lorraine dominates her field and is regularly asked to join industry-expert panels and even judge awards. That wouldn't have happened had she started out trying to 'please everyone'. There's more from Lorraine in Step 6.

When you live and breathe your Dream Audience, walking in their shoes, knowing how they describe their problems, what they have tried, what worked, what they feel guilty about because it didn't work, then you will easily attract them. And they will rave about working with you.

So how do you figure out your Dream Audience?

"Before you build an audience, you need to decide who you want in the seats." ~ Derek Halpern

Well, things have changed a lot since my market research days, when our target audience was defined mainly by social class, geographical location and educational level, with a tiny bit of 'attitudinal' stuff sneaking its way in. Nowadays target audiences are all about behaviours, beliefs, values, identity and the educational levels and income brackets are just a part of it.

When figuring out your Dream Audience, I suggest you start by reviewing your answers to the worksheets on your Big Why, your Big Vision and your Big Message, because it is essential to choose the audience that resonates with your message, rather than changing your message to resonate with the wrong audience.

Even if you have been in business for a while, it's important to sanity-check who you want to serve, each time you're getting ready to step up to the next level. As you expand and grow, your Dream Audience will shift. Here are some questions you can ask yourself, to help you deepen your understanding of who you are here to serve, and why.

Exercise: Who Is Your Dream Audience?

To get the most from this, you need to suspend your logical brain for a few minutes and imagine you can mind-read your Dream Audience's answers. Then, once you have a good idea about it, **it's really worth getting onto Skype with some of your favourite clients** and asking them some of these questions, to get hard data.

There's a worksheet and audio for this, over at the Readers' Club.

- Who do you most love working with?
- What, specifically, do you love about working with them?
- What kinds of results do they get, compared to those who you resonate with less?
- What kind of person are they? Male / female? Age? Kids? What kind of job? Where do they live? *... continues*

- What makes them tick? What makes them laugh? What makes them cry?
- How does their typical day look?
- What is important to them?
- What do they believe… about themselves?
- … about the world?
- … about life?
- How do they love to relax?
- What do they do when they want to treat themselves?
- How do they make important decisions?
- What's their favourite food / drink / holiday destination?
- What keeps them up at night? What is causing those people pain? What stresses them, which they might not even tell their best friend?
- How do they express those problems? What kinds of words and phrases do they use?
- How do they want to feel instead?
- How, specifically, does your solution take them on that journey?
- Where are they hanging out – online and in the 'real world'?

You can add questions of your own, as they come to you. If you need more inspiration – and given that it's sometimes easier to spot what we *don't'* want, rather than what we *do*:

- Who do you least like working with?
- What, specifically do you not enjoy about working with them?
- Who would you rather work with, instead?

Keep this sheet handy. We're going to refer back to it in Step 4, when you create your Visibility Action Plan.

Visual thinkers often find it helps to create a vision board to keep them focussed on their Dream Audience. You might even want to give your ideal customer a name. And then, whatever you're creating, speak to that ONE person, in your mind. You'll be amazed by the difference this makes.

Once you have a clear description of your Dream Audience, a really useful stretch exercise is to try to boil it all down into one sentence and then keep that near you whenever you're working, as a reminder to stay focussed. For example, my one-sentence Dream Audience for this Handbook is:

Action-takers, on a mission to make a difference in the world, hungry to get their message out there, but secretly scared about stepping up to the next level.

As I have been writing and editing this for you, I have kept coming back to that sentence, to make sure I stay focussed, so that the Handbook will (hopefully!) resonate with you. It's the book I wish I had had ten years ago.

We're got a discussion thread in the Readers' Club where you can share your one-sentence Dream Audience description and even a photo of your Dream Audience vision board. There's a short 'how-to' guide there for you, if you're new to vision-boarding.

And I run regular competitions for people who do this exercise and create a one-sentence audience description and a vision board, because it is so important to know who you are talking to, before you grow your business to the next level. I regularly pick someone at random, to win a breakthrough mentoring session with me or to choose one of my online courses, as a reward for having put in the effort to create a vision board, and for having had the courage to share it with us in the forum.

There are also details of an excellent book to read if your major issue is fear of competitors. If that's coming up for you, you either need to tighten your niche and work on Credibility (see Step 4) or you need to create your own "Blue Ocean", which is the title of the book.

What If You're Feeling Confused?

When I work with people, one of the states of mind they dislike the most is feeling confused (and I'm with you on that!), yet it's surprisingly common.

Whenever we want to make a change, there will come a point where you need to stretch that old comfort zone. And we will normally experience one of two things:

1. Totally clear vision that drives us through with passion

2. Total confusion and that listless feeling of a boat at sea with no wind

Both are valid. But here's the rub: you can't 'force' your way out of the confusion. You can't 'think' your way out of it. If you try, you're likely to end up heading at full steam in what might later feel like the wrong direction.

Confusion Is Your Friend

I know it doesn't feel that way when you're stuck in the middle of it. But maybe it's your Soul's way of telling you that things aren't ready yet. Maybe the timing isn't right. Maybe you're not quite ready at some inside level. Maybe you would have been heading in the wrong direction. Maybe you need to rest and build your energy first.

Imagine if a caterpillar tried to push itself out of its chrysalis too early. Its wings wouldn't be fully formed; it would struggle to fly.

Confusion helps us to see that it isn't yet time to press 'go'. But in these days of high-speed-everything and instant gratification, waiting – resting – pausing – isn't trendy.

Confusion precedes clarity

When I was little, and we were learning about butterflies and caterpillars and the whole chrysalis thing, the only way I could get my head round that metamorphosis was to imagine the caterpillar turning into a kind of soup, which got somehow stirred up into a butterfly. Although I have now moved on from that model, you'll be pleased to hear, it is still a brilliant fit for how I view 'confusion'.

Confusion feels, to me, like a murky soup, where I'm being held like a puppet on strings, with my feet off the ground, until clarity comes, to stop me running at full speed in the wrong direction. I'm held, somehow, in that chrysalis until the 'soup' of confusion clears and the butterfly can emerge. Yet I so often find myself using up energy trying to run, trying to get started, before those ideas are fully formed. It's the excitement of starting new things.

From the chrysalis of confusion can emerge the most beautiful clarity, ready to spread its wings and make a bigger difference in the world. But to experience that, you need to honour the 'confusion' process.

Please notice how I said 'honour' and not 'indulge'. This isn't about wallowing; it's about resting and allowing and accepting, if time is needed.

If you're not sure which of these two you're doing, you might find the answers to this statement insightful:

"I can't have clarity, because..."

Look at your answers. Are they coming from a space of genuine 'stirring things up and figuring it out'? Or are they more about being scared to commit, not feeling good enough, or some other inner block?

But what if you've had enough of 'confusion'? What can do you to start to move on through?

Sometimes You've Gotta Shake It Up – And See Where It Lands

If you're feeling 'done' with feeling confused, then you need to get moving. That might be physical movement, to shake off that 'stuckness'. It might be a change to your routine. Or it might be taking a small action, to test whether it feels like the right direction. Or it might be stretching a totally unrelated comfort zone. Doing something different gives you a barometer to measure whether it feels right.

And if your Monkey Mind is too busy telling you 'fed-up-with-feeling-stuck' stories, then ask your body to give you the 'yes / no' answer, instead. It never lies.

If you're feeling stuck or confused over your Big Why, your Big Vision or your Big Message, then mentoring can really help. As little as a single session can give you the breakthrough you need.

And if you want extra help right now, I've got two deep-dive video masterclasses for you over at the Readers' Club. In the Big Vision Masterclass, I interviewed Andre Hartwich, a Clarity Consultant and Coach, on how to get clear about your life purpose, even if you're drowning in confusion. I have worked with Andre, myself, in the past and I highly recommend him, if you feel your Big Why, Big Vision or Big Message need refining. His intuitive ability to compassionately kick you in the right direction is gold dust. He has a knack for asking you the exact questions that unlock your dreams and Dharma.

In the Big Message Masterclass, I interviewed Silke Zanker about how your journey is your message. She is a TEDx Curator and Mentor and a Leadership Consultant. One of her gifts is helping you to unravel how your journey leads into your Big Vision and your Big Message – and how to communicate this in a way that will inspire your audience. The gems that Silke and Andre share with you in these two masterclasses have been described as life-changing, by many who have watched them.

So many of us use lack of clarity as an excuse for not getting started. The world needs your message – your unique voice – today. So once you've played with confusion for a while, please get yourself some support or mentoring, to lovingly kick your butt through to the other side. So many people spend years in limbo because they're looking for perfection in their clarity, which may never come.

Important:

Wherever you are 'up to' with Clarity is just fine.

If you have total clarity, then that's great. If it's all still a bit 'mushy', that's fine, too. Often there are below-the-surface blocks to be cleared, to allow us to truly step onto our Path. And that is what the next phase of this Handbook is for.

All I ask is that you make sure you don't use 'lack of clarity' as an excuse not to move towards your dreams, to make the difference you're here to make. So park your Clarity where it is, for now, and please keep moving forward. You can come back to these exercises again, later, once your blocks have been cleared.

How To Gain Decades Of Hindsight In Minutes

How would it feel if you could benefit from decades of future clarity and hindsight, in the next few minutes? In this next exercise, I invite you to imagine that you can time travel. There's a handy little time machine hanging around in your skull that can zip back to the past or imagine the future, and it's time to take a ride in it.

I'd like you to get to try the current version of your Big Why, Big Vision and Big Message on for size, to see how they fit for you, long term, and which shifts or tweaks might make them feel even better. That wisdom is already inside of you, and the next exercise will help you to tap into it. It is one of my favourite clarity-creating techniques.

There's an audio and worksheet for this exercise waiting for you at the Readers' Club. We're talking about this in a special discussion thread, in the forum.

Exercise: A Letter From The 'Future You'

Sitting somewhere quietly, where you won't be disturbed for the next ten minutes, imagine you can zoom forward in time to your 80th birthday party (or beyond!). Really get a sense for who you are, on your 80th birthday, and how life has been. Allow yourself to suspend any disbelief over this, for the next few minutes.

Now, looking back at the Big Why, Big Vision and Big Message the 'you' in the 'now' has been working on, allow the answers to the following questions to bubble up - and please write them down:

- Standing in the Soul-Shoes of the 80-year-old you, looking back at the future that today's Big Why, Big Vision and Big Message created, how does it feel?
- Which aspects of your life do you love?
- What do you need to do / create, over the coming years, to become that person?
- What kinds of thoughts is the 80-year-old you thinking?
- What did you have to give up, to create your Big Vision?
- What did you gain?
- What did the world gain? What difference did you get to make?
- Who did you need to become, to allow that to happen?
- Which blocks or fears did you need to release?
- Why is the 80-year-old 'you' happy that you did this?
- Was your Big Vision big enough? Or does it need to get bigger? Does it need any tweaks?
- Is there any chance that you're using lack of clarity about your Big Vision and life's purpose as a 'excuse' for not getting started? *Hint: many of us do!*
- And finally, is there any advice that the 80-year-old you would give you? Imagine you can write a letter from the 80-year-old you, to the 'you' in the 'now'. Perhaps start with the opening, "I know you might feel scared or overwhelmed that…. but it was so worth it, because…"

When you're finished, come back to the present moment, giving the 80-year-old you a silent 'thank you'; notice what you have learned from this exercise. What are you going to do, today, to put that advice into action?

What To Do When You Have Too Many Ideas

I have lost count of how many times people tell me they're feeling stuck, because they have too many ideas – for their Big Vision or their Big Message or their product or service. I have experienced this myself, too. It can happen whether you're just starting out or stepping up to expand your offerings, or to reach a new audience.

If this is you, you're in good company. If it's a dose of confusion, then let those ideas sit for a while; try them each on for size, in turn; and notice how they feel. Your body always knows the answer.

You want to pick one that gets you excited, because if it doesn't excite you, it won't compel your audience to take action, and you're unlikely to find the commitment and determination to keep going, once the initial inspiration has worn off.

Remember to play to your strengths – your Inner Genius. And if the big issue is about 'how will I make money with this idea?' that's ok, too. We'll cover that one in more detail in a moment.

You've also got the 80th birthday test that we used just now. Instead of using it to check whether your Big Vision is big enough, as we did then, use it to check which of your options your Inner Wisdom is recommending. Try them out, in turn, and ask the wisdom of the 80 year old you which one needs to come next.

You might want to connect with your Intuition, calming your mind's chatter, so you can get answers. And I'm going to guide you through how to do that in Step 4.

But sometimes the 'too many ideas' problem comes up as a means of procrastinating – of putting off taking action and getting started or stepping up to the next level. If you sneakily suspect this might be you, you can ask yourself the questions:

- What am I *gaining* by putting off this decision?
- What am I scared might happen, if I make a choice?

Let your answers bubble up and write them down, because solutions are waiting for you in Step 2.

And you might find that you need some mentoring, to help you get clarity. If, having worked through this Handbook and the bonus resources you're still not clear, then the relatively small investment that a mentoring session will cost will reap dividends for you, for years ahead.

And if you're stuck with trying to 'find' your life's purpose – that 'perfect' thing you're 'meant' to be doing, then I have a message for you.

You don't find your life's purpose. You choose it.

I spent some time in Assisi, while I was editing this Handbook's manuscript, meditating in St. Francis's cave. He was one of the greatest spreaders of peace and love of all time. But even he initially struggled to figure out what his life's purpose was. He had visions that he thought meant he was 'supposed' to repair the San Damiano church in Assisi, which he did. Only once this was done did he realise that he had been dreaming too small.

His calling was, in fact, to bring the teachings of the gospel to life, as an ambassador of peace and love. 800 years on his message still has a profound effect in the world.

Your Big Vision and Big Message change as you grow. I know that mine will be quite different by the time I'm 90, and that's ok.

So my biggest advice to you is that:

You can't get this wrong.

Just pick the idea that you love the most and get started. It's easier to change the direction of a moving ship.

How To Handle Real Life Vs. Big Vision Dreams

When you get excited about your Big Vision and dreams, reality can come with quite a bump. We look around us and see the day-job or the 'to do' list or the kids screaming or our lack of confidence, or time, or money.

If that is even hinting at happening for you, here are some suggestions to help you to bring your Big Vision in as part of your life, as it is now, whilst you journey towards where you want to be.

I suggest you start by working through this Handbook. It will help you to spot and clear out your blocks, and then to create a practical plan that will move you to where you want to be. Allow whatever transition you might be dreaming of to take the time it needs.

And, whatever your circumstances, look at how you could express your Big Why, your Big Vision and your Big Message, through the life you are already living. You might be surprised by how creative you can get on this.

Many of us feel under pressure to turn our Big Vision into a full-time business. But it doesn't have to be that way. There's nothing wrong with working towards it 'out-of-hours', or building up to work part time in a job and part time on your Big Vision. In our current society, we still need money to put food in the fridge. You're not going to be much use to your Dream Audience if you can't afford to eat.

This is *your* life, and only you have the right to choose how to express your Dharma.

And, once you have a plan, broken down into manageable steps, the techniques in this Handbook will help you with your blocks, your fears, your excuses, and with cranking up your commitment. So you're much more likely to succeed, however many plates you're juggling.

Remember that our lack of time and our sense of overwhelm come from lack of clarity and connection with our Big Why. And they come from the stories we tell ourselves about not having enough time. If you were to take tiny steps, each day, towards your Big Vision, you'll make progress faster than you might imagine.

As the saying goes, "anything you can imagine, you can create." If you really want to do it, you'll find a way, as soon as you let go of your 'how' having to fit with other people's expectations and assumptions of what your journey or destination should look like.

And you are not alone: please make the most of our friendly Readers' Club forum for support, accountability and idea-bouncing.

I'm curious: what might your first step be?

It's Time To Line Up With Your Big Vision, Your Big Why And Your Big Message

In other words, why I don't give two hoots about your mindset - and I don't think you should, either. It's the tail wagging the dog. We've all heard the quote that your success is 20% down to the actions you take, but 80% down to your attitude? Over a decade of mentoring passionate World-Changers has shown me that's no longer true; it's not enough. And I want to share with you exactly why – and what you can be doing instead. And, perhaps surprisingly, the solution is much, much easier.

Now, don't get me wrong, I agree with the concept that your results are governed by something much more important than your 'outside world' actions. But to say that it's all down to your 'attitude' or 'mindset' feels like a risky over-simplification.

Let's start by working with and deconstructing the word 'mindset'. (Thank you Bob Buckley for the nudge on this! Check out his thoughts in the Readers' Club).

The dictionary might define it by talking about our way of thinking and the opinions that we hold – in other words, our thought patterns and our beliefs.

The two halves of the word are 'mind' and 'set'. In English, at a subconscious level, talking about 'mindset' gives our unconscious mind the instruction that this is a 'set' position – something solid, fixed and unchangeable. If you think about 'mindset' and feel it in your body (I know that might sound crazy – please bear with me) then it usually feels solid. And for many of us it produces a contraction and tensing of muscles in the gut or the jaw and throat.

It can trigger sensations of tension and forcing and resistance – taking you out of flow and ease. You're effectively trying to control your thoughts, to 'force' them to line up with how you feel they 'should' be.

In addition, psychologists have known for decades that one of the most important factors for success is a person's level of behavioural flexibility. If your mind – your beliefs, opinions and thoughts – are fixed or set, then your behaviours are very unlikely to be flexible.

Your mindset is about what you habitually think, your beliefs about what is possible, and your choices about what is right or wrong. It is an 'effect' of the stuff below the surface. So if you're trying to control it, without doing the deep-dive work, you set yourself up for a rocky ride.

So maybe we need to look at 'attitude', instead? That gets a similar definition: "a settled way of thinking or feeling about something." In other words, it's another 'set in stone' frame of mind. Is that likely to lead to flexibility? And why do we need behavioural flexibility, anyway?

Psychologist Carol Dweck identified the vital difference between those with a 'fixed mindset' and a 'growth mindset'. Those with a fixed mindset tended to give up, when faced with a challenge. They believed you could either do something or you couldn't, and if you couldn't, then there was little point in trying. Those with a growth mindset tended to see challenges as an opportunity to learn and grow. They would thrive when pushed outside of their comfort zone, though they were just as likely to find it difficult as the fixed mindset people. The difference was that those with a growth mindset had the flexibility to adapt their thoughts and behaviours, to be able to excel, rather than just 'coping'.

If we could completely predict and control life and everybody in it, we would be able to get by with whichever behaviours and habits we're already running and all would be fine. But we can't. Change happens. Things go wrong. Things go brilliantly. Opportunities come up. Some pass us by.

We don't set our course and then keep heading in that direction, stubborn as a mountain goat, forever. Life isn't like that. It would be dull, if it were. We're like ships on the ocean currents, constantly adapting our course, to reach our destination. That requires flexibility of behaviour, which requires flexibility of thinking (a growth mindset), which requires flexibility of beliefs – and ditching those hidden blocks that would otherwise get in the way. We need to allow our 'who am I?' to shift, as we learn and grow.

No amount of positive thinking is going to dig you out of a hole you fall into due to hidden blocks like Imposter Syndrome or following a course that's not lined up with your Big Vision. You need to do some deeper work.

So what can you do instead? You need to get your thoughts and actions to support what you want to create. Clear out your blocks – the limiting beliefs, fears, out-of-date excuses and unsupportive habits. When your 'who am I?', what's important to you, what you believe about yourself and the world, and what you're thinking, all support each other, you can create magic. And your 'mindset' or 'attitude' look after themselves.

If you're trying to think thoughts that clash with your beliefs, for example, or 'pretending' your way into a 'positive attitude' about a project that you're secretly scared of, then you create an inner conflict. You get stuck in the middle of a ferocious tug of war between the part of you who believes you can do it and the part of you that believes you can't.

One of the most effective ways of bringing your Big Why, your Big Vision and your Big Message into your daily life is to consciously 'choose' your mindset, by setting an intention, before you get out of bed in the morning. It can act like a filter in your brain, deciding how you want to experience your day and the role you want to play. Before you get out of bed each day, you might like to ask yourself,

"What's my keyword for how I choose to experience life today? And how would that allow me to express my Dharma today?"

Then, at key points in your day, go back to that word and allow yourself to fully experience the feeling of it, in the context of whatever is happening around you. The shift is so profound, yet so simple to do.

Exercise: Where Am I On 'Clarity'?

To wrap up this section, here's a space for you to jot down notes on where you are up to, so far.

My Big Why is:

My Big Vision is:

My Big Message is:

What have I learned so far? Any lightbulbs? Surprises? Insights?

Which questions do I still have? (Readers' Club forum!)

What action will I take towards my dreams and Dharma, in the next 24 hours?

To support you in your Clarity journey, there is a bonus guided meditation for you in the Readers' Club, to help you get grounded, to clear your thinking and to connect with your Big Why, your Big Vision and your Big Message. It's ideal to do at the start of your day, or before starting work on a creative project.

And now we've done that, it's time to move on to clearing out your hidden blocks. Are you ready?

Clear Out The Blocks

Our deepest fear is not that we are inadequate. Our deepest fear is that we are powerful beyond measure. It is our light, not our darkness, that most frightens us.
We ask ourselves, "Who am I to be brilliant, gorgeous, talented, fabulous?" Actually, who are you not to be?
Marianne Williamson, from A Return To Love

There's epidemic that no one is talking about, which is closing more businesses and squashing more dreams than the financial crisis ever could.

If you have a dream - a Big Vision you want to create - but you're not on track yet, then it's most likely NOT because you're missing skills and tech solution wizardry. It's probably because you're self-sabotaging, running subconscious blocks. And most of us don't even realise that we're doing it.

When you put a dream out there, you need to allow yourself to *become* the person who lives and breathes that dream. Every fibre of your Being needs to *believe* you can do it. You need to take the actions that the 'you' who has achieved it 'already' would take, thinking the thoughts the would think. When you act on that dream from the 'space' of the 'old' you, with the old beliefs, the old limits, the old fears, the old excuses, the old baggage, the old thought habits, you are likely get in your own way and self-sabotage. I'm not judging you in any way on this. We all do it.

- We're too 'busy' to return that call
- We fill our time up with less important things, and convince ourselves they're urgent
- We say 'no' when we secretly wanted to say 'yes'
- We say 'yes' when we know, deep-down, that will fill up too much of our time and make our dreams fall off the table
- We play down our strengths and use false modesty, so as not to shine
- We're easily distracted and struggle to get projects finished
- We leave it slightly too late to reply to that scary-but-exciting offer that would have opened new doors
- We get a new client enquiry, but automatically start offering

discounts, even before they have asked about pricing
- We don't go for that interview, because we're scared we might not get the job - or perhaps that we might

We don't usually do it deliberately. We do it because the little voice inside saying, "I'd love this opportunity!" gets drowned out by the bigger voice telling us all the reasons why we're not qualified or not good enough, and dwelling on everything that could go wrong.

If you step up to do something that's a challenge - something you might feel scared of or not prepared for, then we subconsciously do things that guarantee our failure. Our actions support our inner dialogue and beliefs about ourselves – and how life is 'supposed' to be. We're not usually aware of our hidden blocks and people rarely talk about them. Yet they are the most critical indicator of whether or not we'll succeed with what we want to create.

We get paralysed by our fears and use our excuses to protect ourselves. We subconsciously self-sabotage, to give ourselves the excuse for not succeeding. Alain de Botton (Author and TV Presenter) explains that:

working towards your dreams will finally start "when the fear of doing nothing exceeds the fear of doing it badly."

That's why knowing how to spot your hidden blocks (even the masters of disguise) is essential. In this section we'll do that – and I'll give you a step by step 'how to' for letting them go, in a healthy, empowering, white-wash-free way, so you can step into your future Soul-Shoes and get on with making the difference you're here to make.

I will be sharing with you the exact same strategies that we would use, if we were working one-to-one together, or Masterminding.

So many people miss out this stage. But everyone who is successful has had to do the 'inside work' and deal with their blocks, at some point. Sometimes becoming aware of what your blocks are and deciding that you don't want to carry those bags any more can often be enough to release them. The sense of relief is incredible.

Anything you can imagine, you can create, as long as you give yourself permission.

I want to inspire and empower you to give yourself that permission.

Why Do So Many Of Us Resist Clearing Out Our Blocks?

What is that 'crazy behaviour' **doing** *for you?*

It's not enough, 'just' getting clear your dreams and goals. You might hire a coach to hold you accountable and get you 'pushing on through', with grit and determination, taking 'massive action'. Entire industries are built on SMART[2] goals, which make no mention of pre-empting or clearing out hidden blocks – or the vital importance of the goals being meaningful to you, which is why we started with the Big Why[3]. If you're in the corporate world, then your team will most likely to be able to push through the blocks. There will be processes in place to make sure they do. But if you *are* your business, if you don't clear out your inner blocks, then you're making the journey so much harder than it needs to be – and limiting your likelihood of success.

Your hidden fears, out-of-date excuses, limiting beliefs and old habits mean you'll need to work harder to overcome life's obstacles. You'll need to use more willpower and determination, to get things done. It takes more effort and energy. You'll risk giving up, usually just moments before success was due to show up. You might find you never even get started.

As a species, we have highly evolved 'coping mechanisms' to get us through life's challenges, and these often stem from our childhood. What worked when you were seven is unlikely to be the ideal strategy now you're an adult, when it comes to making a difference in the world. Your inner seven year old had very different thought. The coping choices they made are unlikely to be those you would choose today; with the life experience and world-view you now have. But they're hard-wired into your brain's autopilot behaviours and when the trigger button is pressed, we fire those old patterns off, without even realising.

It means that you risk your inner 7-year-old making your biggest business and life decisions.

But it doesn't have to be that way. We might feel scared of looking in

---

[2] SMART = Specific, Measurable, Assignable, Realistic, Time-Related Goals, initially proposed by Washington. George T. Doran in 1981.
[3] Harvard 2014 paper on setting goals – link in Readers' Club

the mirror and dealing with these out-of-date behaviours because, at some deep level, the thought of letting them go feels terrifying. We might subconsciously feel convinced that if we let go of that belief or fear or excuse, then our world will fall apart. Here's the crazy thing:

*Self-sabotage is **doing** something for us; we're getting something from it. That's what keeps us stuck.*

Whenever someone struggles to make a change, it's usually either because they weren't fully committed to it, or because it was meeting a hidden, unmet need. Yes, I know this sounds crazy, but the destructive behaviour or thought habit or belief that is costing you sleep is, at some deep level, trying to help you.

'Secondary gain' is all about what will we lose if we make the change, if we let go of that belief; if we let go of the excuse; if we make that shift. In any given situation, we're either scared of changing, or we're scared of staying the same. And whichever one risks causing us the greater pain is the one that wins.

At a deep level, each of those blocks has a positive intention. Just as your unconscious mind makes sure you spot the speeding car, before you step off the pavement to cross the road, so it runs those old patterns, to keep you emotionally safe. In some way, your blocks are trying to protect you.

Dealing with them means also dealing with the unmet need to feel safe or protected, in that specific context. Otherwise that 'need' will find another way to be met, by creating another behaviour that holds you back.

For example, we all know someone who knows how to get attention, by creating drama. They might have a need to feel loved and the way they're meeting that need is by creating drama in the life of everybody around them; by being an energy vampire. Until they can meet the need to be loved in a healthy way, they're not going to change that behaviour, no matter how much you yell at them. In fact, yelling at them gives them attention which, perversely, meets their need for drama.

If you want them to change, telling them to change the behaviour simply won't work. It requires willpower. They haven't made the choice and commitment to change. What you need to do instead is to help them to feel loved in a healthier way, then the behaviour will no longer be needed. And to stop dancing the dance with them.

Secondary gain is about what we *get* from a belief, thought pattern or behaviour, even if, to the outside world, it seems bonkers. When you identify the unmet need and deal with it in a more healthy way, then the behaviour, the belief, the limit, the block will float away. You will no longer have to fight it. Dealing with Secondary Gain makes changing your life easier.

It's the easiest way to change a habit. Maybe you've been doing stuff that seems illogical. All that's happened is that good reason has got out of date. It needs an upgrade. And it's ok to accept that – and to forgive yourself. It's in the past and you can move forwards with a clean slate.

If you deny yourself an unmet need, then you're giving your unconscious mind the clear message that you don't deserve to have your needs met or somehow aren't good enough - and that gives your Inner Critic (more soon!) permission to run riot.

How To Spot Your Unmet Needs

There are four questions I normally ask clients when we work on this, and there is an audio and a workbook to guide you through this process, over at the Readers' Club. It's all about identifying what you potentially gain from making a change, but also acknowledging what you are secretly scared you might lose. You can also use them to apply leverage to yourself, to create that 'basta-moment' and kick start your way towards shifting that out-of-date habit.

Exercise: How To Spot Your Secondary Gain

Just let the answers bubble up, without judgement. It's ok if they send your head into a spin; some of them are meant to. There's a worksheet, audio and discussion thread for this, in the Readers' Club.

- If I make this change, what will I gain? How will it help me?
- If I make this change, what do I risk losing? What might I give up? What am I secretly scared might happen?
- What do I gain from not changing?
- What do I risk losing, if I don't change?

Aim to get 3-7 answers to each question. You might be amazed what comes up. Please do this without judgement or analysis - just let them flow up from your non-thinking mind. Sometimes it's amazing what comes up - and those are the gems you can work with.

Once you have the answers to your questions, some of those worries will just fall away, by virtue of you becoming aware of them. Others may need a little work. And there may be situations where your needs clash with other needs in your life. If that happens, then it's time to get creative. For those situations, you can ask yourself:

"How could I meet both of these needs, if anything were possible?"

You might be surprised at the answers.

And for any that you can feel are blocking your path to your dreams, you can ask yourself:

"How could I meet this need in a healthier way?"

There's a special discussion thread for Secondary Gain in the Readers' Club forum and a bonus video training. I'd love to hear from you: how has secondary gain been getting in the way for you? And how might you handle it differently, now you know how to identify those unmet needs and can think of ways to meet them more healthily?

The Real Reason Why Training Courses Don't Create Change

Fact: sticky plasters don't work.

Back in my corporate days, I remember being sent on regular training courses to help me to be 'less impatient'. They didn't work. With the benefit of a decade or more of hindsight, I can now see that what my bosses used to see as 'impatience' was actually tenacity and passion - two of my biggest and brightest qualities. What I needed to learn instead was how to channel these talents, without terrifying my colleagues, rather than getting rid of that quality.

But these courses could never have worked. Why? Because they were sticky plasters.

These courses were trying to get me to change my outward behaviours, but without understanding what it was that was motivating me to think and behave in a way that some others experienced as 'impatience'.

After the courses, I was supposed to have 'changed'; to behave differently. But I didn't. All that happened was I felt bad and judged myself for being 'impatient'. I 'pretended' not to be, but the 'vibe' I was putting out there was the same. And my 'impatience' still drove people crazy.

In fact, it made things worse, because my guilt about my impatience turned into self-judgement and my passion turned into frustration and sometimes anger.

If all you do is try to paint over one behaviour with another, then change hasn't really happened. And if that new behaviour clashes with deeply-held values and beliefs - and who you feel you are - then you can make things worse, by creating an inner conflict.

Whichever need, value or belief that old behaviour was serving will still need to be served, and your unconscious mind will find another way. It's as persistent in protecting you as dandelions are in sprouting through cracks in the pavement.

If you try to force yourself to think positive thoughts, when your mind is racing with everything that's not working or could go wrong, it's a similar thing. Your thoughts are a symptom - an effect - of what is going on deeper down. If you want to think thoughts that make you feel great, then you need to start by working at the level of 'you' that triggers the thoughts, rather than continually chasing your tail to try to change the thoughts you have already started to think. (We'll cover much more on positive thinking, later in this chapter).

Most of us have tried changing our block-driven behaviour, but it didn't work. So, instead, we ignore it and pretend those blocks aren't there. It can be easy to build the idea of 'change' up into something terrifying. We convince ourselves that techniques will work for others, but not us. We turn a transient behaviour into a permanent trait; we turn a belief into a hard fact. It's no wonder we run from change and distract ourselves by keeping busy - taking action - and hoping we won't self-sabotage. We bottle it up, because we're terrified of opening Pandora's box.

Your hidden blocks dictate the boundaries of your comfort zones and limit the amount of difference you can make in the world.

The more of them you can release, the bigger your dreams can become. While we run those blocks, we're subconsciously refusing ourselves permission to succeed.

I often find that clients don't come to me to deal with their blocks until they hit a rock bottom - a point where they tell themselves that 'enough is enough'. People won't make 'inside work' changes while the pain or fear of changing greater than the pain or fear of staying the same.

It might be a fear of the unknown. Or maybe we feel overwhelmed. Or maybe we don't know how to spot those blocks. Or maybe we're not convinced of the benefits of dealing with them. Or maybe we're terrified that dealing with them will cause life to 'fall apart'.

Rock bottom became the solid foundation on which I rebuilt my life. ~ J K Rowling

Until you hit that rock bottom where you make the commitment to change, you're likely to keep heading down that old road. But I don't want you to have to wait until life falls apart to 'find' that rock bottom. You can make the decision, right now, that *now* is where it all changes. And that's where my favourite Italian word comes in.

How My Favourite Italian Word Can Help You To Change Your Life

(And, no, it's not 'vino').

My Grandmother's family comes from Italy and I have always loved the emotional expressiveness of the Italian language.

If you ever feel like you're stuck, going round and round, having the same experiences, but with different people and scenery, then it's time to get unstuck. When you're on that gerbil wheel and nothing seems to be working, then you need my favourite Italian word. It's like a magic wand.

How often do we keep doing the same thing, but expecting different results? Einstein described that as the first sign of madness. But all that happens is that we get deeper and deeper into the 'stuckness', like Wellington boots in a boggy marsh.

Change can feel scary and uncomfortable, and if you haven't yet experienced how great things will feel *after* you have made that change, then it's easy to cling to the status quo. The pain of changing is greater than the pain of staying the same. For change to happen, you need to tip that balance.

Therapists will classically use leverage, to help you crank up the pain of staying the same, by asking you to imagine how terrible it will be, if you keep heading down that road. But if you're secretly scared of changing, then that just sets up a massive internal conflict and can even lead to depression and anxiety, if not handled sensitively.

Over the past fourteen years I have so often seen that people need to hit a rock bottom, before they will consider making those changes. And that rock bottom can be as extreme as losing their business, their job, their health, their home or their relationships. But I don't want you to have to go that far. I want you to be able to turn things around, right now, and that's where my favourite Italian word comes in.

What is it?

"Basta!"

No, it's not a typo.

It's a way of saying to yourself: "Enough!" But somehow the energy of it is much more effective: "I've had enough! This stops now!"

But it's important to say it playfully, with a smile on your face. It's a bit silly and irreverent and it's much better than waiting until you have a life-meltdown.

It's like a magic wand, because when you have a 'basta-moment', as I call them, it's as though you are putting your foot down and telling yourself that you're not dancing that old dance any more: "Here is my new song. Here is my new music. And I'm going to dance to *this* dance, instead."

In using 'basta', you are making a *commitment* to making that change. When you have had your 'basta-moment', the change starts to feel exciting. It starts to energise you. You find yourself taking the new actions you need, moving forward in that new direction. But you need to have that 'basta-moment' first, in order to close the door on the old way of being and walk through the doorway to the 'new you'. Otherwise you'll be pulling all of those old habits and thought processes along with you, and dancing with a foot on both the old and the new dance floors, making your job so much harder.

And the day came when the risk to remain a bud was more painful than the risk it took to blossom.

~ Anais Nin

You can use 'basta' for any situation - a thought pattern you want to change; a habit you want to release; a cycle you're stuck in with someone who bugs you.

For any change you want to create, basta is there to help you. Now, once you have had that 'basta-moment', how long does it take to create that change?

How Long Does It Take To Change A Habit?

I am often asked this one. And researchers seem to agree on the '21 days' time frame. But I, personally, I believe that it's instant. As soon as you have made the decision to make that change - and you have really committed to it - then it will happen. And the commitment – the decision – the choice – is the most important step in creating a change. Changes driven by 'maybe-energy' rarely work. Those triggered by a 'basta-moment' level of decision are near-guaranteed to succeed.

Yes, of course, you need to develop the new habit, which means building it into your rhythm and strengthening the neural pathways in your brain, so that it becomes your new autopilot, and there are many ways to do that.

But changing the habit is instant. It's remembering to do it that takes time.

I remember being a kid, living in Texas, and my Mum went to see a hypnotherapist, to give up smoking. She was nervous about whether or not it would work, and plucked up the courage to ask the hypnotherapist how likely she was to succeed; being a Brit she was concerned about offending him by implying she was doubting his abilities… At the end of the first session he told her that he knew it would work for her - he was 100% certain - even though it didn't work for everyone.

"But how did you know?" she asked.

"Because I could see from the moment you walked through the door that you had made the decision. You had made the choice to quit. So all I have to do is to support you in creating the new habit and handling the withdrawal symptoms. That's the easy bit, once the choice has been made." And, sure enough, she never smoked again, having been a smoker for 20 years.

I have seen many people who didn't manage to create change, and many who have. And the difference between those who did and those who didn't was always the same. Those who didn't make the change hadn't really committed to it. They weren't hungry or fired-up to take the actions that change required of them. They were still in a 'maybe-zone', where both outcomes were possible.

So how do you get to that level of commitment that makes change easier and near-inevitable? I have three steps that I use with my clients - and with myself – you might like to try them out for yourself with a change you are currently resisting.

Exercise: 3 Steps To Creating Change

1. Get totally clear about your Big Why for the change.

Ask yourself: What will this change do for me? How will it help me? How does it move me towards my Big Vision or whatever my dream outcome is for this change?

Then use your imagination to create those new neural pathways, by experiencing how life will feel once you have made the change. Use all of your senses. Feel it. Convince your body to believe it. Notice which thoughts you think and imagine which new actions you're taking.

The more often you practise 'time travelling' and stepping into the experience of having done it, the more quickly it will become autopilot. Rewiring your neural pathways really is that simple.

Doing this for sixty seconds, multiple times a day has most effect. If you imagine walking through grass in a field just once, within a few hours it will have sprung back up. But do it multiple times a day, for a few weeks, and an obvious path will appear. Your neural pathways are similar. They can be changed through your imagination and new "highways" are formed by repetition. That's how a thought becomes a habit, which becomes a belief.

2. Know where you usually fall over when making change and pre-empt the pitfalls.

Are you forgetful? Set reminders on your phone. Are you secretly lazy? Get an accountability buddy (the Readers' Club forum is great for this). Are you too busy? Set time in your diary and make it your top priority. And look at times when you have been brilliant at making changes - what worked? How did you get the support you need? What made the difference? Play to your strengths on this.

3. Celebrate your successes.

We're usually brilliant at beating ourselves up. So train yourself to focus on what you're doing well and the progress you are making towards that change. Perhaps keep a gratitude journal each night (check out the Readers' Club resources), to thank yourself for the progress you *did* make, and the actions you *did* take towards your change, rather than dwelling on the times you might have slipped up. And if you need someone else to celebrate those successes with, sort it, before you make the change. The Dare To Dream Bigger forum is a great place to go for this.

Watch Your Language!

In the coming section, we're going to be talking a lot about 'change'. But research on motivational traits (more in the Readers' Club) shows that over half of the population dives into a physiological stress response, merely at the words 'change' or 'different'. If that's you, then imagine you can do a 'search and replace' and that every time you read or think the words 'change' or 'different', you're in fact seeing words like 'shift' or 'another way' - whatever works for you.

Don't freak yourself out.

If you try to change too much in one go, you'll risk sending yourself into a kind of identity-level shock - and your mind will struggle to cope. It's a source of stress that isn't needed.

Just like a captain steering a ship over the oceans, you reach your destination by making a series of small changes, as the currents and winds affect your direction of travel. There's a good reason why a ship is designed to make a 180-u-turn impossible - it's too dangerous. Similarly, with life changes, it's usually best to create smaller shifts that build on each other, rather than throwing life up in the air, to see where it might land. Incremental shifts tend to create less resistance from your mind than a one-off, big blast. They feel more achievable. And it's important to let change settle, before you start another round of self-work, so you don't send your life into 'shock'.

I strongly recommend that you read this whole section – Clearing Out Your Blocks - and then decide which hidden block to deal with first. Your gut will tell you. It will either be the one you run from or the one that will make the biggest difference for your Big Vision. Let that block go, using the strategies I'll be sharing with you, give yourself time for that shift to settle, and then move on to the next one.

Visualisation alone isn't enough...

As I was editing this Handbook, I was delighted to find that Gabriele Oettingen, Professor of psychology at New York University and the University of Hamburg, had published some research[4] backing up what I have been telling my clients for years – that positive thinking and

---

[4] Links to her research and her book on this topic are in the Readers' Club

visualising, on their own, can actually make you less likely to achieve your dreams. Be warned! It's why the Law Of Attraction so often fails to work for people, even if they're super-keen.

Why is this? Because when we get into the *feeling* of having *already created* that change or experience, our brain gets the same chemical rewards, such as dopamine, as though we had actually created it. But it won't pop up in your physical world unless you actually take action. Professor Oettingen found that experiencing the positive benefits of the change, before it has happened, risks making us less likely to put in the effort – to take the inspired actions – to create the change.

So whilst visualising can rewire your neural pathways and clear out your blocks, you still need to get off your butt and put in the effort to make the 'outside world' change happen.

The strategies we're covering here will work for the vast majority of blocks, but if you find one where you need a little more, the extra resources are there and waiting for you in the Readers' Club. Bear in mind that sometimes a particularly 'stubborn block can benefit from a one-to-one session. But most of the blocks you're carrying can be sorted with the techniques we'll be covering in this Handbook.

You'll find you make the fastest progress if you pick a particular area to work on - setting your ship's course - and then change small aspects of that block. Many incremental shifts create less resistance from your unconscious mind than a big blast - and they're more achievable.

As an NLP Trainer, I was taught (and have seen proven, many times over the past decade) that the quickest way for someone to learn (or change) is to break that journey down into chunks. Those chunks need to be a stretch, but manageable. If you aim for the nigh-on impossible, you'll hit it once in that proverbial blue moon, but most of the rest of the time you'll feel despondent and risk giving up.

If you want to make a change in your thought patterns, for example, rather than deciding, "I'm never going to think another negative thought again," which is a lifelong journey (yes I have met people who wanted to achieve that, especially after reading books like The Secret), then break it down into specific, achievable chunks. For example: "I will work on choosing which thoughts to feed, whenever Fred bugs me in the morning meeting."

That way you can measure your results, you're only looking at shifting one trigger event response, and it's something you could make big progress on in just a few days.

I don't care how you got your block.

One of the things you won't find in this section is navel-gazing about 'why' you have such-and-such a block, or who 'gave' it to you. I also won't be encouraging you to dive into the 'story'. If you feel the need to have your story heard, that's fine. Sometimes it can help. Find someone suitably qualified to listen to you. But then please let it go. When we dive into the drama and emotions of the 'story' and keep telling it to ourselves and to others, it reinforces it in your brain's neural pathways – that footpath in the field turns into a busy main road and then a motorway. It's easy to get attached to the story, until it becomes part of your identity - your 'badge of honour'. And the sympathy you get from your story works wonders for keeping you stuck with it - who would want to give up all of that love and attention?!

So, instead, I'll be encouraging you to learn what you need to learn from your past experience, but to start from where you are *now* and head towards your destination. We can consciously choose the stories we tell ourselves about our past, effectively rewriting it and undoing its effects on our neurological and cellular level biology (more on this from Brue Lipton in the Readers' Club). It's not about denying the past, but it *is* about making choices about your future from the present - with all of the freedom that brings.

And if you dive into needing to understand who 'gave' you your block, then you risk handing that person power over your experience of life and what you can achieve. In some circumstances, it can be useful, especially if you need to come to a place of acceptance and forgiveness. But it risks ending in someone justifying their self-perception as a victim.

It doesn't matter to me whether your block came from something your Mum said or a throwaway comment from a childhood friend or the ravings of a grumpy, overworked teacher. I care about who you are now, and who you want to become – and the difference you want to make. And that's the part of your journey we'll be handling in this Handbook:

"I have this block. It's not serving me any more - it's out of date. It's time to let it go."

That's our mantra. I hope that's ok with you.

Now we've got all of that clear, are you ready to dive in and discover what your hidden blocks are? You're going to feel fabulous, once you have let them go! We're dealing with the two most powerful World-Changer blocks: confidence, in Step 2, and credibility, in Step 3.

Confidence

Confidence means nothing has to feel impossible any more.

Confidence isn't something you're born with. It's something you cultivate. You remember how I promised I wouldn't hold anything back – that you would get the same depth of insights and techniques that I share with my clients and students? Well that means I need to bring in some engineer-approved woo-woo for this section. I thought long and hard about 'dumbing it down' to make it more 'left-brain-friendly' in our analytical, science-based world, but I'd be doing you a disservice.

So in order to share with you what you really need, rather than hiding it, for fear that it might make you run to the hills, you're going to get the Real Deal in this section on confidence. And that means we need to travel back in time about 2500 years. I hope that's ok with you. We'll get to that shortly. But first, we could define 'confidence' as:

having trust in your abilities, in people or in plans; being certain.

But when it comes to making a difference in the world, confidence falls somewhere between 'having the courage of your convictions' and 'believing, deep in your heart, that you can do it'. Confidence shows itself differently in different cultures. And some of the most confident-looking people actually feel like nervous wrecks, inside.

What I want to help you with in this section is that 'deep down inside' confidence, so that it's there for you, whatever goes on. I'm not interested in helping you to create confidence that is 'context-dependent', so that you feel great in your current role or comfort zone, but things fall apart if circumstances change. I want to inspire and empower you to clear out the hidden blocks, so that you line up with who you really are and take a leap towards expressing that, with everything that you do.

I don't mean brash, in-your-face confidence. That kind of confidence may be genuine, but often it's a veneer that is masking deeply-held insecurities and hidden fears. We're going to be looking at the grounded confidence that means you might feel scared about taking an action, but deep-down you know that things will be ok and you still find the courage you need.

The Risks Of Lacking Confidence

Who would you rather do your business with? Who would you rather trust with whatever experience, transformation, or product is being sold: somebody who is secretly scared they're not good enough? Or somebody who is confident, standing tall in their personal power and genuinely convinced that they can help you?

Most of us run our businesses feeling fairly confident, but very few of us feel truly confident, and that is why the second C is confidence. When you've got clarity about who you are, the difference you're here to make, and what makes you different, it's essential to build up your confidence in that dream. If you're not confident in your message, nobody else will be either. But I'm not suggesting that unless you have 100% Rockstar Confidence you should walk away from your dreams. Just the opposite.

One of the things I've had the absolute joy of doing, as I have been writing this book, is interviewing some of my business and world-changer heroes, to talk to them about the blocks they had inside, that they had to clear to grow to the next level. So many of them had limiting beliefs, Imposter Syndrome, self-doubt, lack of self-esteem, self-worth issues, negative thinking, and stories they were telling themselves about how they couldn't do it and they weren't good enough.

Each time they grew to a new level and expanded an old comfort zone, new stuff came up to clear. It's just like your windows. You don't clean them once and then leave them forever. You need to keep cleaning them. It's a regular thing. The two big risks of not feeling confident are:

1. If you're secretly doubting yourself, you are unlikely to take the inspired action that your dreams require.
You're more likely to turn down golden opportunities, miss deadlines, not return that call, miss the interview and subconsciously self-sabotage, playing small.

2. Very few people want to work with somebody who is self-doubting and terrified that they're not good enough.

If you want to earn enough money to put food in the fridge, whilst also helping people and making whatever difference it is you're here to make, you need to deal with your confidence issues.

We have all run a version of this; worrying that we're not 'good enough'. But you are. Your Heart and Soul wouldn't give you the yearning and calling to make the difference you're here to make, if you didn't have it within you to grow into that role.

When you clear out your blocks, when you believe in yourself, and you believe in your Big Vision, your Big Message, and you believe in your clients' ability and responsibility for co-creating whatever it is you co-create together, when you stand in those confident Soul-Shoes and you can see how you can still achieve it, despite having some fears and worries in the background, you will blow yourself away at the progress you make.

And you don't have to wait until you're 'perfect'. You can start from wherever you are, right here, right now, and move from there. Becoming aware of and clearing out even one block will make a massive difference.

Where Did My Confidence Go?

I started studying psychology when I was 14, thanks to a Desmond Morris book my Aunt Hilary and Uncle Stephen gave me for my birthday. I feel passionate about figuring out how people tick – and helping them to feel happier, by letting go of their baggage and being true to who they really are, stepping into their Soul-Shoes and maybe even dancing in them.

Fourteen years of mentoring passionate World-Changers has shown me that the most important factor in your success, once you have clarity about what you want, is confidence. Yet most of us are secretly walking around, feeling like a fraud, scared that someone is going to 'catch us out'. We're terrified of being kicked out, if we dare to make it into life's VIP room.

We might be drowning in little-acknowledged fears. But that confidence is still there, somewhere deep inside. And I want to help you to reconnect with it, in this step.

As a baby, we're curious, but naturally programmed to keep ourselves safe. We have reflexes to alert us if we're going to fall. We flinch at loud sounds. We quickly learn how to get attention, if we're hungry or cold.

As we grow, those self-preservation reflexes expand to cover not just our physical world, but our mental and emotional worlds, too.

For example, instead of flinching at a loud sound (which you may still do), we flinch at other things that scare us; causing us to contract or play small. The trigger might be the imminent stretching of a comfort zone. It might be facing a new challenge. It might be launching a new product or growing your audience. It might be taking your current mission to the next level.

If what you want to do makes you feel like you just flinched - like your body tried to get smaller to protect itself - then it's going to affect your confidence.

Whenever part of your Being is calling you to grow and expand, but hidden fears and blocks are causing you to contract, you'll feel it in your gut, in body tension and your posture will often subtly shift, as you try to make yourself smaller, and your jaw and eye areas will most likely tense up, too.

Once our evolution moved us beyond escaping from sabre toothed tigers, then these protective instincts transferred to our emotional and psychological well-being. At a deep level, we shift to wanting to protect ourselves from the emotional pain caused by, for example, someone's unkind words or our deep-rooted fear of rejection.

Our mind can get truly creative, inventing strategies to keep us safe. These strategies become the foundation for the 'auto-pilot' programmes that run, without us realising, when our 'buttons' are pressed.

So if someone presses our "I'm going to be rejected by this person" button, then chances are we'll instantly reach for our well-rehearsed response strategy, which will often involve either running away (emotionally and psychologically) or attacking, before we are attacked.

The stories we tell ourselves about the past cause these strategies to get stuck in time.

And, when these strategies get stuck, we shut down to other behavioural choices. This 'shut down' is another form of protection mechanism, which has become stuck in time. So, if you were using a strategy - a coping mechanism - designed by the emotional intelligence of your seven-year-old self, this strategy can become set in stone; this response didn't mature with the rest of you. So the 'you' in your thirties, forties or beyond will still be using this auto-pilot programme, even once it's well past its sell-by date.

These 'shutdown' events often cause us to suppress the real emotions we were feeling at the time[5]. They can even lead to vows along the lines of, "I'm never going through that again!" These vows close the door to other choices of how to respond, whenever we encounter that trigger in the future.

We spend our future years creating a supporting network of beliefs, values and external behaviours to match the vow or shutdown choice from the past - without even realising it.

For example, Emma was struggling to speak up in big meetings, especially when Board members were there. She was highly intelligent and had plenty to contribute. In smaller meetings she felt fine - confident and happy, but once there were twenty or so in the room, she would clam up. It wasn't doing her career - or the company - any good.

We worked on this and she identified the 'getting smaller' in her body was a tensing of her jaw and throat and her voice wouldn't come out properly. She often had to clear her throat, before she spoke up in meetings. She also noticed that her shoulders would round and she would look at the desk - classic signs of trying to make yourself smaller.

She remembered early memories of having those same physical feelings, she remembered a particularly grumpy teacher, from when she was about seven, who would get the class to laugh at anyone who got a question wrong in class discussions. Emma quickly learned to make herself 'invisible' during those sessions, and never, ever, ever to put her hand up to speak. It doesn't matter which 'story' or 'memory' her mind had picked. What mattered was giving her a way of connecting her current behaviour with out-of-date choices from her past, so that the part of her that had chosen that original protective behaviour could feel safe to let it go. It doesn't mean that the teacher 'gave' Emma her habit; but Emma needed to reach a place of acceptance, and even forgiveness, of that 'story' to feel 'safe' to move on and let the habit go.

Those seven year-old's survival strategies were seriously out-of-date, now she was in her forties, and no one ever got ridiculed in that way in meetings in her company. But they were still hard-wired in her brain, as an autopilot, self-preservation response.

---

[5] There's a bonus video on why this is so risky in the Readers' Club, along with links to Bruce Lipton's inspirational work on this topic.

Once she was aware of this, it didn't take us long to shift those old scripts and she was free to choose to behave more confidently in meetings - something her boss quickly noticed and ensured she got recognition for.

The impact of the auto-pilot replay of childhood strategies can be that we end up feeling we are the victim of other people's actions. The reality is that these people are simply playing their part (often very well!) in a play that offers us the opportunity to catch ourselves at this game and finally set ourselves free.

None of this 'stuck behaviour' means that we are 'bad', 'wrong' or 'broken'. It is just how we are behaving at that moment in time. Who we really are, deep down underneath, remains unchanged. As soon as we become consciously aware of these behavioural patterns, it means that the underlying cause is ready to be acknowledged, dealt with and released.

And it's important to take action, when this happens. White-washing it and 'pretending' that everything is fine doesn't work.

There's a deep-dive article on why white-washing is such a bad idea, and a video on the modern epidemic of the 'spiritual bypass', over at the Readers' Club.

How To Build Up To Rockstar Confidence

In the rest of this section, I will guide you through questions you can ask yourself, to figure out exactly where you're blocking your confidence, what that's costing you, and then you'll learn what you can do about it.

Once you are aware of your hidden blocks, you can take action to shift them, and I've got plenty of how-to on that for you, too. I strongly encourage you to pick block one at a time, rather than unravelling your entire life-coping-mechanism in one go. That way you'll reduce resistance and you'll find it easier to convince your unconscious mind, step by step, that you can do this.

How Can I Feel More Confident?

You're going to rewire your brain and reprogramme each cell in your body. Don't worry - it's easy, and you already know how. I'm going to guide you through how to figure it out.

My kids (all under 12) are learning Italian, whenever we're in the car, in preparation for going on holiday. (Yes, they already know 'basta'!) Even my four-year-old will walk around the house and suddenly spout random phrases in Italian, usually pizza-related, and I'm pretty sure he knows what they mean. His ability to learn them is really impressive. They're not genius kids; just inquisitive. All they're doing is creating new neural pathways in their brains.

If you have ever learned anything about anything, you've created a new neural pathway, and you've overwritten an old one as you deepen that knowledge or experience. You can do it with learning. You can do it with limiting beliefs. You can do it with blocks. You can do it with fears. You can clear this stuff out. This will work for you.

It doesn't have to be big, and it doesn't have to be scary. You pick one thing, and you deal with it. You build your confidence day-by-day-by-day, with small steps, little and often. And, before you know it, you'll have cleared out loads of old blocks and cranked up the dial on your inner confidence.

If you just pick one aspect of your confidence issues and deal with it for a few weeks, letting it go and releasing it, and then the next one, by the end of two or three months you'll be amazed at how different your life feels. And it all comes down to two little words.

The One Tiny Big Difference

Self-talk.

If you tell yourself stories about being good enough, clever enough, experienced enough, having the connections you need and how it will feel to turn your dream into reality, you sky-rocket your chances of getting there.

If you're drowning in self-told stories about how you're too young or old, how you're not ready yet, you're not good enough and it never works out for you, then that is what you will get.

It's hard to take 'inspired action' if you're constantly beating yourself up.

Your self-talk, your 'Inner Critic', can be used to trash your dreams and cause you to self-sabotage, or you can turn it into your biggest cheerleader, one thought at a time.

But how? As Einstein allegedly said: "You can't solve a problem with the level of thinking that created it."

And here's the problem: self-talk is just the symptom. It's not the real cause. So if you try to change your negative thinking patterns by just thinking different thoughts, it's like putting a sticky plaster over your inner dialogue. Unless you handle the underlying beliefs, values and identity-level 'baggage' that create and feed your thoughts, they're just going to come up somewhere else, shouting even more loudly, until they're heard.

The great news is that spotting those underlying triggers and doing something useful about them is straightforward, when you know how, and that's what we're going to be doing for the rest of this section.

Over the years I have seen many courses on 'positive thinking' and read plenty of books on the topic, which talked about how to change your thoughts. But when you're stuck in a negative thought spiral, it's nigh-on impossible to 'think' your way out of it.

When your inner drama queen is feeding the confidence-killing soap opera storyline that keeps you stuck playing small, he or she isn't going to let up, just because you ask nicely.

So in this chapter, we're going to start with some of my favourite ways to press 'pause' on the inner story, to calm those negative thoughts down. Then we're going to look at longer-term solutions.

How To Spot Your Blocks

Once you are aware of your key blocks, many of them will melt away, just by realising that they're no longer valid. But for those that need a little more work, it's important not to fall into the most common trap:

Most people are fixing the wrong thing.

Most personal development techniques are like 'sticky plasters', covering over the pain of the problem and often failing to produce lasting change. When this happens, it's because:

- They only deal with the symptoms; with the 'effects' of a problem, rather than the underlying root cause.
- They assume you are 'broken', operating from a disempowering belief that there is something 'wrong' with you that needs to be fixed by the technique.

The Symptoms Are Your Signposts, Not The Destination

The 'symptoms' of the problem are the signposts that can lead you to the root cause – or to your true destination.

Back in my engineering days, I worked in the car industry,

specialising in discovering - and permanently resolving - potential quality concerns when manufacturing hugely complex diesel engines. One of the things that was drummed into me was the need to see past the 'effects' of a problem, to identify and deal with the 'root cause'.

The effects - symptoms or visible problems - would lead me to the root cause, if I had the right team involved and asked the right questions. Then it was up to us to choose whether or not to deal with the causal issue. If we did, then we would know that the problem - the effects - could never recur.

If we didn't deal with the root cause, say, due to budget, time or priority constraints, then no matter how much papering over cracks we did on the effects, the problem would eventually come back.

It's the same with unwanted habits, thought patterns, behaviours and emotions.

Strangely, we tend to feel more enthusiastic about dealing with the symptoms in life, rather than the root causes - perhaps because the symptoms always shout loudest and catch our attention, whilst the root causes can hide away, unnoticed, out of sight.

What You Need To Know About Root Causes

Discovering the root cause of a problem behaviour isn't about looking for someone or something to blame. It's not about diving into the story or drama. You don't even need to discover what the story is, most of the time. In fact, getting stuck in the story is one of the most common reasons why we can find it hard to set ourselves free from our past - and its impact on our current experience of life.

We've all heard it:

"My therapist told me I'm depressed, because of the way my mother treated me when I was six..."

"I'm a 'commitmentphobe', because of the way my ex behaved when we split up, ten years ago..."

"I'm no good at presentations, because of what my teacher said to me when I did my first ever presentation at school..."

These might have been strong experiences that had a major impact on us. They might even be the initial trigger for our current issues. But dwelling in the drama of the story never brings resolution or inner peace. It only ever brings more pain. And in this kind of statement, you're giving the power over your present and your future to the behaviour of someone in your past.

Moving away from current, symptomatic behaviour to the older, deeper root cause is about discovering the 'trigger' that sets off our auto-pilot responses - our subconsciously-programmed behaviours. When you identify the catalyst that removes your sense of 'choice' or keeps you stuck, repeating cycles of behaviour long past the point where it might have added any value to your life, then you can release those triggers - and set yourself free.

Let's take the example of an 'angry button' - most of us have one, in certain circumstances.

Dealing with things at a behavioural level, we could get coaching or therapy to help us spot the early warning signs that we're starting to feel angry. Then we can use our willpower to choose a different behaviour - even though the 'angry button' has already been pressed and has fired off the chemical cycle of emotions in our body. It's hard work. You're effectively using your mind to fight your body and your instinctive behaviour. You have to be constantly vigilant, looking out for the trigger's early warning signs.

Alternatively, we can deal with whatever the underlying issues were that created the 'angry button' in the first place. By dealing with the suppressed emotions and experiences at the root cause level, we can dissolve the need for the angry button. That way, when someone comes along to press our button, it's no longer there. The change in our response becomes natural, effortless and permanent.

When we deal with the root causes, our destructive behaviour naturally disappears.

A client of mine experienced this recently. One of her team members was driving her crazy and was causing her huge amounts of stress, through long-term underperformance issues. But she couldn't let this team member fail to the extent that performance management could be invoked, because that would damage the firm's relationship with their clients.

The thing is that you can't force anyone else to change (yes, you can provide incentives, but you can't force them!), you can only change yourself.

So we deep-dived into what was happening 'inside' for my client. What were the buttons that were being pressed for her in this situation? What was important to her? How was it holding up a mirror for her, for her own fears and insecurities?

When we dealt with those - and it took under half an hour. She created an action plan to turn things around with that member of staff. It gave her a huge sense of relief. But the real proof was back at work the following week. Within a few days, she found that staff member no longer pressed her buttons. And their relationship - and the staff member's performance - improved.

That was so much easier than having to spot the button being pressed and choose alternative behaviours, each and every day, for years.

Before we move on to setting ourselves free from the old pattern of behaviour that may have become destructive, I want to talk to you about riding waves and pulling out tent pegs.

Success Isn't A Straight Line

I prefer to think of it as a game of riding the waves and pulling out the tent pegs. During your journey, 'life' comes at us from all angles. Some of it might be brilliant, but some of it might knock you off course. If you stick rigidly to a path, you're going to find very quickly that you are trying too hard and it's not going to work.

Instead, we could imagine that life is like steering a ship on the ocean: when you see somebody steering with and old fashioned ship's wheel, they don't just hold it rigid. They make constant tiny adjustments, because the currents take you one way, and then there'll be a riptide that takes you another. Then the wind will take you another. You have a clear destination in mind, but the route to get there requires small shifts the whole way. If you ride those waves and stop trying to push the ocean, you will get to your destination faster, it'll be more fun, and it'll be easier.

You can't push the ocean, so you might as well ride the waves.

Once we know how to ride those waves, what stops us from reaching our Big Vision destination are the tent pegs that we've banged into the shore, on dry land, to hold our journey back. It's like Gulliver being tethered with pegs and ropes in Lilliput. These tent pegs include our limiting beliefs, our fears, our old excuses and the things that we worry about. If you've got a belief, for example, of "I can't achieve this," then that's a really big tent peg to have holding your boat back. You create this internal tension: part of you wants to sail the ship and ride the waves, but part of you that's saying, "I'm not letting go of this tent peg!"

Limiting beliefs are like tent pegs you bash into the ground that stop you heading towards your dreams.

We defend our tent pegs. Each time we feed the mind-story around a limiting belief, it's like we're banging in a bigger and bigger tent peg, and that's going to make it harder to get to your goal. So I'm going to show you how to become a 'puller outer' of your secret tent pegs.

How Do You Spot Your Tent Pegs?

At a surface level, it's: "I can't do xyz because…."

The because-answers are your tent pegs. As you work through this section, I suggest that you start with the ones that you're defending the most. For example, an incredibly common is, "I can't do this because I don't have enough time."

I was using this excuse recently. My diary was full and I had over-committed on some live trainings I was about to deliver. I was due to go the next week and it was the end of term, which is always a crazy week. I woke up at 3am, silently chanting, "I don't have enough time!"

So my creative 'ship' was happily riding the waves and tweaking its direction, as it needed to. But all the time I was banging in the tent peg of "I don't have enough time!" that tent peg was growing stronger. And the more the ocean pulled me towards my Big Vision's creative impulses, the more I had to defend the tent peg, to stop me getting there, because there was a subconscious part of me that was secretly scared.

Fortunately, I know that being 'time-poor' is one of my favourite tent pegs, so I switched to my time-creating mantra (from Step 0): "I'm grateful for the time I have." That brings me back on course. If I find myself using the biggest sledgehammer I can find to bang in my 'not enough time' tent peg, then the mantra reminds me to pull it back out. Can you imagine any of your tent pegs yet? Is there anything holding you back?

Psychologists warn us about what happens if we reject our 'tent pegs' – the part of us that hammered in that peg digs its heels in more firmly, defending its right to have a tent peg. If you attack the tent peg, you get what Professor Brendan Nyhan of Dartmouth College, USA, calls the 'Backfire Effect', where that tent peg will get defended to the end of time.

If we have a point of view that we're so attached to that it has become part of our identity, then contradictory evidence won't just be rejected, it will trigger us becoming more entrenched, defending that belief. You effectively set up a massive internal conflict between the part of you that wants rid of the tent peg and the part of you that believes it will be annihilated, if it lets it go.

So how do you pull out a tent peg, when it's getting in your way?

To release a tent peg, ask yourself: "What do I want instead?" and focus on moving towards that.

Part of you is ready and willing (desperate!) to let go of that old belief. And that simple question allows the belief to soften; it starts to change the stories we're telling ourselves; it reduces resistance; it prevents us from entrenching.

Then let the tent peg go. When you do, you might want to cut the invisible ties to it, or you might want to imagine yourself pulling it out. If you need someone, in your mind, to go with you to help pull the tent peg out, great. Imagine taking them with you. Feed the "What do I want instead?" rather than feeding the tent peg, because that will make your ocean wave journey smoother - and it will be much more fun.

It's Time To Stop Defending Your Excuses

They say that if you talk to people who are coming to the end of their life, they will tell you about everything they regret, and that their biggest regrets are the things they didn't do - the chances they didn't take - who they did not yet become.

The more we cling to our fears, excuses, limiting beliefs, worries and self-sabotaging behaviours, our tent pegs, the more likely we are to end up with all of those regrets.

But when you spot a block and deal with it, the sense of relief and lightness is delicious - it's the only way I can describe it. The look on someone's face when they release an old block is truly beautiful. They somehow fill the room with a wave of relief. When you let a block go and allow yourself to expand, even just slightly, into being the 'whole' of who you really are, life feels lighter, more fun, easier and less stressful.

When you think about what your blocks are costing you - and how much they are hurting you - financially, emotionally, mentally, and in your ability to create your dreams, surely it's time to give yourself permission to let some of them go?

If you insist on defending your excuses, you'll get to keep them.

I want to make it as easy as possible for you to let go of your old blocks - and pull out your tent pegs - so we're going to go through the five most common areas of blocks that are responsible for the vast majority of self-sabotage. And the tools and techniques I'm going to share with you will work for you, whatever is going on in your life. And here's where the engineer-approved woo-woo bit comes in.

Inner Rockstar Confidence: Clearing Out Five Layers Of Blocks

I don't want to leave you with sticky plasters all over your blocks, so this is where we're going to dive in and deal with the underlying causes. I want to give you as deep as possible an understanding of your hidden blocks and how to develop your Inner Rockstar Confidence.

In this section, I want to take you through some Ancient Wisdom, with a simplified version of what the meditation and yoga world calls the 'five koshas' and how these can help you to release your blocks to making a bigger difference in the world, once and for all.

A 'kosha' is described as being a 'sheath', but I prefer to think of it as being an aspect of the way we experience life, like a layer of Being. They are all connected, so if you create a shift in one, you'll create knock-on effects in the others. For the rest of this section – and the next two – we'll work through the koshas in turn, to help you to boost your confidence, from the inside out. Before we begin, here's an overview – you don't need to learn any of these terms – I'm giving them to you so your thinking brain has 'hooks' to hang the coming strategies on, and in case you feel inspired to find out more about the Koshas.

The Physical Body - Anamayakosha
This is the physical world experience of life. It includes your body, what you consume, your actions and your habits. It also includes material-world 'stuff' like money and possessions. So if you're feeling broke or surrounded by clutter or what you're doing isn't working – or you're doing too much – then this is where to find your answers.

The Energy Body - Pranamayakosha
This kosha deals with your life force – prana or chi – and your energy levels. If you're running on empty, then this is where to fix it. It is strongly influenced by how you treat your physical body (in Anamayakosha), but also by the way you breathe (pranayama is the ancient study of breathing techniques) and the thoughts you think.

Your Mind And Emotions - Manomayakosha

This is the framework behind your thoughts, including your beliefs, values and needs, and also how you process the world, via your senses. It governs your emotions and is responsible for your passion, motivation, illusions and fears. Your Inner Critic hangs out in this layer – as does your Inner Cheerleader.

The Wisdom Body - Vignaanamayakosha

This is about Knowledge with a capital 'K' – that inner wisdom or deep knowing. It's also about your self-awareness and your connection to all other living beings. It's where your business breakthrough ideas come from. We'll cover this in Step 4 on Connection and Step 5 on Creativity.

The Bliss Body – Your Higher Self - Anandamayakosha

This is where you really connect deeply with who you really are – it's a block-free zone. It's where your inner peace and stillness hang out. You might have felt it when you get totally in flow – and that inner joy and excitement bubble up – or when you are meditating or practising mindfulness – or walking in nature. We'll touch on this in Step 4 on Connection and Step 7 on Celebration, and it's covered in more detail in the deep-dive resources.

We're going to look at each layer in turn, identifying its common blocks and how to release them. And then we'll do a wrapping-up exercise where you'll come back up through the layers. It's a brilliant way of making sure you will be supporting the changes you're making, long-term, and aren't just papering over the cracks.

In each section, you'll get a set of questions designed to draw out the blocks at that level. Some of the blocks may feel like they are straddling multiple layers, and that's fine. This process will handle that for you. Then you'll get deep-acting techniques to deal with those blocks, both at the 'help! I need a quick fix' level, and also at the 'I'm done with this – time to let it go!' level.

So let's start with the 'outside world' evidence of what's going on inside: your physical body and your behaviour.

Your Actions - Anamayakosha

I do, therefore I am.

This layer includes your physical body, your physical environment and 'stuff', what you consume, your actions and your habits. When a client comes to me with challenges like feeling stressed or overwhelmed, or not getting the results, despite taking action, or being stuck in destructive habits and addictions, then we'll often start working at this layer.

Your physical world is where the 'symptoms' or 'effects' of your 'inner world' show up. For example, if you're surrounded by clutter or are constantly running out of money, you'll notice it here, but the causes may be in other layers. So some of the work we'll do in this section will be about identifying those blocks, so we can handle them later. Some will be about easing the pain of the symptoms, because that's important, even if it's only a temporary fix. And some will be about changing behaviours that might be holding you back from Daring To Dream Bigger.

Are Your Favourite Habits Getting In The Way?

We're going to start with your actions and habits, then move onto your physical body, and finish off with your physical environment. Blocks in any of these three areas can get in the way of your Big Vision.

Exercise: What Are Your Physical-World Blocks?

Answer these questions in the context of your Big Vision – there's a worksheet and audio in the Readers' Club, as well as a discussion thread in the forum.

- What actions am I actually taking, on a daily, weekly or monthly basis? Draw a table with three columns.
  One has the heading 'moving me towards my Big Vision', the middle one is 'neither towards nor away from' and the final one is 'moving me away from my Big Vision'.
  Split your answers to this question between the three columns.

Continues...

- How am I spending my time? Are any time-thieves getting in the way?
- How much time am I spending on 'small stuff' that isn't really building towards my Big Vision? Or doesn't really need to be done?
- How often do I procrastinate? What kinds of things distract me?
- Am I running a perfectionism streak? If yes, how is it getting in the way?
- How often do I feel overwhelmed at how much there is to do?
- What proportion of my time am I spending on stuff that is in my Genius Zone?
- When did I last do something that made my Heart sing?
- In what ways am I looking after myself and topping up my batteries?
- How often do I feel stressed or exhausted?
- How is money flowing for me? How do I feel about this?
- How much time each day do I spend moving my body, compared to sitting in front of a screen?
- What am I eating? Is that supporting my Big Vision?
- How often do I truly relax?
- How much time do I spend in nature?

You are *not* your behaviour or your actions. These are just outward symptoms of your inner world; your thoughts and beliefs. But our actions and habits give us important clues about what's going on underneath the surface, and for many people, starting with making subtle changes to their outward actions gives them the confidence to do the deeper work.

When we answer the questions in this exercise, one of the things that often surprises us is how few actions we are taking actually move us towards our Big Vision. Our time might feel full, but we're making little progress. The table from this exercise should give you insights about the proportion of your actions that are moving you towards your Big Vision. Are they as many as you would have expected? Which actions are missing?

And the column with actions that are moving you away from your Big Vision – what is in there? Any surprises or lightbulbs? What could you do differently? Topics that often come up in this column include procrastination, distractions, turning down Golden Opportunities and self-sabotage behaviours.

And the neutral column: is it really neutral? Or is the 'doing' of those actions taking up time that could have been used to move you towards your Big Vision? Is any of it non-essential? Is it all really *your* job? How much of it could you ditch or delegate?

Let your actions match your asking.

Our actions often contradict what we think we are asking for. It's one of the reasons why visualization doesn't work for many people. Management and self-help articles often quote the Harvard and Yale studies into the fact that the 3% of graduates who wrote down their goals ended up earning ten times as much as the other 97% put together. It has since been found that neither of these studies actually took place! However, what *has* been confirmed by psychologists is that there is a strong connection between writing down your goals (or Big Vision and Big Message, for us) and actually turning them into reality[6].

And it makes sense. If you are committed enough to your goals to have clarity and write them down, then you're much more likely to have the discipline to take action to move you towards them.

What Is Stealing Your Time?

Let's look at your answers to the next batch of questions from the last exercise, which are all about what is stealing your time – and the habits that feed this.

Procrastination & Distraction

Yes, I know those kittens are really cute and the video has had a gazillion shares, but unless your Big Vision is creating cute kitten videos, then watching five of them a day is not helping. Yes, I'm exaggerating, but you get my point? We all fall prey to procrastination and distraction at times, but it's when it starts becoming a habit that it's an issue.

So what's really going on, when we procrastinate or distract ourselves with stuff that's nothing to do with our Big Vision? There are three main causes:

1. You're not lined up with your Big Why, so you're missing that passion and excitement; you're feeling bored and filling up time, instead of taking inspired action.

2. You're running on empty and feel like the procrastination or

---

distraction dance is topping up your batteries, but really it isn't. You'd be much better doing a 10-minute relaxation or mindfulness technique (more shortly).

3. You've got a below-the-surface block running, telling you that you're not good enough to achieve your Big Vision, so you're distracting yourself from taking action and you risk self-sabotaging.

When you have total clarity about what you want to create in your life – and the lives of others – you value your time more. You'll choose to spend it like a currency – with conscious choices. When you're feeling really excited about your Big Vision, the fluffy kitten videos lose their appeal. It's easy to skim past them. You'll be feeling fired up and confident and blasting through your 'to do' list, with anything non-essential meeting the 'delete button' faster than you can say, "Awww... That's cute." If this is resonating for you, and you need to crank up the passion, then Step 1 will help - and make sure you pay special attention to Step 6: Commitment. It's all about how to have the self-discipline to keep going, even if you're not in the mood.

If you're running on empty, feeling stressed and exhausted, then filling your time with small-scale actions – especially if it's more screen time - will drain your batteries further, frittering away what little energy you had left. You would be much better off taking ten minutes out to relax and recharge your batteries and then come back to your work feeling alert and refreshed. Ten minutes of walking can help with this, too, as can mindful breathing or even deep relaxation. And I have some extra resources for you in the Readers' Club, if running on empty is a common theme for you, including a bonus 5-day energy-boosting challenge. And we're covering it as a separate theme, in a few pages' time.

You don't have to keep yourself busy or put off getting started because there's a part of you that secretly believes you can't do this. The techniques in this Step will set you free from that.

Are You Running A Perfectionism Streak?

Perfectionism is one of the most common causes of procrastination. I had to deal with this at regular points, as I was writing this book. I ran a pattern of feeling like each chapter should be the 'definitive' chapter on its topic. But if I created that, you wouldn't be able to lift this book, it would be so big and heavy, and it would have taken too many decades to write. To get through this, I reminded myself that this book isn't about me or for me - it's about *you* - and *for* you. And as soon as I focused on that again, the words would start to flow.

Perfectionism means we risk holding ourselves to an impossible standard. It's easy not to get started, because part of us believes the goal is unachievable, so why bother?

It's important to remember that perfectionism is just a symptom and that the cause lies underneath.

Exercise: Getting To The Root Of Perfectionism

You can figure out what's really going on by asking yourself:

- What would happen if I believed this didn't have to be perfect?
- How does insisting on this being perfect help me?
- What does it allow me to avoid?
- What do I risk if I let it be 'good enough'?
- If someone else did this and it weren't perfect, what would I think about them?

Gaining awareness of what's driving your inner perfectionist is often enough to press pause on the behaviour. And the following sections give you practical tools to handle the deeper causes.

Overwhelm

Do you ever feel so overwhelmed that it seems your 'to do' list is closer to that needed to host the Olympic Games, rather than creating your Big Vision? If yes, then the table you filled in at the start of this section is vitally important for you.

Sometimes we fill our time because we are subconsciously scared of having free time – just as we fill our world with noise, because most of us are scared of silence. Being too busy to work towards our dreams is a wonderfully effective form of subconscious self-sabotage.

It's essential to make sure you're focusing on the actions that will make the most difference; ditching or delegating the rest. When you're lined up with your Big Why and your Big Vision, then taking actions towards them will energise you. If your 'to do' list is stressing and exhausting you, instead, then there's either a hidden block running (read on) or you're miles away from your Inner Genius. Here is a reminder of some of the resources we have already covered or which come in future sections:

- Dealing with your 'time stories' – see 'Before We Get Started'
- Clear-out and declutter exercises in Step 0, especially 'spinning plates'
- Your Inner Genius – see Step 1
- How to connect with your Dream Team – see Step 4
- How to overcome your fear of delegating – see Step 4
- Mindfulness and stress-busting resources – later in this section
- Bonus podcast: the dangers of multi-tasking – Readers' Club

And I've got an inspirational video Masterclass for you with Rachelle Strauss, who is a specialist in helping you to ditch overwhelm and get the 'to do' list clarity you need. It's packed with practical strategies and you can find it in the Readers' Club.

Not Hanging Around In Your Genius Zone

If you're stuck spending most of your time doing things that really don't need to be done by you - which don't allow you to hang out in your Genius Zone - then you're in great company. It's an epidemic. And from what I have seen over the years, it either stems from self-doubt - not really believing that you're as good at being 'you' as you are, or from fear of asking for help and support.

One of the things that the EU VAT Action Campaign taught me is that if you don't have support, you drown. And I also know that delegating can be scary.

If the thought of hiring someone to help you with your dreams is secretly freaking you out, then I have make sure you catch the interview with Penny Pullan, author of Virtual Leadership. You can find it in Step 4 – Connecting with your Dream Team.

If the issue is not feeling up to living in your Genius Zone, then keep reading - help is coming.

Self-Care Isn't Selfish - It's Essential

Is it time to top up your world-changer batteries? You are your Big Vision's greatest resource. Yet if we looked after a laptop the same way most of us look after ourselves, we wouldn't expect it to last long. Looking after yourself isn't selfish. It's essential. It's time to stop beating yourself up, and look after yourself, instead.

If you're feeling stressed and exhausted, then it's really hard to connect with your inner passion and inspiration, let alone find the energy to take action. Looking after your physical body is essential, if you want to make a difference in the world, yet so many of us put it last on our 'to do' lists, paying little attention to our health.

In Ancient Sanskrit, there's a holy word called 'ahimsa', meaning non-violence. It's something that Gandhi talked about a lot. But it doesn't just apply to peaceful protests. It also applies to how we live our lives - and how we treat ourselves.

For many people, being kind and compassionate towards others is relatively easy. Being so towards yourself can present more of a challenge. There are two ways you could apply non-violence towards yourself – we're covering the first one here, the second one will come later:

Ahimsa: Non-Violence Towards Your Body

I visited the 800-year-old hermitage of St Francis of Assisi again this summer. And when you sit in his meditation cave, there's no doubt that a spiritual being resided there. It is a wonderful, inspirational place, which leaves you with n feeling of profound peace.

One of the things that St Francis said, as he neared the end of his life, was that he wished he had better looked after his physical body. His neglect of himself caused him to die much younger than he need have done and he realised that he could have helped more people, had he been able to hang around for longer.

Whatever your mission, looking after your body will give you the energy to connect with and help more people, avoiding burnout, and still having time for yourself and your loved-ones.

It's a choice. And nearly everything you can do to look after your body is free. Yes, there are supplements and gym memberships you could pay for, but they're the icing on the cake. Making healthy food choices, drinking enough water, taking gentle exercise, breathing properly (most of us don't), taking time it to rest, allowing your adrenal glands the chance to heal and recharge, avoiding strong stimulants such as coffee or sugar, which offer a temporary boost, but pack as heavy a punch as a clenched fist – all of these are free or very low cost.

Sometimes we're running limiting beliefs that get in the way of looking after ourselves; maybe we don't believe we're worth it, or it would be selfish, or we don't have enough time, or we don't have enough money.

Exercise: Why Is Self-Care So Hard?

You can unpick these beliefs by finishing the sentence:

I can't look after my body, because...

Allow at least seven answers to bubble up. Jot them down and keep them handy for when we reach the limiting beliefs section, soon.

It's important not to let perfectionism get in the way of looking after yourself. Every little thing you to do look after your body will help. Just because you can't do enough 'gym hours' doesn't mean you wouldn't benefit from walking up the stairs, instead of taking the lift, for example. Just because you don't make it to 10,000 steps in a day doesn't mean you failed – celebrate the number of steps you did achieve! Beating ourselves up over our self-care doesn't make us any healthier.

This is such an important topic that I interviewed Heather Bestel for you on it. She is the founder of The Happiness Garden and teaches internationally on the topics of self-care and how to be happy.

Heather has realised that people – especially women – don't take self-care seriously. We put others' needs first and consider looking after ourselves to be something we can do once everything else has been done, as though it were fluffy or frivolous.

We believe that we don't need it, and yet it is the sacred foundation for the work we are here to do. We need to start seeing our health as something to maintain, rather than waiting until we collapse with burnout before taking action. Small, consistent actions will quickly have a major positive effect.

If we're going to have the energy to make a difference in the world, then we need to learn to put our self-care needs first – not last. It's not selfish. You shouldn't feel guilty. Whether you're a stressed-out parent, a CEO or a presenter standing on stage, if your batteries are empty, you're unlikely to be able to help those who depend on you. If we keep putting others first, we end up resenting them – and those receiving our prioritised attention are often totally unaware of the problem. We have to learn to put our own oxygen mask on first.

Heather helps people to figure out why they are resisting looking after themselves. She helps them to learn that meeting their own needs is not just safe, but essential and positive. And she encourages us to teach our loved-ones that our self-care is important – helping them to respect our needs and boundaries.

Above all, if you're running inner blocks that make looking after your body seem somehow selfish, she suggests a reframe: instead of doing it for yourself, how about you do it for your loved-ones? After all, they will benefit from your increased energy levels, your happier frame of mind, your longer fuse before getting angry and you're also setting them a wonderful example for how to live a positive, healthy life.

What could you do *today* to crank up your self-care? Which small step could you take? There's a discussion thread for this in the Readers' Club, as well as the video version of Heather's full interview.

There are some extra resources waiting for you, too, including a bonus 5-day challenge I run, teaching you ways to de-stress and top up your energy levels in under five minutes and how to ditch your energy vampires. There's also a bonus article on whether your Monkey Mind is telling you the truth about stress, and a range of meditation and mindfulness resources, which can make a profound difference to your physical, emotional and mental wellbeing, in as little as ten minutes a day.

Why You Need To Relax

Most of us run on adrenalin, moving from deadline to meeting to mini-crisis, fuelled by caffeine, wheat and sugar and collapsing into bed at the end of the day, only to wake up tired again. Our systems are full of the stress hormones cortisol and adrenalin and our adrenals get fatigued, leading to long term illness and burnout.

On-going stress also makes it harder to think clearly, because your sympathetic nervous system (the bit responsible for the fight-flight-freeze mechanism) prioritises the primal survival part of the brain, diverting blood flow from the pre-frontal cortex where you do rational thinking and can see the consequences of actions. After all, that sabre-toothed tiger wants its dinner now, not once you have figured out the next five contingency steps in your escape plan. But this is also why we end up with such a short fuse, fire-fighting and making decisions when we're stressed out that later seem crazy.

How Stress Levels Build Over Time

If you keep running on low-level stress, never relaxing to rebalance your nervous system, then the effects build up over time. For example, your stress levels go up with the morning rush, when your inbox sends you a Harry Potter-style 'howler', in the queue in your lunchbreak and then in traffic on your way home. If you take sixty seconds to relax, at key points of your day, the stress never builds up. If you don't, then your cortisol and adrenalin levels stay raised and each new stress-trigger makes it worse, until, by the end of the day, you're exhausted.

Learning how to relax only needs to take a few minutes of mindful breathing. It's fast and effective, when you know the techniques. It can:

- slow your heart rate back to normal levels
- rebalance your nervous system

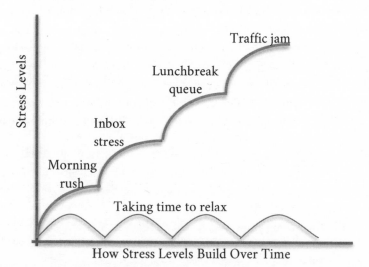

How Stress Levels Build Over Time

- have a healing effect on the body
- help the digestive system to work efficiently
- rebalances your stress hormones
- help you to think more clearly and to concentrate

Surely that's worth a few minutes of your time? If this is an issue for you, then make sure you sign up for my free 5-day challenge on how to de-stress and boost your energy levels in under five minutes (see the Readers' Club). It has already helped thousands of super-busy people to kick their stress-habits and learn quick-fix relaxation techniques, as well as to deal with the root causes of those stress triggers. There are also details of my book *52 Mindful Moments*, which shares techniques to help you cut your stress levels in under sixty seconds. And there is a bonus gift for you of a 20-minute guided deep relaxation MP3, to help you to recharge your batteries and feel full of energy again.

Movement – As A Means Of Releasing Blocks

If you're feeling stressed, overwhelmed, irritable or bored, then the likelihood of you connecting with your inspiration and Daring To Dream Bigger is near-zero. But it can be quite hard to 'think' your way out of those mental states (after all, your brain is the bit that got you there). So when those moods hit, you need to drag yourself out of your stress-head and back into your heart and body.

How can you press 'pause' on stressful thoughts and emotions? By getting active in your physical world.

It might mean dancing to your favourite music or going for a run or taking the dog for a walk or doing your favourite exercise. Being right here, right now, in your body, gets you out of your thinking mind and sets you free from the stories you're telling yourself.

It's why I start any meditation or yoga workshop I run by getting people moving and dancing. It brings you out of your worries and back into the moment, in your body, rebalancing your nervous system and releasing your body's feel-good hormones. If you'd like some inspiration on this, there is a video of a great five minute activation workout waiting for you in the Readers' Club.

The worst thing you can do if you're feeling stuck and stressed is to keep sitting at your desk, thinking about feeling stuck and stressed... If you find you're feeling 'stuck' and you need to tap into some flexibility, then I've got a short bonus video for you in the Readers' Club with a Dru yoga technique called the 'spinal wave'. When your spine is flexible, it allows the body's fluids and energy systems to flow, it oxygenates your brain, and – remember mind and body are linked – increasing flexibility in your body will help your mind's flexibility. It's well worth sixty seconds of your time.

Is Your Stuff Getting In The Way?

When our physical world is already full, we're 'carrying' too much stuff. There's no room for growth and expansion. Sometimes we run from our fears by trying to make ourselves feel better with 'stuff'. We compulsively shop online, getting excited about each big sale and filling our lives with things we didn't really want, that we might not even be able to afford. But it only satisfies that deep inner need for a short while. It never fills the emptiness of being off-path; of not following your Dharma.

We might be hoarding through fear of lack – 'But I might need that someday". It's giving out a silent message that we don't trust our needs will be met. Or it might be fear of letting go of the past. Or guilt that means we hang on to gifts we no longer love, or never liked. So we drown in stuff. We pay for storage for that stuff. We fill our homes with stuff. Our cupboards are bulging. Our shelves are covered in dust. And we wonder why we don't have the headspace to think about our dreams, in order to expand and grow and make a bigger difference.

If this is resonating for you, please revisit Step Zero on *Clear-Out And Declutter*. It could make a transformational difference for you, if you let it.

Putting Food In The Fridge

One of the most common fears that gets in the way of us making a bigger difference in the world is money. "How am I going to make a living?" Money worries hang around in the bottom layers of Maslow's 'Hierarchy of Needs' model, meaning he believed we couldn't move on to 'self-actualisation' – living our Path – until our physiological and safety needs were met. In the yogic tradition, 'money worries' hang around in your bottom two chakras (energy centres) and can block the flow of creativity and inspiration.

Whatever you want to do with your inner genius, whatever difference you want to make in the world, you *do* need to have a plan to be able to feed yourself, and anyone who depends on you. For example, how many struggling artists have we seen, whose brilliance was clear, but who had no plan for how to actually sell their work? This is such a key issue that I interviewed Crista Cloutier for you. She is the founder of 'The Working Artist' and specialises in guiding through creatively-minded people to design a business plan that means they can live what they love, without having to be destitute.

Crista had a successful career, and had worked internationally, but she had a bigger dream. She wanted to pursue her creativity, full time. And whilst she was good at what she was doing, she found herself turning to shopping and other habits, to fill the 'emptiness' that not following her passion was causing. Of course, it didn't work.

So Crista took the dramatic step of selling everything she owned, to clear her debts and to fulfil her creative dreams. Her 'stuff' had been getting in the way. She was hungry to set herself free.

As Crista lined up with her passion, she realised that the difference between successful creatives and those who were struggling to buy food, was an attitude. Those who were flourishing had stopped waiting for a 'fairy Godmother' to come along and sell their art *for* them; they had developed business and marketing plans; they were proactively getting their name known, reaching an audience that valued what they were creating.

So Crista set up The Working Artist, guiding hundreds of artists through how to create a highly effective business plan, in a way that suits their life vision and what is important to them. To get her started, she took the unusual step of using crowd-funding her business, which worked brilliantly. She is passionate about helping people to figure out what a 'meaningful life' would be for them, and to build that around their creative genius.

"I'll never make any money," is a belief, not a fact. You can learn how to make money through your creativity; it's a skill, like any other.

Crista helps people to understand that there are many ways to turn your creative dreams into reality and they don't have to involve moving to a derelict garret in the right part of Paris, giving up your 'day job'. When you shake up what life 'should' look like, and pull together a practical plan that inspires you, you set yourself free to express your creativity *and* still be able to put food in the fridge.

What Ya Gonna Sell, Dude?

If your business isn't turning over enough for you to pay yourself, then it's not a business; it's an expensive hobby. To make it sustainable, you have to put food in the fridge and avoid running up debts. Yes, it takes time to make money, but you have to have a plan to take you there, unless you have other income streams.

So when you're taking that inspired action, at the back of your mind there needs to be a sanity-check, to make sure this action will, somehow, allow you to live, financially.

A few years back, I spent time with Mark Boyle, author of "The Moneyless Man". He is inspirational and spent three years, living without money, near Bristol in the UK, to prove to himself that it could be done. But at the end of it, he concluded that, in the society in which we currently live, money is not optional. He went to extremes, to try to achieve it. But, as things currently stand, most of us can't.

I feel so sad when I see brilliant entrepreneurs going back to day jobs, if it's not what they really want. There are so many ways to be an entrepreneur; it doesn't have to be a full time occupation. And you don't have to quit your day-job tomorrow. If you have clarity and focus and have sorted your time-wasters, you might be surprised how you can ramp up one avenue whilst still working in the other.

A client of mine recently received an email complaint from someone who had been a long-term subscriber to her newsletter. Having received years of free content, my client had sent an email to her readers, asking them to sign up for a paid programme she was running; it wasn't a high cost. The email complaint's main message was, *"I can't believe you charge for your courses!"*

It hit all of my client's hidden 'guilt' and 'resentment' buttons. Once we had dealt with those, here was her response (reproduced with permission):

> "Well, there's this crazy thing that I have to put food in my fridge, or my kids would be taken away from me by social services. And then my team - get this - they insist on me paying them. And I offer a bursary programme, so I have never, ever, ever turned anyone away, based on money.
>
> "And I'm guessing you don't just walk into the supermarket and take food. And you don't expect to get your boiler fixed or your hair cut for free. My courses are no different, especially when you consider the difference they can make for you, and it lasts much longer than a haircut."

Until you value your work, no one else will. Often, "I can't afford it" simply means, "it's not important enough to me." And if your audience doesn't value your work enough to want to make an energy exchange for it, then it's time to change your audience. There is a discussion thread for this topic over in the Readers' Club forum and you'll find a full podcast interview with Crista in the Club, too.

As our Grandmothers used to say: "If you don't value yourself, no one else will."

One Of The Most Potent, Yet Simple, Body-Layer Solutions

When did you last get grounded? As an engineer, I studied the effects of static electricity build-up on machine components and we knew that if we didn't earth the machines, there was a strong chance that things would go wrong with the electronics. It's the same for your body. Coming 'back down to earth' is a vital way of letting go of stress and tension, getting out of your head, back into your body – in this moment. And that's where your power of choice lies.

I often teach the yoga posture *Tadasana* (mountain pose) with a grounding breathing technique, even at the start of business-related workshops. When you know how to stand in your personal power, with the strength and groundedness of a mountain, but the flexibility of a tree in the wind, then life flows around you. It is transformational and you can practise it anywhere, even standing in a queue or sitting in a meeting. If you would like to discover how this technique could boost your confidence and cut your stress levels, there's a short audio to guide you through it, in the Readers' Club.

Spending time in nature, especially if you can go barefoot, helps you to let go of worry-thoughts, rebalance your nervous system, calm your mind and feel more connected with the world around you. Mindful walking is a wonderful way to do this. And there's a guide to this in the Readers' Club, as well as details of Thich Nhat Hanh's beautiful book *Walking Meditation*.

Two other books that I have found really helped with 'physical body' blocks are also listed in there: "Wheat Belly" by William Davis MD and "Revive" by Dr. Frank Lipman. Both of these helped me to understand the role of what I was eating on my physical, mental and emotional health, and my energy levels. If you're running an Adrenal Fatigue pattern, they are well worth a read.

To wrap up this section, I'd love to hear from you: which of these physical-world level blocks have you been running? How were they getting in the way for you? And what are you going to do about them? Let me know via the Readers' Club forum discussion.

And now it's time to move on to the next layer: your inner energy.

Your Energy – Pranamayakosha

I breathe, therefore I am.

This is where your energy levels and life force hang out. If you're running on empty, then this is where to fix it. It is strongly influenced by how you treat your physical body (in Anamayakosha), but also by the way you breathe (pranayama is the ancient study of breathing techniques) and the thoughts you think.

I don't know about you, but I have found that 'feeling exhausted' is one of the most effective ways for me to self-sabotage my dreams. After all, if I have no energy left, I can't take that inspired action, can I?

And I have noticed that the more tired I tell myself I am (more on that in a moment!), then the more I distract myself with social media and Facebook, and the harder I find it to concentrate. But, in over 15 years of working in the online world, I have *never* boosted my energy levels by sitting at my desk, staring at a screen, yet that's what I can end up spending hours doing, when my batteries are at their lowest.

It's hard to feel confident and upbeat and full of passion for your Big Vision, when your inner batteries went the wrong side of the red zone years ago.

Your prana, or life force, is your fuel for getting stuff done. In each moment, we're either topping that life force up, or using it up. It is meant to be used and replenished in a fluid way, but in these fast-paced days of multi-tasking and pushing-on-through, it's common not just to use up your daily energy, which gets topped up each night as you sleep, but also to deplete your longer-term back-up energy stores. And micro-biologists are now finding that the mitochondria in our cells, responsible for energy production[7], are increasingly unable to produce and store energy, because they have become so depleted.

What Drains Your Energy?

If you have been running on empty for a while, pushing yourself to keep going, then your body will be physically exhausted, but you are also likely to be feeling mentally and emotionally exhausted, too. Adrenal

---

[7] See Readers' Club for research and more explanation on this.

Fatigue is a modern epidemic (there's an excellent book on this by Dr James Wilson - details in the Readers' Club). Common energy drains cam quickly empty your inner batteries, and it can feel hard to top them back up. These might include the food we eat, the news we watch, those crazy-difficult people we sometimes have to hang out with, the gossip we share, the thoughts we think, our exercise habits, the stories we tell ourselves and the worries we worry at 3am. The thing is:

No one and nothing can 'steal' your energy, without your consent.

Energy is like a currency, and we can consciously choose how to 'spend' it. When we let it drain away with habits we know feel self-destructive, with food that leaves us feeling exhausted, with thoughts that make us feel terrible, then it's nearly impossible to top it up fast enough to be able to confidently stand in our Soul-Shoes and make the difference we're here to make in the world.

For the rest of this section, I'm going to share with you the main ways to stop draining your energy, and the main way to top back up your energy levels and boost your confidence. And we'll wrap up with a 3-minute guided visualisation and breathing technique for reclaiming your power to choose, if an energy drain is taking over. It's a quick fix that you can use any time, any place.

What's Your Biggest Energy Drain

I mentioned earlier in this section that our self-talk is one of the most potent ways of empowering or disempowering ourselves. But your thoughts are just surface-level symptoms of what's going on underneath. Our self-talk comes from the below-the-surface levels of our beliefs, fears, worries, values and sense of Self. So in this section we're going to discover how to handle your thoughts, if they're getting in the way.

I remember about 15 years ago sitting with a Buddhist Monk who was attempting to persuade my then-chattering-mind to learn how to meditate. I was a classic, compulsive over-thinker.

He was trying to get the group of us to sit silently for twenty minutes and my mind was screaming its objections so loudly that I was sure he must be able to hear them. After a few minutes of him sitting serenely, ignoring my vibes of frustration, I started to feel really angry. And when he told us that any thought or emotion, left to its own devices, will pass on through in sixty seconds, I was ready to yell at him.

I wasn't impressed. And I wasn't convinced. I was determined to prove him wrong.

I had the gift that most of us have - I knew how to make a thought or emotion last not just for minutes, but for hours or even days and weeks. I could go back to that thought and needle it and prod it and poke it and examine it from every angle. I was great at letting the thought trigger more thoughts - memories of each and every time something similar had happened to me in my life - and I would retell myself those stories, indulging in the drama, embellishing the details and cranking up the emotions.

The thing is that your body can't tell the difference between what is happening now, in the 'outside world' and what's happening 'inside'. It's all 'real' to your body. It dutifully triggers the required physiological responses, to support the instructions it's getting from that thought, as we have already discussed. These body-chemistry changes support your emotions, which trigger more similar-themed thoughts, and so it becomes self-perpetuating.

The idea of somehow being able to 'let go' of a thought and not get stuck in that cycle was incomprehensible to me, back then. But, a few years later, when I was training to become a meditation teacher, I realised that the wise old monk had been right.

You can choose which thoughts to feed.

I promise you - it's true! And you can slow them down. And you can make them quieter, so they don't get in the way so much. You can even retrain your brain to get off the complaining train and to think mostly thoughts that make you feel great, instead. And I'm going to show you exactly how. Just imagine how transformational that could be!

When I'm meditating, especially if I get into the habit of doing it daily, I can get to the stage where my thoughts switch off, if I want them to. I can just sit there and wait for the next thought to come along. But when I'm feeling stressed, especially if I'm not meditating regularly (yes, even Meditation Teachers can fall off the wagon), then my thoughts can take over, triggering worries, anxiety, self-sabotage and generally feeling grumpy and irritable.

But as soon as I remember that I am not the 'victim' of my thoughts, and that I have the power to choose which thoughts to feed, I set myself free again. And when I choose to feed the thoughts that make me feel good, the stress-thoughts melt away. In as little as a couple of minutes, my body's physiology comes back into balance, my emotions calm down and I can think more clearly.

Exercise: How Are Your Thoughts Helping Or Hindering Your Big Vision?

Before we dive in, let's figure out the kinds of thoughts you're thinking, so that you can measure the changes you're making:

- What happens to my thoughts when I think about my Big Vision?
- What kinds of thoughts do I think when I imagine achieving / creating my Big Vision?
- As I take action towards my Big Vision, what kinds of things am I thinking?
- What speed do my thoughts run at?
- What volume and pitch are they using?
- Are there any images? What are they like?
- What tone of voice are they using?
- How do I *feel*? Which emotions are these thoughts triggering or feeding?
- What do I notice in my body?

Now you've got that awareness, I want to take you through how to press 'pause' on those thoughts, so they don't get in the way of your dreams.

How To Press 'Pause' On Negative Thinking

Why does negative thinking have such a major effect on our success? Thinking stress-thoughts or worry-thoughts or I'm-not-good-enough thoughts will stop your success in its tracks, unless you have a fabulous team around you, to pick up the pieces. The occasional stress-thought is survivable. But if it's the soundtrack on your favourite inner radio station, then it will sabotage your best efforts.

You'll struggle to grow a successful business or make the difference you dream of in the world, if your self-talk is constantly telling you that you can't.

If your heart is calling you to achieve or create or change something, but your mind is reminding you of all the reasons why you can't, you'll create an inner conflict between your heart's dreams and your thinking mind's permissions. That leads to stress, subconscious self-sabotage and a major case of 'getting in your own way'.

As Heather Bestel said during our interview: "Would you talk to your best friend the way you talk to yourself?"

Your thinking doesn't get in the way of your dreams, unless you believe the stories you're telling yourself.

But most of us don't realise that we can choose which thoughts to feed. In fact, the first time I experienced it, it blew me away. I had lived for decades thinking I had no choice over my thoughts. Once you realise you're in the driving seat, then picking thoughts that make you feel great can become addictive. Of course, there are still times when I dive into the drama, especially when I'm feeling stressed and I secretly want it to be someone else's fault. I don't try to suppress 'sad' emotions. Indeed, choosing which thoughts to feed allows you to experience life more fully, within the entire emotional spectrum. When I find myself indulging those stress-stories, sometimes I press pause, and sometimes I don't; but I know I can always choose, as soon as I'm ready.

Many years ago a dear friend of mine had been reading The Secret. She was inspired and could totally understand how her thoughts were creating her experience of life - and deciding what she could or couldn't achieve. But I remember her sitting on my sofa, in floods of tears, as she asked me, "But how on earth do I change what I think about?! Those thoughts just arrive and I have no control over them. So my life will always be a mess."

The problem isn't the fact that we think. It's that we believe the stories we tell ourselves. And that we believe we have no control over them.

You are responsible for your experience of life. You can't always choose your circumstances, but you can always choose how to respond. And we do that by choosing which thoughts to feed. I want to share with you what I shared with my friend that day.

Exercise: How To Press Pause – And It's Never Too Late

- I'm curious: in the context of your Big Vision, how do you behave towards yourself? Are you pushing yourself hard and driving yourself into the ground? Or are you making sure you're in flow, topping up your batteries regularly, and looking after your business's biggest asset?

- What kind of thoughts are you thinking about yourself, as you step out of your comfort zone, to make the difference you're here to make in the world?

- What do you believe about yourself, your abilities, and your likelihood of achieving success? And I mean what do you *really* believe - I don't want the sanitised public-facing beliefs - I want to know what's running under the surface.

- How are you doing about what's important to you in your life?

- And when you look at all of this, how does it feel, to be on the receiving end of your thoughts and beliefs about yourself? Is it boosting your confidence, or trashing it?

- Is that what you really want?

Shall we do something about it? (*Hint: you can - and by the end of this section you'll have already created lifelong, positive shifts*).

If you're feeling ready to reclaim control over which thoughts you feed, or just curious to feel how it works, here is my deceptively simple ABC process for turning things around. I have taught this to many thousands of people and they are usually amazed by how easy it is, and yet how effective it is.

ABC

The A stands for Awareness.

They say that 'Awareness is the key to change'. If you don't realise you're thinking and feeding thoughts that make you feel bad, then you're not going to be able to do anything about them. So it really helps to pay attention to your body and your emotions. If you notice that you're feeling grumpy, stressed, tense, miserable or whichever other flavour is running, pause for a moment and notice which thought you're currently thinking.

Become aware of it, without trying to change it or judge it or tell yourself stories about how [*insert your favourite self-judging attribute here*] you are. Allow yourself simply to observe this thought.

B stands for Breathe.

Yes, obviously I know you'll be breathing, because otherwise there wouldn't be much thinking going on. But this is about using your breath to get out of your stress-head and back into your body, getting grounded and coming back to this moment.

So gently close your eyes (assuming it's safe to do so) and become aware of your breathing. If it feels comfortable for you, move your breathing from your upper chest back down to your upper belly / diaphragm area. Relax your shoulders, jaw and neck.

Now allow yourself to become fully absorbed by your breathing and the physical sensations of it as you breathe in and breathe out. If you're feeling really tense, you might find that the first few breaths help you to let go if you sigh as you breathe out.

If your mind needs a job, it can recite the following mantras, silently:

In-breath: *I breathe in.*

Out-breath: *I breathe out.*

Do this for at least ten breaths, allowing yourself to let go of any physical tension with each out-breath.

You'll probably find that your breathing rate has slowed. After a minute or so of this, you will have started the process of rebalancing your nervous system and your thoughts are likely to have slowed down. You'll probably find that the tension in your solar plexus area has decreased, your jaw has relaxed and the area around your eyes will feel softer.

And now C is for choose.

When you're in this calmer place, choose to let go of the thought that had been making you feel bad. You might want to imagine it floating across the sky like a cloud, or perhaps sitting on a conveyer belt, moving into the distance. Let it go. It is in the past, now.

And when you feel ready, pick a thought that lifts your spirits. You might want to think of something you feel grateful for, saying a silent, heartfelt 'thank you'. Or perhaps choosing to re-experience a happy memory.

Or maybe you'll just wait to see which thought bubbles up next.

Do this one thought at a time. There's no judgement. And the more often you practise it with slightly annoying, niggling thoughts, the easier you'll find the process if a biggie comes up. It's amazing how quickly this can shift your experience of life.

If you found this process useful, there's an MP3 guided meditation that takes you through it, in the Readers' Club, as well as a highly-effective grounding exercise that really helps when your mind is running wild. You might want to download these MP3s to your computer or phone, so that they are there for you, whenever you need them.

How To Handle Sticky Thoughts

What do you do when a pesky thought just won't move on? Remember the section on 'secondary gain', on page 84? Although it sounds crazy, at some level, that thought is giving you something that you want.

Here's the magic question I use when a thought gets stuck, especially if it's a thought about something that has gone wrong or could go wrong:

- What do I want instead?
- And then feed thoughts that move you towards that.
- There are two essential elements to you answer on this.

Firstly, you need to make it something that is potentially within your control to influence or create. You can't change others; you can only change yourself. So if your 'what do I want instead' requires someone else to change their behaviour, it's not likely to happen and you're not likely to feel better. It can be easier to identify what we *don't* want, rather than what we *do* want.

If that comes up, just ask yourself again: 'what do I want instead?' and tell your mind to come up with something that's within your sphere of influence.

Secondly, you need to make it something positively-phrased, because your unconscious mind cannot process a negative. It first has to imagine the thing you don't want and then adds a token 'not', which gets lost at the end.

For example, if a teacher yells in the playground, "Don't run!" then the child first has to imagine 'running' and then - if there's headspace left - might process the 'not'.

You can try it on for yourself, right now.

> ### Exercise: The Dangers Of 'Don't'
> Whatever you do, don't think of a purple donkey sitting in a pink tree playing a shiny blue saxophone.
> What happened?
> I'm guessing you imagined the purple donkey sitting in a pink tree playing a shiny blue saxophone and then tried to get the image and sounds out of your head, and you might even have been wondering how on earth the donkey got into the tree, how it holds a saxophone and whether or not it's feeling comfortable. I'm curious: which tune was it playing?

The same goes for our thoughts:

"I don't want to mess up today's presentation" is received by your unconscious mind as: "I want to mess up today's presentation - not." In other words, you're going to be subconsciously imagining all the ways you could mess up the presentation, reinforcing those neural pathways and autopilot behaviours, triggering the body's stress responses, and you're risking *increasing* the likelihood of messing up the presentation.

What's the alternative? Phrase it positively: "I want to enjoy today's presentation" or whatever works for you. The key is to aim for a phrase that you believe is possible and which creates a sense of relief, allowing you to let go and expand.

One of the keys I learned when I started meditating regularly is that it's much easier to choose which thoughts to feed, if you're having fewer of them. So if your mind is constantly racing and dragging you into your stress and worry-zones, it's worth experimenting with meditation and mindfulness, to give you tools to slow your thoughts down, day-to-day.

If the idea of this resonates with you, I have some deep-dive resources for you in the Readers' Club, including details of my 28 Day Meditation Challenge and 52 Mindful Moments books, which have helped thousands of people, across the world, to tame their monkey mind and think thoughts that make them feel better. There's also a bonus 20 minute deep relaxation MP3, which can help you to calm a chattering mind, while you recharge your inner batteries.

It's Time To Get Off The Complaining Train

No one is quite sure where our thoughts come from, though neuroscientists and spiritual-seekers alike have their theories. But one thing that most of us instinctively know is that our thoughts have a core theme, which is different for each of us. Some people think lots of thoughts that make them feel happy and empowered. Others think mainly thoughts that lead to overwhelm, anxiety and stress. We all have our pet themes, and they can change over time.

One of the most common themes is being stuck on the 'complaining train'. In the UK, where I live, it's part of our national identity. We find it hard to talk about things going well (I'm massively generalising here!) and it's not politically correct to stand tall and be proud of your achievements. If someone dares to stand tall and 'own' what they have achieved, they can find themselves shot down. And we love to gossip, which is a way of spreading stories that produce an emotional response, usually at the expense of the lead character in the story.

Regular doses of complaining and mentally criticising others sets the frequency of your inner radio station so that you attract more thoughts that are about complaining. It also creates strong neural pathways in your brain, so that if something even slightly bad happens, you dive into your well-rehearsed negative-thinking complaining response. It gives your mind the clear instruction that judgement is the way to go, so you risk creating motorway-speed autopilots that give your Inner Critic (who we'll meet in more detail in the next section) permission to judge you, as well as encouraging you to judge others.

A belief is a thought that crystallises as fact.

The more you indulge complaining-style thoughts, the more you will be forming and supporting beliefs that filter out the good bits in life and show you the bad bits, wherever you look. I'm not suggesting that you white-wash or pretend that everything is ok. But there are ways to get off the complaining train, no matter how subconsciously addicted to it you might have been.

And one of my favourites is gratitude.

If you get into the habit of thinking about things you feel thankful for, you are 'rewiring' your brain and positively affecting your nervous system, cutting your stress levels. Neurological and psychological research has shown that as little as three weeks of keeping a gratitude journal, for example, can have a measurable impact on the tone of your thoughts and your emotions, and can alleviate mild depression[8]. In my

---

[8] See Readers' Club for sources.

experience with my clients and students, it can be take even less time than that.

If you want to increase the probability that the thoughts that bubble up are generally positive and make you feel good, then practising gratitude at regular points during your day can help you make that difference.

I've got some bonus techniques, videos and articles for you in the Readers' Club on this, as well as details of my best-selling journal: A Year Full Of Gratitude and a deep-dive online course: Getting Started With Gratitude, which is a 21 day programme for you to make gratitude part of your daily life, no matter how busy you are. There are also short training videos on how to shift the tone, the volume, the speed and the feel of your inner voice, and how to press 'pause' on those thoughts, if you're feeling stressed, and a 5-minute bonus video-guide on practical ways to get started with 'gratitude', even if you're a complete beginner.

There's also a bonus workbook on why positive affirmations don't work, and what you can do, instead. So there's plenty there to support you with getting off the complaining train, if that's what you want! I want to make it as easy as possible for you.

It's time for you to reclaim the power to choose which thoughts to feed. I strongly encourage you to play and experiment with the strategies in this section, to find out what works for you. Please let me know how you get on, via the forum in the Readers' Club.

Are You Throwing Your Energy Away?

Recent research showed that adults typically spend five hours per day watching TV, listening to the radio and surfing the internet, in non-work-related activities. In those hours, we are bombarded with other people's opinions; with headlines designed to wind us up to get us to click; with sensationalist news stories of doom and disaster; of gossip and ridicule of those we only yesterday put on pedestals. It convinces us that the world is a terrible place, to be feared, where standing up for what you believe and making a difference feels impossible.

Remember we talked about how your body can't tell the difference between reality and your imagination? Well, those stories you're watching, reading and listening to can trigger your stress hormones, as though they were actually happening. The emotion-rich news that fills our screens can make it nearly impossible to feel happy. Neuroscientists have even shown that regular consumption of violent news and computer games can shrink the area of the brain responsible for compassion, which is a scary prospect.

"Good news doesn't sell." That's what Geri Weis-Corbley was told, back in her days in TV news broadcasting. It drove her to create the Good News Network, back in 1997 – to help redress the balance in the media we consume. With her hugely-popular website, she collects positive and inspirational news stories from around the world (more in the Readers' Club).

How often do we actually *choose* what to consume; be it a newspaper, magazine, book, news programme or website? And how often are we consuming on autopilot? When you consider the potential effects on our body, thoughts and emotions, surely it's worth exercising a little more choice? And in a world where we feel so time-poor, could you cut out some of your 'consuming', to free up time to work towards your dreams?

There's a discussion thread in the Readers' Club for you, on what we consume and why – and how we might motivate ourselves to change those habits.

The Energy-Boosting CEO Mindset Shift

Running a business doesn't mean you have to be 'busy' all the time. It's one of the fastest ways to drain your energy: keeping going, despite being exhausted, pushing yourself to hustle, when your body, mind and Soul are screaming for a break.

I remember one of my earliest mentoring clients, MD of a division of a large international company, telling me that he never felt bad about going to the golf course on workday afternoons, because that's where he came up with his 5-figure+ ideas. I know, personally, that I can create a whole training course in a day, if I'm away from my 'normal' routine, especially if I go somewhere warm and sunny, where I feel 'looked after'. It's why I love running business breakthrough retreats. Inspiration and ideas flow.

As your business initially grows, you'll start by doing most things yourself, unless you have funding for a support team. But there will quickly come a time when that is no longer sensible. You become the biggest block to expansion and to delighting your customers. You can't do it all yourself, any more.

I talked to Adam Dobay about this. He has a background in film and storytelling and has held over 400 talks on how stories resonate with people. Together with his wife, Livia Farkas (we meet her soon), they run Cabbit Supreme, which helps digital entrepreneurs to connect with their audiences, on a human level. They have to work especially hard on work-life balance, because otherwise their business would take over all aspects of their lives. Here is some of what Adam has learned:

> Just because you have 'some time', don't fill it up with work. It's essential to create work-free time, to rest. It's even more important, if you live with your business partner! But you have to plan it in or it won't happen. When you're into the 'hustle' of working 'in' your business, it's easy to forget how many hours a week you just worked.

> If you wake up at 3am with a brilliant idea, by all means get up and scribble notes. But then you need to make sure you take time out to rest, later in the day.

> To help make sure they don't let their business take over, Adam and Livia schedule regular time when they go out and don't talk about their businesses. They find this really helps them to remember that there is life 'outside' of their business life.

> Adam sees the shift from solopreneur to CEO-mindset being, in part, about valuing your time. He says it's important to look at what your time is worth and to invest it wisely. There's no benefit in you spending, say, eight hours transcribing videos, when someone else (better at it than you!) could have done that for you, freeing up your time to do something else that you're great at.

> And it's not just about work. Going to a café for three hours can be a worthwhile investment, if that gives you the headspace you need to come up with new ideas. Sometimes you need to get out of your home or office, to somewhere that you are choosing to focus on just one project, to get maximum value from your time.

> If you're doing things you don't enjoy, it will divert your energy from the actions where you can make a bigger

difference. So if that means getting help with your cleaning or cooking or your or your website maintenance, do it. Although the costs are a factor, if you are using that freed-up time to move your business forwards, it will pay back.

Adam has found that letting go of the need for things he delegates to be 'perfect' has helped him to free up more time and energy. The way he sees it, if he delegates a task and it comes back 80% right, then he needs to put in maximum 20% of the original effort to make it 100%. It is often cheaper to delegate the things you don't want to do any more than to do them yourself. That balance is an essential skill, as you move from solopreneur to CEO.

Adam and Livia's full interview is in the Readers' Club. Their story about relocating from their native Hungary to the UK is a shining example of having courage in your Big Vision and taking inspired action to make it happen.

How Can You Top Up Your Energy Levels?

One of the most potent ways of building up energy – your prana - is silence; quietening your mind and turning off outside-world distractions, such as TV, computers, phones and radio. When you go on a meditation retreat, chances are there will be some silent time, outside of the meditation sessions. This is because you need to build up energy to concentrate, which is a step on the journey towards meditating. Chatter and noise deplete our energy, so spending time in silence, even in the company of others, helps to replenish your stores.

You can experience this for yourself by taking quiet time each day. You might choose to meditate for ten minutes (suggested resources are in the Readers' Club) or go for a mindful walk, or just sit with your eyes softly closed, letting your awareness gently rest on your breathing. These are all wonderful ways to increase your energy levels and even boost your confidence, because that quiet time calms your mind, rebalances your nervous system and tames your Inner Critic.

Have You Forgotten How To Breathe?

The breath is the bridge between the body and the mind. ~ Chris Barrington

When we feel stressed, our breathing moves to the upper chest area, the shoulders and the throat, and you're only using a tiny proportion of your lungs, restricting the oxygen levels in the body. This drains your energy and makes it hard to think clearly. It triggers further stress responses in your body and leaves you feeling exhausted.

When you feel confident, you stand tall, your posture is strong and your breathing comes from your belly. When you lack confidence, your posture is likely to get 'smaller'. We tend to slouch and round our shoulders, which triggers the same stress-related breathing patterns.

Since mind and body are linked, you can shift the mind's thoughts and emotions through changing your posture. You can also build up your energy levels through special breathing techniques, called Pranayama.

In my workshops, I teach a wide range of these tools, whether you're coming to me for meditation or for senior management training – they are so powerful. And in this section, I want to share with you two techniques. We'll cover a third in Step 5.

The first is alternate nostril breathing, which is simple to do (you can even do it in a meeting) and it brings the two main aspects of your nervous system into balance, allowing you to be relaxed, but alert. It helps you to calm your mind, to feel more grounded and confident.

The second is the classic Deep Yogic Breath, which helps you to calm your body, mind and emotions, and encourages you to use your full lung capacity. The inner stillness this gives you can boost your confidence.

I have videos for you explaining both of these techniques, which are fantastic energy-boosters, in the Readers' Club. I strongly suggest you pop over there now and experience these for yourself.

How could you find five minutes a day to top up your energy levels with these (or other) breathing techniques? What action do you need to take, to mark that time in your diary? Let us know, via the discussion forum, how you get on.

We are just scratching the surface of Pranamayakosha (your energy body) and how it can help you to make a bigger difference in the world, but I hope you have found it useful so far. If you want to know more, I run regular retreats on these techniques, where we get to dive in more deeply.

Your Mind And Emotions - Manomayakosha

I think, therefore I am.

This layer is like the spark to the fuel in your energy body, telling it where to focus and igniting your passion. It includes your thought pattern habits, beliefs, values and needs, and also how you process the world, via your senses. It's also the home of your Inner Critic – and your Inner Cheerleader. Your emotions hang out here and they drive your passion, motivation, illusions and fears. Manomayakosha provides the energy and framework behind the thoughts that we think and triggers the stories we tell ourselves. It is the home of your Will – your determination. Manomayakosha is where we find the root causes of many of the symptoms from the first two layers. So shall we dive in?

Wave Goodbye To Limiting Beliefs And Self-Sabotage

Let's start with beliefs. Our beliefs can empower or limit us. And we rarely consciously choose them. They are sometimes formed by thinking a particular thought over time, or they can be 'facts' we're presented with, which we choose (at a deep level) not to doubt. But even the most empowering belief can become limiting, over time, as you learn and grow.

Beliefs are like boxes, within which
we experience life.

And they are real - being part of the Reticular Activating System (RAS)[9] in your brain, which is the portal through which nearly all information arrives in your brain, and it filters out most of the data that comes in, so we don't get overwhelmed. It's really useful.

Imagine trying to walk along a path if you were consciously aware of each step, which muscles were being used, your heart rate, your blood pressure, the oxygen levels in the air around you, whether or not you were allergic to the various pollens in the air, the air pressure, the moisture levels, the temperature, the length of the toenail on the little toe on your left foot? You'd never leave the house. Yet your body is - at an unconscious level - noticing all of this. It needs this information to know

---

[9] See Readers' Club for more information

how to keep you safe and healthy. But your RAS filters the information out of your conscious awareness, because you don't need to know it.

The filters in your brain govern what you notice in life. That's why, if you have programmed them to find things to complain about, as in our last section, you'll spot more things to complain about. You have trained that part of your brain to let that information through. It's the same as when someone buys a red car, suddenly every car on the road seems to be red.

Our brain gives us information that backs up what we believe and what is important to us.

It's one of the reasons why being a researcher or a scientist can be so challenging. Collecting truly unbiased data can be difficult, because our brain tends to discount information that doesn't fit with what we believe. So researchers have to be trained to be open to disproving their own hypothesis.

Our beliefs create our expectations and govern our comfort zones. If you believe you're not good at something, you'll find evidence to support that belief, you'll think thoughts that perpetuate that belief, and you'll take actions that prove you're right.

Similarly, your expectations about how something might happen or how someone might behave will filter the information you notice about that situation, and you tend to get what you believe. If you believe that Dave is going to be difficult to work with on a project, then you will notice all the things that prove you are right, and you'll subconsciously filter out all the time he is neutral. And if he dares to be *helpful*, you'll risk writing it off as a fluke.

Your beliefs are neural pathways in your brain. Just as you can create new neural pathways if you learn a new fact or skill, so you can rewrite those belonging to your limiting beliefs. Your limiting beliefs are responsible for your:

- Comfort zones
- Excuses
- Inner Critic - that voice in your head that tells you all the reasons why you're not good enough
- Self-sabotage, where you turn down golden opportunities
- Key decisions - you're unlikely to make an important decision if you don't believe that choice is possible

- The actions you're prepared to take, towards your dreams
- The extent to which you connect with people and magnetise your dream team and audience
- Your expectations of your performance - and that of others
- How much money you're prepared to earn
- Whether you'll accept publicity opportunities
- How much success you can handle
- Whether you'll feel happy or guilty about your achievements
- How big a difference you will make in the world

You get what you believe. As Henry Ford famously said:

"Whether you believe you can, or you believe you can't, you're right."

People sometimes try to dispute this using examples like, "if you believe you can jump off a tall building and fly, you still won't be able to!" And I agree with them. But there's a difference between a belief and a crazy state of self-delusion. And sometimes, yes, we can achieve things that we didn't believe were possible, particularly if it's lined up with our Big Vision. But don't underestimate the power of your beliefs to determine the level to which you achieve your dreams.

Who Is Making Your Major Life Decisions?

Most of us like to believe that *we* are, unless we're running a victim-pattern, in which case most things in life feel beyond our control. But our decisions are often not made by the grown up version of us.

The biggest decisions in your life are probably being made by your inner seven-year-old.

When we pick up a limiting belief and run with it for decades, it becomes a guiding principle for life, onto which we hang other beliefs and decisions. These beliefs are called 'core beliefs'. And if you're running a core belief of, for example, "Things never work out for me, so it's best not to try," then it's unlikely that you'll take actions that you feel could be risky. But it's not the 'adult you' making that choice - the one who has succeeded, even when the stakes were high and times were tough - it's the 'younger you'. Our choices get limited by a belief that got stuck in time, meaning we're effectively using the thought processes that belonged to our inner child, who accidentally picked up that belief.

Our beliefs shut down our options, usually without us realising. And that's how your inner seven-year-old (or younger!) accidentally ends up making some of your biggest life choices.

By the time you have finished this Handbook and its bonus resources, it won't be that way for you any more. So let's start by figuring out how to spot some limiting beliefs.

Exercise: How Do You Spot Your Limiting Beliefs?

Here are some of the questions I would ask you, if we were in a one-to-one mentoring session together. There's a worksheet and audio for this exercise, at the Readers' Club.

Take a deep, sighing breath, to settle yourself back into this moment. Then, thinking about your Big Vision, ask yourself:

- What do I believe about my ability to achieve my Big Vision?
- Am I the kind of person who can achieve this? Yes / no, because…

And now complete the following statements – listing multiple answers to each, if they come up:
- I haven't done it yet, because…
- I can't do it, because…
- I'll never achieve it, because…

Keep going with your answers to these statements until you have at least ten responses to each - some may be the same – and some might feel a bit mad, but that's ok. It's important to let them 'bubble up', without judgement or editing.

If you feel you get stuck at four or five, take a deep breath in and breathe out with a sigh, then add some more. The gems are the ones below the surface, which are usually towards the end of your list. If you get stuck and your thinking mind objects, this phrase often helps:

"And if there *were* more, what might they be?"
It opens it up to the possibility of diving in more deeply.

These are the limiting beliefs, excuses and comfort zones that are running behind the scenes. And there's nothing wrong with them, if they're genuinely making you happy and allowing you to express who you really are. But if they aren't, then it's time to wave them goodbye.

Now, this is the point where many people trip up. It's easy to try to find someone or an event to 'blame' for 'giving' us that old belief. Whilst this can sometimes be helpful as part of a therapeutic intervention, especially if it's combined with forgiveness work, it's also a great way to keep yourself stuck feeling like a victim, abdicating your power over who you become in life to that person from your past. So please resist the temptation to apportion blame - especially to yourself. And if you need extra help with this, please get professional support.

How To Handle Your Limiting Beliefs

Once you're aware of them, many of your limiting beliefs will melt away just by looking at them, on paper, and realising that they're not true. It might have applied to the seven year old you that picked up that belief, but you can see it's not true now. I call it the 'Duh! Test'. It's a face-palm moment when you look at the belief objectively and, by seeing that it's patently not true, it melts away. If any of those in the exercise fit that category, draw a great big line through them now.

For others, they'll need a little work.

It's really important that you allow your limiting beliefs just to melt away or soften and dissolve, rather than forcing them and trying to get rid of them. As Carl Jung said, what you resist persists. So if you fight against that old belief and try to destroy it, you're actually giving it all of your attention - and potentially your power. Also, it has been part of you for so long, and rejecting yourself is a great way to get your Inner Critic yelling at you again.

Exercise: How To Handle Those Limiting Beliefs

Here are some of my favourite mentoring questions for this. I strongly suggest you start with one belief at a time, perhaps one that's a 3 or 4 out of 10, so you learn the process for handling them and get used to the idea of shifting them.

...Continues

Remember: for anything really big or yucky, get yourself the support that you need, please. You can do this. And sometimes having someone to guide you makes it so much easier. There's a worksheet and audio for this at the Readers' Club.

Pick a belief that made it through the 'Duh! Test', answer these questions:

- Is it really true?
- Who says?
- Is that what I want to believe?
- What do I want to believe, instead? (Follow the tips for the 'what do I want instead' question at the end of the ABC technique on page 131)
- How could I collect evidence to support that new belief?
- Which thoughts might I think?
- Which actions might I take?
- How does it *feel*, having let go of the out-of-date belief?

For the 'what do I want to believe, instead?' it's important to make it something that your body tells you is possible. It can be hard to replace "I can't" with "I can". If saying that new belief to yourself causes your body to tense or constrict, then your mind hasn't accepted it and you need to do some of the work in the rest of this section, first.

For any beliefs that are feeling 'sticky', there's a five minute guided MP3 in the Readers' Club, which people have found really helpful. It's normally something people pay for on my website, but it's yours as my gift, to help you to release stuck, out-of-date beliefs. And, remember, you might have a belief that would benefit from some mentoring or other professional support. When you consider the benefit that releasing it could have on the rest of your life, it's worth the investment, rather than spending decades feeling stuck and playing smaller than you need to.

Why 'Can' Is Not The Opposite Of 'Can't'

There's no such thing as "can't". But that doesn't mean you can.

My Great Aunty Yo was famous for being a teeny bit dotty, but she had a secret that she shared generously, with all who would listen. I remember the "no such thing as can't!" message being thrown back at me, every time she spotted one of my excuses, as a kid. Back then, I didn't appreciate her secret much. "What's stopping you?" Couldn't she see? Of course I couldn't do xyz, because…

Then, as I got older, I started to understand. She wasn't trying to tell me that, at 5'2" tall, there was nothing stopping me from being an Olympic high jumper. She just wanted me to see the blindingly obvious truth:

"I can't" was my excuse for anything I didn't want to do - or didn't believe I could do.

At a gentle level, she was helping me to learn that there are only two things that risked getting in my way in life:

1. What I believe is possible or impossible.
2. What I choose to do / not to do.

For those of us who are used to positive thinking and all its friends, you might think that the fix for this one is to replace "can't" with "can". But it doesn't work… You're trying to do a U-turn flip from a negative to a positive and your Monkey Mind will go all-out to resist that, digging its heels in, to defend the decades of evidence it has collected. Instead, you need to soften and shift old beliefs, letting them go, rather than kicking them out in fit of rage.

If we have invested time and effort into creating a belief that we can't do something, simply picking the positive affirmation that we 'can' do it doesn't change that belief. Instead, it sets up an internal conflict:

Our thinking mind tries to say yes. Our unconscious mind (which runs the show), says no.

All that is likely to happen is that you'll feel frustrated and miserable. If you try it out now on one of your "can't" beliefs, you'll probably notice that it causes physical tension, too. So what's the answer?

Maybe. Perhaps. Might.

Think of that "can't" belief. Instead of forcing it to be a "can", try softening things with, "perhaps I might…"

Can you feel the difference? You're opening up the possibility –

gently and without creating resistance. As your old belief dissolves and you collect evidence to support the new belief, then, 'maybe' will naturally shift into 'probably'; soon to become a 'can'. Imagine that ingrained belief softening and melting, like an ice cube in the Indian sun, until it finally disappears. Doesn't that feel easier than trying to smash it with a hammer? Isn't that a kinder way of making changes in your life? And I've got a bonus mentoring process MP3 waiting for you in the Readers' Club, to help you to really try that new belief on for size, and to fast-track its journey to becoming your new 'normal'.

Don't Get Rid; Release And Let Go

It's really important to truly let go of those old beliefs. Although it no longer serves you, it has been an important part of who you have become now, a vital part of your journey. Acceptance of the part it played in your life is an important stage of moving on.

It's important to accept and forgive yourself for the thoughts and actions that old limiting belief triggered in you. There's no point in letting go of that belief, only to fill its space with regret and guilt. Honour the journey those beliefs triggered; the personal growth that happened. welcome the 'new' version of you that feels more free and empowered.

To set yourself free from the old 'energy' of that belief, you might want to imagine a giant pair of scissors cutting any invisible ties you had to it. You will also find it helpful to spend a moment quietly reflecting on what you learned from having that belief; perhaps even giving gratitude to the lessons it taught you. It can really help to write these down.

If there's a belief you're hanging on to, it's worth revisiting the section on 'secondary gain' on page 84 to find out what it's 'doing' for you.

And if you can find a way to accept and forgive anyone else involved, over time, too, that will truly set you free. There's a bonus video for you in the Readers' Club on why forgiveness is the key to freedom – and how it's not about pretending that the other person's behaviour was ok.

If you're stuck with one of your beliefs on this, then EFT (Emotional Freedom Technique; 'tapping') is an effective way to release those old ties. I have pulled together some of 'how-to' videos for EFT for you in the Readers' Club, including the basics of getting started, from Brad Yates. And there's an inspirational interview with Joel Young, on Non-Personal Awareness: a technique I have found life-changing. There are are also suggestions for yoga postures that can help to release attachment to the past, enabling you to move forwards, with newfound confidence.

How To Support Your New Belief

This is one of my favourite ways of working with hidden belief blocks with clients. Did you know that your beliefs are context-dependent? We tell ourselves stories about them that make them feel like a Universal Truth, but actually a belief is only valid in the context in which it lives.

If you try to bully a belief into disappearing through contradicting it, you'll hit the 'Backfire Effect' (see page 106), when that belief will dig its heels in even more deeply and get entrenched in defending its point of view. But if you present your mind with evidence that it already accepts as true, from a different context, then you reduce resistance.

For example, you might be great at being organised at work, but your home life feels chaotic. If you want to feel more organised at home, have a chat with your unconscious mind (yes, you can do this – just imagine it in your head!) and ask the bit of it responsible for feeling organised at home what it could learn from the bit of you that manages it at work. Look at what might be different between the two contexts, and what is the same.

Which thoughts and actions could you shift at home, which would allow you to bring home the skills you clearly have at work? Then pick one element of these and do whatever it takes to make it your new-best-friend habit for the next week. And then pick another element. And another. And make sure that when you tell yourself old stories about being badly organised at home, you press 'pause' and show your mind the evidence that you *can* do this, even if it's in a different context, so it must – somehow – be possible at home, too. Have a play with this and let me know how you get on, via the Readers' Club discussion thread.

Juliet McKenna, a best-selling Science Fiction and Fantasy Author, shared a practical example of how she did this, when I interviewed her for this Handbook. (We'll meet Juliet again in Step 3). She was Co-Founder of the EU VAT Action Campaign – a role that took the whole team out of our comfort zones, as small business owners, when we suddenly had to debate the minutiae of European VAT law with people who had lived and breathed such topics their entire career.

Holding your own in a meeting in Downing Street or the European Commission takes guts, especially when people don't want to admit the extent of the problem you are there to tell them about.

As an Author, accounting wasn't Juliet's forte, and she could easily have allowed herself to feel intimidated by the behaviour of the key decision-makers. In fact, she admits that she initially felt way out of her depth. So she made a choice: to show courage, despite her inner fears, because hundreds of thousands of micro businesses were relying on the campaign. And, to find that courage, she looked to other areas of her life.

Instead of focusing on what she *wasn't* good at, she built on her core strengths. She gave all her energy to what she *could* do. Her college days had taught her how to analyse and construct a narrative argument, that allowed people to move from one point of view to another, backed up by evidence. And she knew a huge amount about how the publishing industry worked, and how the new rules could inadvertently devastate it, so she was able to share compelling case studies to back up her position.

For her confidence, in the face of disbelief and defensive contradiction, she drew on her grounded calmness from her Aikido background. Juliet is a 3rd Dan Black Belt and she anchored herself in her confidence from Aikido, whenever she needed to stand in her Truth.

Her advice to you is that, whatever you want to achieve, you *do* have transferable skills. If you are feeling inadequate or lacking in confidence, look at the skill or belief you need, then find somewhere in your life where you have demonstrated a similar quality, and bring that into your new project. If you can't think of an example, then go and create some! Pick an area unrelated to whatever is scaring you, build up your confidence in yourself in that context, and then bring that confidence into your Big Vision.

In the NLP world, this is about 'mapping across' your inner qualities, so that they are available to you in any context. A single mentoring session can make a profound difference, if you need support with this.

This is just the beginning of what we could cover with limiting beliefs and I hope you have found the techniques helpful so far. As with so many of the topics we're covering in the Dare To Dream Bigger Handbook, it could deserve to be an entire book on its own, so to make sure you have everything you need, there are some additional, transformational resources waiting for you in the Readers' Club. There's a deep-dive video masterclass on how to handle limiting beliefs and there's also a full hour-long video training on how to set yourself free from old comfort zones, without freaking out or life falling apart.

The Two Most Dangerous Words You Have Used Today

These two words will either trash or create your dreams. Each and every day we use them, telling the world who we believe we really are – these are like super-belief statements and they talk to your unconscious mind at an identity level. When you make shifts to what happens at that deep level, it creates knock-on changes in every area of your life.

These two little words either open up the possibility of creating your dreams, or make double-sure they'll never come true. I'm guessing you've probably used these words many times already today:

"I am..."

Here are some really common 'I am' statements:

- I am bad
- I am exhausted
- I am not good enough
- I am too busy
- I am too old / young
- I am not qualified enough
- I am bored
- I am fed up

- I am sick and tired of…
- I am angry
- I am an addict
- I am a failure
- I am worried
- I am rubbish at…
- I am sad
- I am stressed

As soon as you use the words "I am", you lock whatever comes after it. It becomes part of your identity. It is taken by your unconscious mind as a statement of fact - an instruction - with which it must comply.

We equate our outward behaviour - the symptom - with who we really are. And we do that for others, too. Think about the way we give feedback, especially to children:

- You are so clumsy!
- You are so naughty!
- You're no good at that!

Not convinced yet? Want to try it out? Here's a classic exercise that NLP Trainers love to run:

Exercise: The Power Of 'I Am'

Sitting on a chair, recite out loud: "I am tired and weak!" Put some conviction into it. Keep saying it as you allow your body to shift into a position that fits with what you're saying. Really mean it.

Now try to stand up.

Hard work? Shake it off!

Now sit down again, and this time recite out loud: "I am powerful and strong!" Really mean it. Allow your body to move into whatever position it wants to, as you keep saying the phrase. And when you feel ready, stand up. Did you fly across the room?

That only took a few seconds. So can you imagine the effect that decades of "I am" statements could have on each cell in your body? On the neural pathways in your brain? On your values? Your beliefs? Thoughts? Actions? Your body is the barometer of whether your 'I am' statements are empowering you – or trashing your confidence.

Exercise: Your Body Is Your Barometer

Here are some simple, 'I am' statements for you to play with – they're the kind of thing we use daily:

"I am cross."　　　　　"I am angry."　　　　　"I am fed up."

There will be a physical reaction in your body.

Now try these:

"I am happy."　　　　　"I am excited.　　　　　"I am passionate"

There's a different physical reaction in your body, depending on the kinds of 'I am' statements you're thinking to yourself, or telling to others. That physical reaction and those thoughts are connected; they feed each other.

Most of us use 'I am' statements without even realising. When you spot an 'I am' statement in your head, press that pause. As a 'first aid' technique for times when your mind is racing with self-judgemental chatter, remember to use the 'ABC' method we used for self-talk.

Exercise: Spotting Your 'I Am' Statements

Which 'I am' statements do you use in a typical day?
Which of them make you feel great and confident? Which make you feel bad? How about jotting down some of your favourites in the margins here or in a notebook, before we carry on?

How To Change Unsupportive 'I am' Statements? Do the A, B, C:

Accept: Ok... I used an "I am" statement.
Breathe: Coming back into your body and out of the mind.
Choose: Is that an "I am" statement that makes me feel great? Does it open me up? Does it allow me to have possibilities to expand, or is it one that makes me feel bad? Choose which one to feed.

Do I want to keep feeding that "I am" statement? Yes? No? You can choose. If the answer is no, just let it drift on by and pick another one. It's that simple. And I'm going to share more deep-dive techniques with you, in a moment.

Beware The Label...

As soon as you give yourself a label (the bit after the 'I am'), you are defining the box within which you are going to live and experience life. Even positive 'I am' statements can restrict you, as you outgrow them, over time.

We even do it with psychological profiling. By simplifying behaviour into a 'model', we gain insights into our actions, habits and preferences - and those of people around us, based on certain assumptions. It can help us to make changes. But there's a drawback: most of us use these models, with great enthusiasm, to put ourselves into boxes.

How often have you heard someone come back from a personal development course, proudly proclaiming, "I'm a [insert newly-chosen label here]....!"

That's when behaviours - something that can be changed at will - get mixed up with personality or identity - which most people in our Western culture believe is unchanging.

Back in my corporate days, I remember enjoying a course on Myers Briggs Personality Types (originally based on the work of the Swiss psychologist Carl Jung). As a tool to understand behaviours and why some people get on well with each other, whilst others don't, it's a really valuable resource. But only if you understand that a person is *not* their behaviour and that behaviour can change. All a 'personality questionnaire' can ever test is your behaviour – your choices in certain contexts. And, as we have discussed, our behaviour is different, in different circumstances. It changes, over time.

A personality test can only tell you about your
behaviour. It can't tell you who you really are.

For the next few weeks at work, the office was full of everyone saying things like, "I'm an INFP!" or "I'm an ENTJ!". It had been decreed on the course that women who ran an ENTJ behavioural preference (which I did at the time – though I don't now) would find it hard working with strong-minded men, as the men could feel threatened. So a female-only ENTJ support network was created. Talk about reinforcing the stereotypes, the fears and the excuses! We were even told by the trainers that our Myers-Briggs 'type' was 'set in stone' and would never change.

The problem with all this is that the model's labels become our 'reality'. The label can keep us stuck. It tells us that things are black or white, rather than shades of grey. We have picked our box and now it's time to live in it. Instead of helping us to see how we currently behave, so we can become more flexible, the label can become our excuse for not changing.

"But I can't do it that way. That course said I'm a ... person! It's just who I *am*."

"Of course I'll never get on with him. He's a ... and I'm a ..., so we're always going to clash."

We believe the label and often modify our behaviour
accordingly.

I have lost track of how many mentoring clients I have seen do this, after being sent on courses at work or reading influential self-help books. They change their behaviour to fit the identity given to them by their new box. Rather than expanding their comfort zones and increasing their behavioural flexibility, it can create new beliefs that limit their potential for change.

But you *can* shift this, almost instantly, without white-washing or pretending that everything is great. And it's not about heading for the opposite; remember the unconscious mind can't process a negative (how's that donkey doing with his saxophone playing?). Doing a U-turn only leads to internal conflict and stress. So how do you create the shift?

It's Time To Get Your Verb On!

When you use *I am* followed by a noun or adjective, you freeze time. It's an identity-level statement that will never change, unless you put in some conscious effort.

To shift it, all you need to do is to get some movement back into your language. In engineering terms, it's like the difference between static friction and dynamic friction. To get an object that's standing still to move takes more effort than to keep a moving object going.

So if you want to make changes in who you are telling yourself that you are, the first step is to turn that solid-object-statement into something that is flowing and moving, because then your mind starts to believe that change could be possible.

All you need to do is to use a verb: verbs imply movement and action, so they'll get you unstuck.

Let's start with the statement "I *am* exhausted". It's as though you're telling yourself that this is *who you are*, and it's *how life is* and will always be. How about, instead, telling yourself, "I *feel* exhausted." Can you feel the difference? One has the finality of a fist thumping on a meeting room table. The other is softer and has the feeling that it's a transient and perhaps changeable state, rather than a forever-fact.

Instead of "I'm not good enough" you might play with, "I notice that I'm *thinking* I'm not good enough." So the statement is that you're *thinking* it, rather than *being* it. It opens the door to this not being a permanent state, which gives you back your power to choose.

Instead of "I am worried", how about "I worry, that..."?

Can you feel the difference that ditching "I am" and bringing in a verb makes? It often allows your body to release tension and can bring with it a sense of relief.

How To Use This To Create Deep-Acting Change

The power of 'I am' is one of the reasons why positive affirmations so often don't work (there's a whole video masterclass on this in the Readers' Club). It's the flip flop phenomenon again.

If you are used to telling yourself that you are not good enough, and then try to tell yourself that you *are* good enough, then your mind will object. It has invested decades in telling that story and collecting evidence and nurturing beliefs to support that identity-level statement. The new belief feels like a lie.

There will also be a decent dose of secondary gain running. So affirmations that directly contradict your long-cherished status quo are likely to be met with a pantomime-style yelling match of "Oh yes I am!" and "Oh no I'm not!"

What can you do instead? Choose your 'I am' statements with care and make them expandable. You don't want to replace one frozen-in-time identity statement with another. So instead you could choose phrases like:

"I'm not good enough" => "I am good enough" => "Each day, I learn to value my positive qualities more."

"I'm exhausted" => "I am full of energy" => "Each day, I take actions to build my energy levels."

"I am rubbish at..." => "I am great at..." => "Each day, I improve at..."

These phrases allow your mind to gently release its old beliefs and habits, whilst building up evidence - over time - to support your identity shift. Here's an exercise to help you create phrases of your own.

Exercise: Unfreezing Your 'I am' Statements

There's a worksheet and audio for this exercise in the Readers' Club, as well as a discussion in the forum.

- Taking some of the statements you jotted down earlier in this section, how might you play with them, to shift them from facts to verb-based sentences?
- How could you turn them into empowering affirmations, to create deep-acting shifts?

- What happens when you make them 'expandable'?
- What do you notice shifting in your thoughts?
- In your body?
- In your emotions?
- How might you remind yourself to use these affirmations?

Reclaiming Your Personal Power

No one can make you feel inferior, without your consent. ~ Eleanor Roosevelt.

Your belief in and acceptance of who you are is the source of your personal power and your confidence. In this statement from Eleanor Roosevelt, she is reminding us that no one can *make us* do or think or feel anything. The choice always lies within us, though sometimes the provocation can be intense!

So when we use phrases like, "He *made* me so angry" - risking more rotten tomatoes here - no he didn't. He did or said things that pressed your 'angry-trigger', but only you had the power to dive into that emotion, as your response.

The more comfortable you can get in your own skin, and the more you clear out the blocks to expressing who you really are, the less the behaviour of others will bother you.

For now, I'm going to suggest you use incidents like that as a chance to practise choosing to reclaim your personal power, to choose how to respond. But there's a full section on 'how not to strangle the people who are driving you crazy' in Step 4 - Connection.

The Curse Of The Green-Eyed Monster

One of the most common ways we give away our personal power is through comparing ourselves to others, and feeling jealous. As soon as that happens, we are giving our Inner Critic permission to remind us of all the reasons why we're not good enough, or at least not as good as that other person. Our confidence takes a dive, we throw a bath full of freezing cold water on the flames of our dreams. We grind to a halt on inspired action. That effectively give power over what we will achieve and create to the person we compared ourselves to. And they never even asked for it.

You'll never live up to your dreams while you're obsessing about what others are doing.

The more you deal with your Inner Blocks, and the more confident you get in your Big Vision and why you are the ideal person to spread your Big Message, the less comparing yourself to others will bother you. When the buttons are no longer there, they can't be pressed. And that's what we're doing, with this Handbook.

Comparing yourself to others drains your energy. And there's another risk that most of us don't realise: resenting their success. It is so easy to fall into that trap – so human. If comparing yourself to someone and judging yourself lacking is bad, then what is even worse is telling yourself 'it's not fair!' stories about their success. These stories come from a fear of 'lack', that there's somehow not enough 'success' to go round.

They give your unconscious mind the clear signal that 'success' is 'bad' because it will bring judgement and resentment from others, so you're more likely to self-sabotage. But if that inner button has been pressed, and those thoughts, emotions and body-chemistry reactions are in full-flow, what can you do?

There's a way to find the silver lining to this cloud, so you reclaim the personal power you didn't even realise you were giving away, and so you can use those feelings of jealousy to set yourself free.

Try out this exercise with a 3 or 4 out of 10 'jealousy' block, to experience for yourself how you *can* turn this around and even learn and grow from it; boosting your confidence.

Exercise: Turning Jealousy Around

If you find these emotions coming up for you, press pause, using the A and B from the ABC technique (Accept, Breathe). Then there are two stages to turning this around.

1. Find out what is 'really' going on: ask yourself the following questions (worksheet and audio in the Readers' Club):

* What is *real* in this? And what is my projection or story?
* What might I need to be doing, thinking, or believing different, in the context of my Big Vision, so that this 'comparison' won't bother me any more?
* What am I 'gaining' from these emotions? What do I get to avoid doing or being?
* Is there a message that my Soul is trying to get me to hear, through my emotional reaction to this person's success?
* Is there a block I need to release, as a result of this? What will I do, to let that happen?

2. Reclaim your confidence:
* What am I doing well?
* What do I feel grateful for in my life, at the moment?
* What do I appreciate about myself and how I am serving my audience?

3. The icing on the cake:
* Go and do something that makes your heart sing – ideally involving movement – for ten minutes. Dance to your favourite music. Walk in nature. Do whatever you love doing, to fill your body with its happy-hormones and to let go of the icky emotions.

That ten minutes is a wise investment, when you consider the risks of letting the feelings of jealousy and inadequacy carry on for hours – or years...

There's a special discussion thread in the Readers' Club for this, as well as a bonus podcast on how to handle the green-eyed monster, to stop it from trashing your confidence.

Remember That Perfectionist Streak?

Perfectionism is just your Inner Critic in a smart suit.

Perfectionism isn't just responsible for your addiction to procrastinating. It's also an identity-level issue. And it's one of the fastest ways to kill your dreams.

I'm a member of a social media group for business owners who want to launch membership sites. And as I was drafting this section of the book today, I popped in there during one of my breaks, to help a few people out. Nearly every post in there from the past 24 hours mentions perfectionism. And they all had the same theme:

"Perfectionism is killing me!"

"I put this project off for years, because of perfectionism."

"I finally got past perfectionism and launched the programme - and people love it!"

"I'm a perfectionist and I was so scared that people would say this site isn't good enough - I nearly didn't launch it."

Feel familiar? Fear of potential criticism freezes us into non-action or we subconsciously self-sabotage.

One of the most common symptoms of an inner perfectionist is waiting until you feel ready or good enough, before getting started. But here's the thing: for most of us, that time may never come. And the world needs you now - not at some unspecified future date when you have finally stopped telling yourself off for not being perfect!

Each time I read a book that affects my life, I remember that the author will have had to deal with their fear of not being good enough, before they could publish it. What if they hadn't? I'd have never been able to read that book and my life wouldn't have been changed. And I send them a silent 'thank you'.

So many of us let perfectionism get in the way of living the life we're really here to lead. But who told you that you had to be perfect? Chances are that no one did. So where does it come from?

It's a choice we make, when we were young, to try to win approval. But what started out with being a 'good girl' (or boy) grows into being 'good enough'. Then, as we move into adulthood, we see how those in the public eye are judged and ridiculed for the silliest things and 'I have to be good enough' morphs into 'I have to be perfect'. Another 'victim' of perfectionism is born.

I suffered from perfectionism at many points during the writing of this book. There's something so 'final' about putting ink on paper in a gorgeous cover and sticking it on a shelf - virtual or real-world - for someone to buy. I wanted each section to be 'perfect' for you. And there are some sections that took months to get written, because I didn't spot myself playing the avoidance game. But the moment I let go of the need for them to be 'perfect' or 'the definitive' essays on a topic, and I remembered my Big Why and my Big Message for this project, the words flowed and inspiration flooded my laptop.

But I had to spot myself playing the game, before that awareness could help me to let go of the hidden block.

When you believe that you *are* your external behaviour and that people will only accept you when that conforms to an unspoken set of rules, then you run the risk of perfectionism.

How Can You Set Yourself Free From Perfectionism?

Turn it into a game and stop believing the stories you're telling yourself! If you spot yourself diving in to perfectionism procrastination again, press pause and choose to remind yourself about things you do well and your positive qualities.

You could meditate and ask yourself what's driving that behaviour? What are you really scared of? What is it doing for you? Deal with that and the perfectionism will melt away.

I've got a bonus article for you on this, in the Readers' Club: "The Simple Mindset Shift That Could Change Your Life – And Business – In A Heartbeat", all about perfectionism.

And, of course, you could also deal with your Inner Critic, which is what drives perfectionism. Shall we?

5 Steps To Taming Your Inner Critic

We have already mentioned self-talk - our Inner Critic – a few times in this Handbook, but now you have the tools to deal with it. Our self-talk is the symptom, not the cause. If you change your self-talk without dealing with the underlying beliefs, values and identity-level stuff, you'll just find your Inner Critic seeks out other ways to get your attention.

Over the years I have realised that the Inner Critic stems from our identity-level 'I am' statements and it dictates everything from believing that we're not 'good enough'; through to lack of self-esteem, confidence and self-worth; through to whether or not we achieve our dreams. The work we have done so far on our habits, self-talk, limiting beliefs, hidden needs and "I am" statements forms the foundations for taming your Inner Critic, making the job surprisingly simple. That's why I have left it until now to open this particularly unappealing can of worms.

How Can You Tell If Your Inner Critic Is Trashing Your Dreams?

We all know that feeling. You're totally fired up. You're about to start doing something really important. You know it's a bit of a comfort zone stretch. But you're feeling excited.

And then a little voice in your head starts talking. It tells you all the reasons why you won't be any good at it and how you're never good at anything anyway, and you're not ready. Maybe it is telling you that the timing isn't right, and you should just leave it for now. We each have our own favourite self-talk stories on this.

You feel that tightness in your stomach. Your body tenses, and you might even feel fear and panic rising.

But it doesn't have to be that way. You don't have to live at the whim of this Inner Critic, of its voice, its negative self-talk. You can tame it.

You see, it's just a habit. And like any other habit, it can be changed. It's surprisingly easy when you know how. So I want to take you on a whistle stop journey of how to spot your Inner Critic, what to do about it, and how potentially to turn it into your biggest cheerleader.

Most of us have an Inner Critic - pretty much all of us. I did meet somebody once who didn't have one, a wonderful 17-year-old German girl. She was really confused when I was talking about Inner Critics. But, in 14 years of serving the audience I serve, she's the only person I have met without one. The most common side effects include:

- **Lack of self-esteem and low confidence levels**
  We beat ourselves up when we try to do something important. Your Inner Critic is fantastic about reminding you about your mistakes.
- **Stress**
  Your Inner Critic is responsible for the vast majority of stress in your life due to the stories it tells you.
- **Self-sabotage**
  When you're just about to achieve something you've been dreaming of, your Inner Critic leaps in and pulls the rug from under you. Or, maybe it creeps in quietly around the corner.
- **Insomnia**
  If you're lying awake at 3:00 a.m., then chances are it's your Inner Critic choosing the bedtime stories. Maybe you're feeling exhausted. Your Inner Critic is running the show. That keeps you running your sympathetic nervous system, the fight or flight, meaning you've got too much cortisol and adrenalin in your system. That exhausts your adrenals, and it's really going to hit your energy levels and maybe even your physical, emotional, and mental health.
- **'Okayness'**
  Your Inner Critic is the biggest single reason why most of us put up with a life that's okay rather than great.
- **Guilt**
  Your Inner Critic is so good at reminding you about all the things that you did or didn't do and ways you let people down. Those are its words, not mine.

Some of my clients and students go so far as to call their Inner Critic their own worst enemy. It's strong stuff.

It's really important not to beat yourself up about your Inner Critic. Your Inner Critic criticising you for having an Inner Critic feels like an infinite-loop – the thought of it makes my head spin! And this is where we can come back to the Ahimsa (non-violence) from page 116. In addition to non-violence towards your body, you can choose to express non-violence towards your mind – your thoughts.

One of the three keys to successful meditation is acceptance (the others are relaxation and concentration – more details in the Readers' Club). To sit quietly and meditate, you need to accept your body, with its aches and pains, and your environment, with its sensory interruptions. But you also need to accept your mind. If you try to meditate whilst fighting your thoughts, you will struggle.

Given that some of the benefits of meditation include connecting you with who you really are, with your inner stillness, helping you to see life as it is, rather than as we think it *should* be, criticising your mind for thinking, during your normal day, moves you away from that. It moves you into your fight-or-flight stress response. At a deep level, you are rejecting yourself.

Consciously choosing to experience Ahimsa towards our thoughts is life-changing. Choosing to no longer feed the thoughts that make us feel bad, or with which we beat ourselves up, is transformational. So in this section on taming your Inner Critic, I encourage you to make it a playful process, celebrating your successes and laughing about the times where you spot, after the event, that the Inner Critic ran riot.

If any of this feels familiar, and you're feeling fed up with that Inner Critic, then I want to share with you five techniques you can use to start taming it today, and even start to turn it into your Inner Cheerleader.

1. A Simple Mindset Shift

There's a fact I need to tell you here: *you are not the same as your Inner Critic*. It is just a train of thought. It is just a soundtrack that we're used to playing. No matter how real it might feel, it isn't actually real.

When you realise that, it gives you the power to make changes. You can choose which thoughts to feed, as we have already discussed. One of the best ways to do this is with mindfulness and regular meditation (there are resources to get you started on this in the Readers' Club). When you're falling into the trap of believing that you and your Inner Critic are one in the same being, then it will always hold the power. If you make it real, it will feel real.

Instead, when you feel an Inner Critic thought coming up, press pause. You can do that. Remind yourself: *this is not who I am. This is a thought I am thinking.* And let it go. Do the ABC. Feel the relief bubble up.

2. Don't Fight It

I am not suggesting you indulge your Inner Critic's every whim, but it doesn't help if you reject it, fight it, or try to get rid of it. Why? Surely we want to get rid of our Inner Critic? Remember Carl Jung's "what you resist persists"? That goes for your Inner Critic, too. If you fight your Inner Critic or try to get rid of it, you're resisting it. That means you're giving it all of your attention, 100% of your headspace, rent-free, and you're spending time telling yourself stories about it, which just makes you feel worse.

I'm a mother of three young boys, so I know that, like a grumpy child, if I feed my Inner Critic and give in to it, it will learn to do more of what it did to get the attention it wanted. This is why I talk about taming it, rather than getting rid of it. It's about accepting that it's there. There's a part of you that wants, at some level, for you to see the risks, for you to make sure that you're not taking really crazy actions. At some level, it wants to protect you, no matter how mad that might feel when it's in full blown character assassination mode.

If you reject a part of yourself, it will only ever lead to pain and conflict. Instead, you can retrain the part of you that runs your Inner Critic to be more supportive and empowering instead.

When your Inner Critic starts ranting, stop what you're doing and notice that it's there, so that it doesn't have to shout so loudly, if it feels heard; it can relax. Say a silent thank you, even if you don't feel like it, but it's the opposite of rejecting it; at some level, it has been trying to help you. Then consciously choose a happy thought to feed, instead.

3. Stop Feeding Its Pesky Stories

Your Inner Critic loves drama, and the nation's favourite soap operas look dull, in comparison with the stories that are going on in our heads. We love to gossip. It's why we love to share stories, and the more dramatic the better. Embellishing is completely okay in the Inner Critic's world.

When it comes to negative self-talk and your Inner Critic's stories, the more you feed them, the worse you will feel, and the further you will move from the amazing life you've been dreaming of; you'll be trashing your confidence.

Researchers have shown that, the more we repeat a story, the more we convince ourselves that it's true, including the embellishments and the 'what if' scenarios. Put enough subconscious effort into it and you can even pass a lie detector test. So it's essential to make sure you choose whether or not to feed your Inner Critic's stories.

When you feel an Inner Critic conversation coming on, press pause, and consciously choose whether you want to dive into that drama or whether you want to focus on something else instead. Ask your Inner Critic what the facts are, and stick to discussing those. And please don't beat yourself up if you catch yourself 'doing' the drama and emotions -

I've got a secret for you: it doesn't matter how far you've gone down the drama track before you realise. You can always press pause and come on out again.

Just because your Inner Critic tells you something,
it doesn't mean it's true.

If you're feeling stuck, then gratitude is a fantastic antidote. Right now, grab the nearest small object to you, pick it up in your hand, and really see it. Notice how the light reflects off it, how the shapes and contours give it form. Feel the weight of it in your hand. Notice the textures.

Then, this is the icing on the cake, take a moment to connect with that object from your heart and to thank it for whatever it does for you. And imagine each person who was involved in getting it to you - from the person who first imagined it through to the people who made it, the distributors, the shop and the delivery people. It's amazing to get to say 'thank you' to each of them, too. If you aim to do this for about a minute in total, it will physically shift the biochemistry in your body, releasing endorphins, rebalancing the parasympathetic and sympathetic nervous system, and helping you to feel happier.

4. Let Go Of 'Shoulditis'

Deleting the word "should" from your vocabulary is one of the best ways to tame your Inner Critic, though it's a biggie for many of us.

How often do we use the word "should" (or its friends) in a typical day?

"I should do such and such."

"I ought to go to that meeting."

"Even though I don't really want to, I should offer to help Fred with his project."

"I have to…" "I must…"

If you pause for a moment and notice how "should" makes you feel, I'm guessing it might be triggering some kind of a sinking feeling in your stomach - a tightening. Usually there's a slouching of the shoulders and your back, as they pick up the additional weight of the world, a frown on your face, a tensing of your jaw and a furrowed brow. The Inner Critic is addicted to "should".

If you feel "should" coming up, pause and ask yourself, "Who says? Is that really true?" Let the answer bubble up. This isn't about apportioning blame. It's about pressing pause on the 'should'. Notice what comes up for you and use it to gain insights into those old, autopilot behaviours that might be keeping you stuck. Remember: awareness is the first key to change, and you're reclaiming your personal power. Instead of 'I have to', you can play with 'I choose to'. It sets you free from shoulditis and cuts your stress levels.

5. Turn Down The Volume

I've got another secret for you: you don't actually have to pay attention to your Inner Critic. Most of us listen slavishly to that negative self-talk. We replay it over and over in our heads, especially when we're stressed. But just because you're having a thought, it doesn't mean you have to tune your inner radio to that frequency for the whole day. You can choose to turn down the volume and just let your Inner Critic get on with whatever it's complaining about, in the background, while you stay focussed on heading towards your dreams.

Imagine that you're watching a comedy show. Maybe one partner is ear-bashing the other for some minor mistake they've made. The partner who is being yelled at carries on reading the newspaper and nodding politely. When the ear-basher has fully vented their spleen, they demand to know what their partner thought of what they said.

"That's nice, dear," is the only response they get. The person on the receiving end doesn't get rattled. They don't argue back. They ride the wave of the other person's drama, refusing to dance the destructive dance – accepting it's happening but choosing not to engage with it.

Now, what would happen if you were to play that game with your Inner Critic once in a while, giving it a good old, "that's nice, dear. I hear you"? Once it has paused, you can ask it a question about something that moves things forwards in a different direction such as, "So I'm wondering, what do you want me to do instead?" And watch what happens.

Do you notice how much easier these techniques feel, having covered the earlier techniques in this section? That's why we have waited until now, to start taming your Inner Critic.

I really hope you can feel the difference already. The key to taming your Inner Critic is 'little and often'. Don't beat yourself up if you accidentally indulge its stories – just press pause and play with one of these techniques. And in Step 7 I'll show you how to turn your Inner Critic into your biggest cheerleader.

If you want to deep-dive on this, then tools like meditation and gratitude work can make a powerful difference for you. They can help you to calm a chattering mind, making it easier to choose which thoughts to feed, and help you to more easily tell the difference between the projection of the mind's beliefs and stories, versus the perception of the truth of a situation, which is a fabulous way to ditch the drama. I've got plenty of extra resources waiting for you over at the Readers' Club.

Getting Off The Emotional Roller Coaster

Your emotions are either a powerful enabler of your dreams, or a ruthless saboteur. They dictate how motivated you feel and can empower or block your success. But here's something I didn't realise until I started training to become a meditation teacher: an emotion is just a chemical reaction in your body.

Woah! So how can an icky emotion last for hours, days or weeks, then? Because of the stories we feed. Remember that mind, body and emotions are linked. Our thoughts trigger changes in our body chemistry, which shift our emotions, which affect which thoughts we choose to feed. Press pause on the story and the emotion will pass on through in just a few minutes. Feed the stories and that emotion could become the theme song for your experience of life.

As we discussed in Step 1, there are two primary emotions: love and fear. Love enables. Fear blocks.

And common fear-based emotions have a flip-side love-based emotion that goes with them. For example, anger and passion are the dark and light sides of each other. Motivation and apathy can be flip sides. It's so hard to describe emotions with words.

I remember when I lived in Germany that the German language felt much more precise when describing emotions. For years afterwards, I found myself struggling to find an English word to match the nuance of what I was experiencing. Trust your body, instead.

Here's an exercise to help you tap into its messages:

Exercise: The Difference Between Fear And Excitement?

Here's a fun test: for most of us, the difference is about two inches.
If you think about something you were scared of doing (make it no more than a 4 out of 10), close your eyes and notice where you feel this in your body. Notice how your posture shifts. Shake that feeling off.

Now think about something you were excited about doing. Close your eyes and notice where you feel that in your body? Notice what happens to your posture.

For most of us we feel fear and excitement in our gut, and if you get a room full of people to do this exercise, getting them to point to where the centres of those emotions were, their fingers only move a few inches. You can use this to your advantage.

Remember how hard it can be to stop a thought-train, once it has left the station, but how moving your body can press reset? Well, you can do the same with emotions.

If you have something you want to do, but you're feeling a bit scared, change your posture to be the same as it would be if you were feeling excited. Then take a finger and place it on your body where 'scared' was and move your finger over your skin to where 'excited' hangs out. Most of the time this is enough to shift the emotion.

You can play with this technique at random points throughout your day. If you notice an emotion getting in the way, ask yourself, "How would I like to feel, instead?" Then hold your body the way you do, when you're feeling that new emotion and move your focus to the point in your body where that emotion concentrates. Allow your thoughts and body chemistry to gently shift, to support this move.

I'd love to hear how you get on with this and how you use it – there's a discussion thread over in the Readers' Club forum. There's also a deep-dive course on Mastering Your Emotions. But my personal favourite technique for getting off the emotional rollercoaster is regular meditation. It helps me to keep things in perspective and to ride the emotional waves of life, with less effort. My students tell me they feel the same way, too.

Five Common Fears That Can Sabotage Your Confidence

Don't get me wrong; I'm not 'anti-fear' and I'm certainly not suggesting you should pretend you never feel scared. Fear is hard-wired into the brain to keep us alive. It's one of the reasons why our species has survived. But there are two types of fear: legitimate fear and 'mind-story' fear. Legitimate fear is the kind that stops you walking off a cliff path or taking a corner too fast in your car. Please pay attention to your legitimate fears. They can save your life.

'Mind-story' fear (which can still feel very real) is one that comes from the stories we are telling ourselves about what might go wrong, but which are 'just' a projection of our mind's beliefs and worries. That doesn't mean you should ignore them, but it does mean it's time to stop believing in them and letting them run your life.

Fear makes you flinch. And flinching makes you play smaller.

When we feel scared about something we're going to do, we tense up. Most people hunch their back and shoulders, as though trying to look smaller and to hide from a potential predator. We dive into the sympathetic nervous system's flight / flight response. We entrench in our 'safety' zone..

Your brain prioritises its blood supply to the primal, survival part of your brain, meaning that your focus is here, in this moment, ready to react. You are likely to feel tense and anxious and to be emotionally volatile, overreacting to stimuli. If you are presented with facts and figures, that primal part of your brain can't process them, so you're likely to dismiss or misinterpret them. Strategic thinking goes out of the window.

That's not a great space to be in, if you've got Big Vision decisions to make and inspired action to take.

When it comes to your mind-story fears, in the context of Confidence and your Big Vision, I'd like to suggest a reframe:

Fear is a way of letting us know we're stretching a comfort zone. Fear isn't a problem until we allow it to change what we do – what we create – and who we are.

Here is a tour of five common fears that I see derailing many a passionate World-Changer - and what you can do about them.

1. Fear Of Failure

We can be so paralysed by our fear of everything going wrong, that we never get started. And if we feel scared of being *blamed* for things going wrong, then that's a potent demotivator. But things are rarely as bad as we fear they might be. If you're a natural-born worrier, then I've got a bonus guided visualisation technique for you in the Readers' Club – I call it my 'Magic Wand For Worrying'.

To train yourself to get past fear of failure, here's a question I often ask my clients (and myself): **"If I couldn't get it wrong, which action would I take today?"** Then imagine yourself having taken that action and anchor yourself into how good that feels. Then take the first step towards that action.

If you want to know what's driving that fear, you can add in: **"And I haven't taken that action yet, because…"**

Run your answers through the processes we have covered in this section – or get some one-to-one mentoring to clear that block. Your Big Vision is worth the effort and investment.

2. Fear Of Success

This particular fear sits squarely in the 'secondary gain' camp; it is protecting us from losing something important to us. Sometimes we're scared that success might cause us to not have enough time for our loved-ones, or maybe we're worried that our friends will reject us, or that we'll be criticised, or that everyone will beg us for money.

Whatever is driving that fear, you can uncover its hidden 'positive intention' by asking yourself: "What is this fear doing for me? What is it allowing me to avoid? What is it protecting me from?" Then run those answers through the techniques in this section.

3. Fear Of Criticism

In this internet-age trolls are a fact of life. And that can make it feel hard to step up and be authentic in your message. So I've got a whole section for you on 'how to handle haters' in Step 3 on Credibility, as part of your visibility action plan. If your fear of criticism is from the 'real world', there's help in that section for you, too, on how to try that 'feedback' on for size, before you let it trash your dreams.

Fear of criticism is a powerful deterrent, because the criticism doesn't actually have to occur for the fear to set in. ~ Seth Godin

Remember: our biggest critic is the one inside us. And we've just been learning how to tame it. When you feel confident and have cleared out your blocks, it's harder for the 'trolls' to find buttons to press.

4. Fear Of Rejection

We're hard-wired to want to belong – to be part of the Tribe. Nearly all of us run a fear of rejection, at some level. But you need to deal with this, to be able to feel confident and authentic in your message. It can help to bear in mind that how someone reacts to you says more about *them* than it does about *you* (unless, of course, you were behaving like a complete idiot). The more you can connect deeply with your Self (see Step 4) and clear out your inner blocks, the less this fear will bother you.

5. Fear Of Lack Of Money

Maslow put money in the bottom area of his pyramid for his famous Hierarchy Of Needs. The Ancient yogic model of the chakras would put it in the bottom chakras, too, because our current Western society means we need money for safety and security – for our home and our most essential needs. If fear of lack of money is an issue for you, it's one of the fastest ways to take the fizzle out of your Big Vision dreams.

Money fears are blocks, just like any other, and the techniques in this Handbook will all help you to get past them. To further support you, there's a special discussion thread in the Readers' Club forum, where you can find inspiration from others who have made it past this block, and get answers to your questions.

Fear is the emotional symptom of an underlying belief or block. Your fears dictate your limits.

The name of the fear doesn't matter. What counts is what you do about it. Deal with the hidden block and the fear can melt away. But if you don't spot the fear, it can keep you stuck playing small, blinding you to the Truth and the possibilities of positive outcomes.

"Feel The Fear And Do It Anyway?"

By all means 'think' it, but 'feeling' it will kick off your body's fear-based hormonal reactions, so there's no point in doing that, unless you really want to. Yes, if you ignore the fear, it risks shouting more loudly for attention; after all, it's trying to protect you from a perceived threat. But if you indulge it, it will keep you stuck and you'll feel miserable.

Exercise: Fear-Releasing

Play with this with a fear that's low on the scale, so you get to experience the process. Then make any tweaks you need, so it works beautifully for you. Pick one that's currently getting in the way of your Big Vision.

1. Identify a fear that you're ready to release. Acknowledge it. Remember the ABC process from earlier in this chapter? Do the A and B – Accept and Breathe.
2. Ask yourself – honestly – what is *true* in this story? And what is projection and drama and conjecture?
3. For each element of the true stuff, look at what actions you could take to deal with those blocks. The rest of the story isn't true anyway, so you can let that go.
4. For that fear, finish the sentence: "I feel this fear, because…" and aim for at least 7 responses.
5. It's time for C – Choose. Reclaim your personal power by answering the question, "What do I want instead?" Remember the guidelines for this that we talked about on page 133.
6. Watch out for your stories on this – turn it into a game, to spot them and press 'pause'. And pay special attention to any 'I am' statements (see page 151)
7. Moving from your mind's stories back into this moment, in the physical world, "What actions could I take, so that this fear doesn't matter so much any more?"
8. And finally, make a commitment to yourself:
"Despite this fear, which actions am I going to take – today – to move towards my Big Vision?"

There's a special discussion thread for you on this in the Readers' Club forum and there is also a bonus 5-minute fear-releasing MP3.

It's Not About You

If your fears are firmly standing in the way of you taking action towards your Big Vision, then it's time to remember that this journey isn't about *you*; it's about the people you want to make a difference for. When we shift the focus from our own worries and fears and move it to how those we want to help will feel *after* we have got past our blocks, that usually gives us the leverage we need – the motivation that inspires and empowers us to keep going, despite the stories the mind tells us; despite the worries that it might go wrong. When you focus on the difference you make, rather than your 'inner world', then your fears and mind-stories still exist, but they lose most of their power.

So I don't recommend 'feeling' the fear and doing it anyway – that's a horrible place to be and your stress hormones will make inspired action nigh-on impossible. Instead, I suggest you 'think' the fear and do your inspired actions, anyway. Cut out the emotional response to your fears and you'll find they shrink fast. Choose which thoughts to feed, as we practised earlier in this step, to regain your perspective. Then, if there is something that needs to be done so that the fear-voice can calm down, do it. If not, ABC it.

Why turn the orange into a lemon because of fear born out of what might be to come? We can't always choose what situation we are in, what the body is going through, or what is happening to us. But we can decide, every moment again, how to experience it and where to put our focus. ~ Bertram van Alphen

The Best Bit About Your Big Why

It burns through your fears.

When you line up your actions, your thoughts, your beliefs and your emotions with your Big Why and your Big Vision, then you're more likely to achieve what you're dreaming of. The passion you will ignite inside yourself will give you the strength to make it past your fears. Your Big Why and Big Vision will burn through those blocks, giving you the leverage to take action *despite* perhaps feeling scared. And the more you do this, the smaller the role your fears will play. They may even disappear.

How To Make Change Last

The pond allows the ripples to effortlessly flow.

Nature abhors a vacuum, so let's fill it. I promised that we would go down through the layers and back up again. You'll be pleased to hear that the 'back up again' is really quick.

Once you have made a change at one of the levels in this step, it's important to allow that change to integrate and settle, which is why I recommend making just one shift at a time. It's also important, though, to support that new 'you'. And that's where walking back up the through the layers comes in.

Exercise: How To Make Change Last

Pick one of the aspects of your confidence that you have chosen to work with in this step and answer the following questions – which will become your action plan (worksheet in the Readers' Club):

- Which 'I am' statements am I going to replace? What do I want to tell myself instead? How will I remind myself to do this?
- Which stories do I want to change?
- What is important to me in the context this change?
- What will it *do* for me?
- What will it *do* for others?
- What will I miss out on, if I *don't* make this change? (*This is your leverage!*)
- Which needs do I have, in the context of this change?
- How can I support those needs, in a healthy way?
- What are my beliefs about this change?
- Do any of these need clearing out or changing? How and when will I do this?
- Which thoughts will support this change?
- How will I remind myself to feed these thoughts?
- Which actions would someone who has made this change take?
- Are there any of my old habits that need to shift?
- How will I make sure this happens?
- And when?

Celebrate the changes you make. Give them time to become part of your rhythm - second-nature - before you move on to the next one. Be kind to yourself. And let us all know how you get on, over at the Readers' Club forum.

And Finally...

I'm so excited for you, now you have worked through the Confidence section. Please remember that your inner confidence is a journey, not a destination, and that you can play with these techniques, whenever you need them. Each and every change you make will have a positive knock-on effect, for decades to come.

And to help you even more, I've got three bonus resources for you, in the Readers' Club.

The first is a five minute guided visualisation, to help you to connect with your "Inner Rockstar" confidence. It's an MP3 visualisation that you can download, so that it's there for you, whenever you need it. The second is a video training on how to handle change, when the thought of it freaks you out. People have found this hugely helpful. And the third is a video training on how to hold onto hope, when the brown-stuff hits the fan. This one went viral when the surprise outcome of the UK's Brexit vote was announced and has been watched many thousands of times.

These trainings build on what we have covered here and can help you to create deep-acting shifts, while you're watching them. I strongly recommend you taking some time out, in the next week, to make the most of them. They won't just help you in your Dare To Dream Bigger journey – they can help with any area of your life.

And I want to let you know how proud I am of you. Whether you just skimmed this section or whether you worked through each and every exercise, you have just done more inner work than most people ever get the chance to do. And it will have a profoundly positive effect on your confidence in your journey to Dare To Dream Bigger and make the difference you're here to make in the world. Congratulations! And thank you!

Now it's time to move on to Step 3 – Credibility.

Credibility

Credibility puts an end to shouting to be heard above the noise; you magnetise your Dream Audience, like moths to a flame.

Credibility is the key to growing a movement and making a difference. It doesn't matter how wonderful your Big Vision is, or what is motivating you, if people don't see you as a credible expert in your field. They're less likely to listen and take action, and your Big Message will fall on deaf ears.

But don't worry - being credible doesn't mean you have to be *the* biggest ever expert. Don't let perfectionism get in the way of your credibility. Being credible means giving people a reason - a 'why' - to trust you; to pause their busy lives and listen to what you have to say.

As part of writing this Handbook, I interviewed people about what makes somebody an expert in their eyes. And the answers were surprising.

There were three key elements needed for credibility, and they weren't what they used to be. In the 'olden days', what mattered most was your qualifications or your job title. Psychologists did reams of research into 'white coat syndrome', where the mere wearing of a white coat and an authoritative tone was enough to get people to obey. That still applies, but the underlying rules of the game have changed.

In this Step, I'm going to take you through the three key elements to establishing your credibility, why some of us resist it so much, then we'll explore the biggest barrier to your credibility (and it's not what you might think). We'll talk about the vital importance of authenticity, and how pretending to be something you're not, even subconsciously, can capsize your business boat. Then we'll deal with the two biggest 'inside work' hurdles on your credibility journey and I'll share with you the same deep-dive stuff that my Masterminders and Dare To Dream Bigger Academy members enjoy. After that, you will know exactly how to create your own credibility-boosting action plan.

Before I share the results of my research with you, let's figure out what 'credibility' means to *you*.

Exercise: What Does 'Credibility' Mean To You?

There's a worksheet for this over at the Readers' Club. Just let the answers bubble up to these questions.

- When you come across someone who wants you to listen to their message, what makes you trust them enough to feel inspired and to hear what they're saying?
- Is there anything blocking you from standing in your 'expert shoes'? Not sure? You can check this by finishing the following statement - and aim for 7-10 answers:
  "I can't / don't want to be seen as an expert, because…"
- How do you currently *feel* about the idea of being a credible expert in your field?

What Is 'Credibility' And How Do You Get It?

We could describe 'credibility' as the ability to "be believable; to be convincing; to be capable of persuading people that something is true."

When I was creating the outline for this book, I thought long and hard about where 'credibility' needed to go. It waltzed with 'connection' for a while, and eventually ended up just before it, as part of clearing out your blocks, once I had gone back and reverse-engineered what has worked best for my clients, for me and for my heroes. Why? Because so many of us run hidden blocks that stop us from standing in our 'credibility shoes', but without credibility, the difference you get to make will be much, much smaller.

Connection without credibility won't grow your business or change the world.

You're unlikely to be able to persuade or convince people of anything life-changing. That requires at least a sprinkling of leadership, and if you don't have credibility, you'll meet more resistance and objections. In fact:

Credibility means your message cuts through resistance and background noise like a hot knife through butter.

And in a world where most people are overwhelmed with information and advice, being able to get your message heard, without having to yell, lie or manipulate, is essential. To make the difference you're here to make, you need to allow yourself to become the go-to person in your field.

There's a good reason why, in this process, credibility comes after getting total clarity on your Big Why, your Big Vision and your Big Message. You need to be 100% clear on what you want to be credible about. You also need to know who you're serving, because becoming the go-to person in a tight niche is much easier than trying to be Oprah. I know that sounds crazily obvious, but you'd be surprised how many people miss out these steps and try to fall back on the credibility brought to them by their historical qualifications - or glossy sales pages. Doing it this way round allows you to gain credibility by being authentic and in alignment with who you are, and with your Soul's Path.

And there's a good reason why credibility comes after Step 2's confidence work. How often have you heard, say, a professor being interviewed on the radio, but they're clearly not confident in their message and they fumble their words, even though they are one of the world's experts on their subject? The credibility brought to them by lecturing at a University topples and falls, as their lack of self-confidence becomes the main thing we remember.

It doesn't mean you need to be the most confident person on the planet before you take action on your credibility, but you *do* need to be convinced about your message, to know who your audience is, and to *believe* that you can create the experience, product or transformation you offer.

Whether you're a yoga teacher, the CEO of a start-up, managing someone else's business, a dentist, an author, a coach, making widgets, a creative freelancer, growing a business from hobby to business to legacy, or on a mission, if you want people to hear your message and feel inspired to take action, you need to consciously choose to become a credible expert. So why do we resist it so much?

Why Do We Resist Being Seen As A 'Credible Expert'?

When we founded the EU VAT Action Campaign, we soon realised that we needed a group of experts to advise us. Although we knew our stuff about how the new laws would affect micro businesses, we needed support from people who could give us the hard facts about things we didn't have the time - or inclination - to study.

We created a social media group where we could hang out together and all was going well, until we changed the name of the group to include the word 'expert'. That's how we saw these people, who were the top in their field. But, for some of them, it's not how they saw themselves. And calling them 'experts' definitely pressed trigger-buttons for some of them, who objected strongly to being given that title.

From the work I have done over the past 14 years, some common themes have emerged in our resistance to being seen as an expert:

- Fear of responsibility - you don't want to raise your head above the parapet, in case someone shoots you down - and it can feel scary, having people actually act on what you're saying
- "I'm not good enough" running as a below-the-surface belief
- Perfectionism - "I can't be a credible expert until I'm absolutely perfect or at least the best in my field"
- Not wanting to feel different from your peers or friends
- "Who am I, to…?"
- "I'm not ready"
- "It's all been said and done already. No one will want to listen to me."

When you look at your answers to the exercise at the beginning of this step, are there any that might benefit from some of the techniques in the Confidence step? And later in this step, we're going to look at the two biggest barriers to feeling and being credible, so by the time we're done, you'll be ready to dive in and make progress. If any of your blocks are in the "I'm not ready / good enough / who will listen to me?" category, remember:

The world needs your voice; your mission; your message. And it needs it now. That's why your Heart has been calling you to step up and Dare To Dream Bigger.

That's why it's vital to uncover any hidden blocks at this stage - and deal with them - because otherwise you'll subconsciously self-sabotage your credibility efforts.

So shall we start by looking at the Credibility Equation?

The Credibility Equation

Can you 'buy' yourself credibility? Strange question? Maybe. But for many people this strategy is working. They plunge thousands of dollars a day into highly-targeted Facebook adverts, for example. Their publishers buy their way onto the New York Times best-seller list. They run crazy promotions on Amazon to hit the top of their category for long enough to call themselves a best-seller. They offer 50% commission to their Big Name affiliates, so that everyone on the planet seems to be promoting their latest offering.

None of this is 'good' or 'bad', it's just 'business'.

And, yes, part of the credibility equation is that people see your name or hear it in places that they trust. It has long been known that articles and interviews trump adverts for credibility, which is why big companies love advertorials so much.

In his book *The Millionaire Messenger*, Brendon Burchard talks about there being three types of expertise, essential to credibility.

He describes the Results Expert (the been-there-done-that-got-the-t-shirt role model), the Research Expert (who has studied everything published on a topic) and the Role Model Expert (someone to whom everyone seems to go for advice).

Ideally, he suggests you want to be a blend of all three.

When I was writing this book, I did extensive research to find out what is going on with 'credibility' in the entrepreneurial community these days. It turns out that the three types of expert from even just five years ago when Brendon wrote his book are no longer enough to give you credibility, though they're still a great place to start.

Traditional credibility-builders like endorsements, testimonials and adverts are still important, but they're losing their power and are no longer unconditionally-trusted. They still need to be there, but they're not enough, on their own.

Even qualifications and awards are becoming less important, in the decision on whether or not to work with you. Of course, there will be minimum qualifications required for some fields, but traditional expert-status-builders are less important.

We had a history-making experience of this in the UK's 2016 EU referendum. The Remain campaign wheeled out its experts and published its data, which it said had been vetted. With hindsight, much of it has been shown to have been correct. So why didn't that 'data' from the 'experts' change the outcome? Because being an 'expert' is no longer enough to change someone's mind.

Instead of 'facts', the Leave campaign 'sold' passion and a vision for the future. It created campaigns that resonated with people's worries, dissatisfaction and frustration. It made extraordinary promises, to gain attention and change people's minds, to create an emotional connection. It didn't matter that many of the key promises were, even at the time, unrealistic, and some were impossible. Most people weren't voting based on cold data. The traditional 'experts' made little difference.

In response to all of this, the Remain campaign brought in yet more experts and published yet more data. But it didn't work. Research at the time showed that the data wasn't majorly influencing people's voting preferences; the promises and the passion and the vision for the future were.

The 'Backfire Effect', which we have already discussed (see page 106), meant that instead of being influenced by the 'experts' and the 'yet more data', that contradictory data caused people to entrench more deeply, to defend their strongly-held views.

This is supported by research done by Dr Tom Stafford, Lecturer in Psychology and Cognitive Science at the University Of Sheffield and author of Mind Hacks. His research, with Dick Eiser in 2009, concluded that expertise is not enough to ensure people will trust you. Instead, he found that people trust those who they believe have their best interests at heart. His research showed this was three to four times more important than perception of expertise (details in the Readers' Club).

And this ties in with what my research on credibility found, in the micro business community. People told me that, in order to find someone credible and trustworthy, they want to connect with the 'real you' - not the 'persona' or facade.

Of course you need to be an expert, but that's not enough. They want to *feel* your passion and excitement for your subject. They want to *feel* comfortable around you; to be able to connect with you. They want to know you care about *them*, not just about yourself. They want to matter. They want to *feel* your confidence, so that they can let go and trust you.

Calling yourself an 'expert' triggers their mistrust button. They want you to *show* that you're an expert; not just tell them.

Want credibility? Prove it, don't preach it.

Your audience wants to understand your journey, how you figured out what you now know. They don't want you to pretend to be perfect.

We idolise celebrities and put them on platform-heeled pedestals. But would we trust them with our deepest dreams and hopes? We want our experts to be human. We want to identify with them. We want them to be 'real' and authentic.

We want to see where they fell over, and how they picked themselves up - or how they helped others to do it.

Perfection makes you inaccessible. Authenticity makes you irresistible.

I remember a 'Happiness Consultant' a few years ago, marketing herself as being 'always happy, perfectly happy'. She went on to tell us how she wanted that for us, too. Firstly, it's not believable. Even Enlightened Masters feel sad emotions. Secondly, it set the bar so high that there was no way you could imagine wanting to work with her, for fear of being judged if you ever dared to have an unhappy thought.

When your audience knows you're 'real', that you have walked a mile or ten thousand in their shoes, they will feel connection with you; there's rapport between you. And if you can remember what it's like to stand in the shoes of someone who hasn't yet figured out how to solve the pain point you fix, then you'll be able to lead them on their journey in a way that will inspire and motivate them. You are a living and breathing example of what can be achieved. You are the authentic expression of what you stand for - and your Big Message.

Whether you're über-qualified and have helped thousands, whether you've been through the crisis and come up with your own solution, or whether you're the best-read pro in your niche, your authenticity and passion are the key to your credibility. Without these two, your publicity and visibility strategies will ring hollow.

So the three-part Credibility Equation is:

Expertise + Passion + Authenticity = Credibility

When I started in this industry, in 2002, what you needed was confidence and paperwork, and that was it. If you were confident, you were big and bold on stage, and you could talk the talk, you were seen as an expert. But these days it's no longer enough to talk your Big Message. People demand to see you walking it. So many of people I spoke to in my research on this said, "I don't care if somebody says they are really good at what they do, or they've got loads of certificates. I want to see they are living and breathing their message."

Let's start with passion: if you don't have clarity on the difference you want to make, and you're not confident, then you're not going to be able to access your passion. You'll risk coming across as bored. If you're stressed and overwhelmed, you're not going to have that excitement and energy. You don't have to be a high-octane Tony Robbins, but you do need to be able to connect with your inner excitement about your Big Message, even if you're just talking to someone about it in a lift. Otherwise, you won't be able to inspire others to take action.

Your expertise is essential; you need to be able to do what you say you can do. Certificates are no longer enough. Your customers want to see evidence that you can really do it.

Authenticity is about walking your talk - being a living example of the work you do or the Big Message you stand for - and allowing people to connect with you; the real you, not just the veneer.

To help you really 'get' this - and to kick your backside into allowing yourself to be seen as a credible expert, we need to deal with the single biggest barrier to your credibility.

The Biggest Barrier To Being Credible

Now you've got the credibility equation, I hate to break it to you, but there's only one thing that can stop you from becoming the credible, go-to expert in your field… And that is you.

If you have worked through Step 1 and identified your Inner Genius, who your dream customers are, and how to solve their burning problems, then being seen as an expert is near-inevitable, as long as you don't get in your own way, which is what Step 2 was all about.

There are a three main ways we can self-sabotage our credibility efforts.

The first one is something I call "the Oprah Complex", which we talked about in Step 1: trying to help everyone and therefore trying to become a worldwide credible expert.

The second block applies to so many of us and it is Imposter Syndrome. You might experience this as 'feeling like a fraud' or 'inferiority complex' and you can spot it by watching your self-talk. Are you saying things like:

- Who am I, to…?
- But who will listen to me?
- What if they 'find me out'?
- If I do XYZ then they'll spot that I'm not good enough.
- I don't feel like I'm 'meant' to be here.
- I don't 'belong' here.
- I feel like a fraud!
- I wish I could do it like he / she does.

I had never heard of Imposter Syndrome until I started one-to-one client work, back in 2002, and my very first Executive Mentoring client had a massive case of it. And the next. And the next. And then I realised I had it running, too. It is crazily common. Many of the most successful people in the world have had to deal with their fear of being a fraud and not being good enough.

I see people having three main reactions to Imposter Syndrome:

1. They get scared and defensive and behave like bullies, projecting their fears of being inadequate onto their teams.

2. They run and hide and never step outside of their comfort zone - ever - ideally shrinking it, if they can get away with that.

3. They self-sabotage, semi-intentionally screwing up, so they don't have to be put in the spotlight again.

You can imagine how Imposter Syndrome might make it hard to step up and claim your credibility, can't you? But don't worry - I have a fabulous solution for Imposter Syndrome for you, later in this chapter.

The third block is (and - confession time - it nearly meant this book didn't get published!) fear of 'haters' – negative feedback.

The internet has a lot to answer for. It has brought us gifts like the ability to quickly grow a business or share a message internationally, breaking through historical trade and cultural barriers, and being able to help people, even while we sleep.

But it has also brought us trolls.

No longer are trolls the preserve of fearful fairy tale goats, foolishly crossing rickety bridges. Now they wield keyboards instead of clubs, but the trail they leave behind them smells just as foul.

And our obsession with celebrity perfection and gossip means we, as a culture, love to tear people apart for the slightest misdemeanour or mistake.

I vividly remember an old business I used to run, back in 2008, getting some national media coverage as a result of an interview I did. It had felt completely natural and comfortable to do it, and the newspaper was beloved of my dream customers. But then I read the comments for the online version of the article.

Back in the 'olden days', the only way to respond to an article would have been a 'letter to the editor'. These, whilst often controversial, were always vetted by someone with sufficient brain to ensure they were civilised and didn't fall into the realms of libel.

Alas the mostly-unmoderated world of website comments is a free-for-all for people whose sole purpose in life seems to be attacking and destroying the confidence of others (we'll look at why people behave that way in the Connection section in Step 4).

And that's what happened to me with my interview. The trolls kicked in and I still shudder at some of what was written - all conjecture, all hugely personal and insulting. Once the trolls had claimed their turf, no sane person would dare to write a sensible comment. I had to ask the newspaper to delete the discussions. And it took 7 years before I agreed to be interviewed by a national newspaper again - as part of the EU VAT Action campaign. One thing that has taught me is never to read the comments on an interview I have been published in. I have a Dream Team to do that for me. They let me know about anything that's important and they handle the rest!

The lessons I learned and the techniques I used to go 'visible' again are waiting for you, later in this chapter. But first I want to talk to you about the hardest part of the Credibility Equation.

What's The Hardest Part Of The Credibility Equation?

The hardest part isn't developing your expertise. You either have that or you don't. It's not connecting with your passion – your Big Why does that for you. The hardest part is being authentically, awesomely you.

As tiny children, we are totally authentic. We fully express who we are (often very loudly, at 3am) and connect deeply with the world around us. But as we grow up, things happen to cause us to shut down; to believe that somehow it's not 'safe' to be 'you'. We compare ourselves to others and find ourselves lacking. We cover ourselves in protective layers, until, one day, the 'outside world' version of us is almost unrecognisable. But when we allow ourselves to be authentic - to be fully present, in this moment - as who we really are, we magnetise those who have been longing to hear our Big Message. They can connect with us – deeply. We get to inspire them.

A friend of mine on Facebook posted recently that he was on the metro in his home town when he saw an amazingly beautiful woman, and he was trying really hard not to look at her, because he didn't want to stare. She came over and chatted to him, because he had his diving kit with him and it was a hobby that interested her.

As she started asking him about diving, and he looked at her and he thought, "Well, you know, she's pretty. She's nicely dressed," but there was nothing that could help him understand what it was that magnetised him to her. Afterwards he realised that it was just something about her 'Being'. She was clearly 'happy in her own skin'. She didn't have to be a raging beauty by modern media standards. He found her irresistible because she was in love with herself and allowing herself to be who she really was, and that was shining through every pore, every action, every word, every movement.

Sometimes it takes you a long time to sound like yourself. ~ Miles Davis

When you know who you really are, and you clear out the blocks to being that beautiful version of you, and you allow yourself to be authentic, those who are hungry to work with you, who are lying awake at night right now wishing you could help them, will come and find you. When they find you, they will say yes.

You know they say that dogs can smell fear? Well, humans can smell fake. If you're not being true to yourself and you're not being authentic, people will suss it. Yes, there are those who are going to go for the snake oil merchants, and that's their choice. It's their money. But what we want nowadays is people we can connect with, who have walked in our shoes, and who can prove that they can do it.

> *Do what you do best, and do it well.*
> *Do what **you** do best, and **do** it **well.***
> *~ Robert Smith*

This is the mantra that Robert Smith, my mentor from my NLP Trainer's Training, used to throw at me whenever I doubted myself. Authenticity is about doing what you do best and doing it well; being who you really are. The minute you stop pretending to be somebody that you're not and you really step into your Soul-Shoes, and start allowing yourself to love being who you really are, you will transform your life. Even a tiny step in that direction will make a huge difference.

If you only take one thing from our time together, please let it be this:

> *Be yourself, in everything you do, totally authentic,*
> *and your Dream Audience will love you for it.*

My clients and Dare To Dream Bigger Tribe members consistently report that when they have the courage to step up and be vulnerably authentic, they get a hugely positive response from their audience.

Yes, I know that being totally authentic can feel scary. So often when we connect with people, we put up the barriers first, as though we need to protect ourselves, as though we're scared what they will really think, and we're only safe if we wear that invisible mask.

Here's the thing: in this Photoshopped and Instagram-filtered online world, very few people are who they really seem. We no longer keep our masks in the jar by Eleanor Rigby's door. Our social media logins do that for us.

> *It's time to stop comparing yourself with glossy*
> *strangers on the internet.*

Behind that gorgeous-looking website might lie a nervous wreck, with a great graphic designer. Please don't change who you are, because comparing yourself to someone else made you feel somehow less worthy. Only you have the unique set of gifts and the unique message you feel inspired to share. And the only person you need to compare yourself to is yourself.

And just in case you have been tempted to hide your light under that proverbial bushel, or to change how you come across, to please your audience, I've got a bonus article for you on this in the Readers' Club: Don't Let Other People's Expectations Change Who You Are.

We have all done a version of this, at some point in our lives. I have met health gurus who are secretly addicted to the very foods they teach you to avoid, and are using out-of-date photos in their publicity, to hide the fact that they're no longer fit and healthy. I have met business coaches who are constantly broke, but still claim to be doing six or seven figure launches. Inflating results, Photoshopping out wrinkles and waistlines, and embellishing facts is rife in the online world. And, as a friend of mine remarked the other day about meeting the keynote speaker at a networking event, "I actually recognised him from his Facebook profile photo. I told him how rare that was!"

I'm not saying this to judge anyone – we're all doing our best; it's how people are cope with their inner blocks and insecurities. They may be suffering from fear failure and rejection, if they allow the real 'them' to be seen. They deserve our compassion. I'm sharing this with you because we need to let ourselves off the hook, too, so we don't fall into the traps they did. So please stop comparing yourself with the highlights from someone else's life.

You are good enough, just as you are.

Our natural fear of rejection, combined with dollops of Imposter Syndrome and inferiority complexes, means that we constantly compare ourselves to others, especially those who look successful, on social media, the internet and in magazines. And when we do that, it's like we step out of our own Soul-Shoes and try to squeeze into someone else's.

At best, we risk becoming an insecure shadow of who we really are. At worst, we end up feeling jealous and inadequate. And we might even be tempted to copy that other person, which can lead to ugly law suits.

That's why I'm risking annoying you, by asking you to get clarity and then clear out the blocks, before we move on to the juicy bit of taking inspired action, so you can take the next step on that journey towards falling in love with being who you really are.

I want you to feel safe, being Authentic.

Exercise: What Is 'Authenticity'?

There's a worksheet and an audio for this exercise in the Readers' Club. I invite you to take a few minutes to explore these questions and write down your answers. It will help you with creating your Credibility Action Plan, at the end of this step.

- What does 'authenticity' mean to you?
- What would happen, if you allowed yourself to be totally, authentically 'you'? And allowed others to see that in you?
- When you imagine that, what happens in your body? To your posture? To your breathing? To your emotions? To your thoughts?
- And now I want you to imagine wearing the mask that you normally wear, instead. How does that feel? What happens in your body? To your posture? To your breathing? To your emotions? To your thoughts?
- Now I have four questions for you. They might send your thinking mind into a bit of a spin, and it's ok if they do. It's their job. Just write down your first responses, without analysing or judging.
- What *would* happen, if I *do allow* myself to be authentic?
- What *won't* happen, if I *do allow* myself to be authentic?
- What *would* happen, if I *don't allow* myself to be authentic?
- What *won't* happen, if I *don't allow* myself to be authentic?

What did you discover? Any lightbulbs? Surprises? Questions?

Before we move on, give yourself a bit of a shake and shrug, to let go of any emotions that came up in that exercise that are less-than-helpful. And give me a big smile, please. I don't care if you're just grinning at a book. It will release the endorphins your body so loves, helping you to feel more positive and energised.

I'm curious: what could you do to step into your authentic Soul-Shoes, to allow yourself to be even just 1% more of who you really are, that beautiful, bright, shining light of your inner being? Standing in your Truth, with confidence and self-belief; just feel that for a moment; 1%.

Connect and feel it expanding. Breathe into that feeling and know that with each and every breath you can allow that to effortlessly grow.

*If you're not standing in your Truth, you're standing in
lies; according to my 9-year-old, that stinks.*

Open-hearted, authentic communication unleashes your passion and your ability to make a difference in the world.

The Two Biggest Threats To Your Credibility

We've already mentioned these, but now I want to deal with them in more depth. The two biggest threats on your credibility journey are your fear of haters and Imposter Syndrome.

I have seen these two derail so many passionate world-changers. It makes them turn down golden opportunities, not return that life-changing call, self-sabotage on dream projects, not take action on their inspiration and dream smaller than the world deserves.

So in the final part of this section on credibility, before we dive in with your credibility action plan, we're going to take a tour through how to spot these silent saboteurs and what you can do about them. And I'll share with you some deep-dive resources that you can find in the Readers' Club, in case they're a key issue for you.

It's Time To Stop Feeling Like A Fraud

Confession: even as I have been writing this book, I have had regular bouts of Imposter Syndrome. I have even felt like a fraud, for feeling like a fraud! How do I know it's running? Usually procrastination and self-distraction. I would suddenly get writer's block or try to over-think things. It's amazing what suddenly becomes desperately important, when Imposter Syndrome wants you to avoid doing something that secretly scares you. Anything from checking the news to painting your toenails can get in the way of taking inspired action, if you're running a deeply-held fear of being caught out as a fraud.

But the fact that you're holding this Handbook in your hands proves that I dealt with those fears and got on with creating it. And I am going to share with you exactly how I did it.

Imposter Syndrome could be said to belong in section two, under 'confidence', but I have given it a home under 'credibility' instead, because it deserves its own space. My personal experience and my mentoring clients have taught me that, once we have clarity and confidence,

Imposter Syndrome is the most common final hidden block that causes us to self-sabotage. And it usually hides until it's time to stand in our 'expert shoes' - when you're moving into the credibility zone. But what is Imposter Syndrome? And how do you spot it if you have got it?

I was working with a client recently who has been running their own business for many years. They felt frustrated at how they were able to quickly grow to a certain level, but then always got stuck, no matter what kind of project they were working on.

Their Facebook groups never grew beyond a certain size. Their courses never had more than a certain number of students. They always reached the same, familiar old point in a corporate pitch process and the emails would dry up. Their competitors seemed to be enjoying huge success. But despite doing all the right things, this person wasn't getting the results they knew they deserved.

Why? Imposter Syndrome. They felt like a fraud. They felt terrified they might get 'caught out' and people would see that they 'didn't really belong' in the 'VIP lounge'. The crazy thing is that this person is hugely talented. Nearly every successful business owner and executive I have ever worked with has been held back, at some point, by this pattern.

It's so common that 'Imposter Syndrome' has now become a clinical term, used by psychologists, who describe it as the fear of being unmasked as the incompetent person that you secretly believe you are. Ouch! Some of the most successful people on the planet are suffering from this. So if you are, too, then you're in great company.

> *Whether you believe you're good enough, or you believe you're not, you're right.*

… because we get – or subconsciously create – what we believe, even if we don't consciously realise that we believe it.

As we have already discussed, your brain has filters that are governed by your beliefs, so that you don't get overwhelmed by the gazillion bits of information flying around in its subconscious awareness at any point in time. So, for example, if you believe you're rubbish at presenting, you'll spot the feedback from the audience that confirms this, but you won't notice all the positive feedback that confirms you did a great job.

Imposter Syndrome is how we accidentally create self-imposed glass ceilings and self-sabotaging behaviour. When we're running a case of Imposter Syndrome, one of the biggest risks is we'll create conditions that allow us either to under-perform or to self-sabotage. We find a valid excuse to say no to that opportunity. Or we leave it just that little bit too late to return the call, or reply to the emails. By allowing the opportunities to lapse, we don't have to stretch ourselves out of our comfort zone. Most of the time, we don't consciously realise we are doing this.

When you find Imposter Syndrome rearing its fairly ugly head, it is important to realise this is ok. You're not broken. You're completely normal. As I said, you're in good company. And the work we did in Step 2 (Confidence) will already have helped. It might require some kind of one-to-one work to uncover what the underlying issues are and deal with them, but you *can* deal with them.

If you're feeling like a fraud, it's actually a positive sign, because it means there's a comfort zone that's being stretched, which means you've got the chance to grow beyond it. By that point, you then won't feel like a fraud doing that any more. You'll feel confident, and you'll have proved to yourself that you can do it.

Exercise: What Is Imposter Syndrome Really Costing You?

We often don't notice how much Imposter Syndrome is costing us, because we pretend we don't have it. Instead, we'll use excuses like being too busy or a dream project not being a good fit. Here is how to spot the tangible and intangible costs of Imposter Syndrome, for your life, your happiness and your business:

- Which opportunities have you turned down?
- Which projects did you not start – or not complete?
- How many hours have you lost due to stress or worry or emotions linked to your negative self-talk?
- How many times have you felt demoralised, by comparing yourself to others and fearing that they are better than you?
- And just imagine, if you do nothing and keep running this pattern, how much will that cost you, over the coming months and years?
- Now you know what your Big Why, your Big Vision and your Big Message are, how would it feel if you let Imposter Syndrome get in the way of you taking massive action?

Why Is It Important To Deal With Imposter Syndrome?

The world needs your Light now, whether or not you're scared of feeling like a fraud!

And even if you now WISH you had done something about Imposter Syndrome years ago, remember that, according to the Ancient Chinese:

The second best time to plant an oak tree is today.

And it's not just about you! Here are three reasons why your Dream Audience WISHES you would deal with this:

1. Negative self-talk keeps you stuck playing small...

... when they need you most, which means that many of your Dream Customers will be missing out on you completely.

2. You can't do your best work...

... in flow and connected with your inner genius – if you're reciting mantras about how rubbish you are.

3. They want and need to believe in you...

... so that they can believe in themselves and the transformation you provide, whatever that is. That can't happen unless you believe in yourself.

All of these stories about what we can or can't achieve – or who we can or can't be – are just thoughts. They're not the Truth. They are simply symptoms of an Inner Critic – a disempowering internal dialogue – that is scared of either failure or success.

It's easy to run from dealing with Imposter Syndrome - it can seem big and scary, but actually it's not; I'm going to share a process with you that can start getting things sorted in under ten minutes.

Setting Yourself Free From Imposter Syndrome

What can you do?

Well, to start with: put a name to it. It takes the power out of the internal dialogue: "Oh – that's just Imposter Syndrome come out to play."

Can you feel the relief? It takes the drama, emotions and potential victimhood out of the discussion. It stops the story in its tracks. It sets you free to make other choices. If you find yourself diving into the drama, revisit the techniques from Step 2 on limiting beliefs and taming your

Inner Critic. Asking yourself what is 'Truth' in the story, versus what is conjecture, is a great way to turn that mountain back into a molehill.

Here's another top tip: this one's from the world of yoga. Movement is the key to change. You can't shift anything by standing still. Want to sort out your internal dialogue? Then move – physically! Take action. Stop being stuck. Dance to your favourite music. Go for a walk. Do whatever works for you, to shift your mood and your self-talk. You will never set yourself free from Imposter Syndrome by sitting at your desk and worrying about it.

Forget the old saying, "If at first you don't succeed, try, try, try again."

If what you're doing isn't working, try something different.

Thousands of my clients, students and readers over the past 10+ years have proved to me that you CAN choose which thoughts to feed. You CAN set yourself free from Imposter Syndrome. And you can even tame your Inner Critic – retraining it to become your biggest cheerleader, as we started in Step 2 and will continue in Step 7.

Remember, you've got the A, B, C method from Step 2. You can let those thoughts pass through on the conveyor belt without diving into the drama. It's not a soap opera. You've got all the tools from Step 2, to help you figure out the underlying limiting beliefs and even the meditation MP3, to help you deal with any fears.

And, if Imposter Syndrome is a big issue for you, there's a video in the Readers' Club of a guided visualisation technique you can use in under ten minutes, to set yourself free from feeling like a fraud, so you can feel confident and happy again.

I have seen so many people suffer from Imposter Syndrome – and I have experienced it myself, and refined the strategies for moving beyond it. I want that for you, too. So this video pulls together the gems from thousands of people's journeys; the common thread techniques I have used to help them. It works so much better as a video than if I transcribed the text here. Have a watch and you'll understand why. Hula hoops will never be the same again…

How To Handle Your Fear Of Haters

As I mentioned earlier, there have been times during the writing of this book when I have been so scared of trashy reviews and trolls that I nearly didn't publish it, even though I knew I would be doing everything I could to make sure this book is great, and to road-test it with my R&D team of entrepreneurs.

Of course, I didn't consciously use that excuse. Instead, I convinced myself that I was 'too busy' or 'too tired' or had 'other priorities' (and I got very creative in creating yet more 'other priorities'). But underneath all of these 'little lies' lay the Truth: I was terrified of trolls.

A friend of mine who is a fiction author says she actively avoids telling people about her books, because she is scared they won't like them, even though they're international best-sellers. She and I both describe the process of having a book published to be a bit like being called to the Head Master's office, each time someone reads it, not knowing whether you're about to get smiles or shouts, and knowing that the whole world is watching.

Allowing yourself to be seen as an expert in your field means you need to stop being 'beige' (toning yourself down to be 'neutral', so you don't offend anyone) and you need a dose of Marmite-appeal (see Step 1).

Marmite has played for years on its "love me, hate me, I don't care" image. If you want to become a credible authority in your field, you've got to be so confident and comfortable in your own skin that the occasional adverse 'Marmite response' doesn't bother you.

When recently talking to a group of business owners, we all realised how the business world has changed over the past few years – and how many people are out there on the internet saying things they would never dream of saying to your face.

A straw poll quickly showed that fear of criticism from 'Trolls' and 'Haters' was one of the biggest secret blocks, holding us back from being truly authentic and taking the leap outside of our comfort zones – to grow our businesses to the next level.

In fact, the fear of being criticised, in general, was one of the biggest barriers to taking leaps and creating business breakthroughs.

Whether you've already had your first 'hater' or you're just worried about what might happen, if that time comes, there are simple things you can do to stay sane and keep smiling, no matter what they throw at you.

So in this section I'm going to share with you some of the most helpful strategies I developed over more than a decade as an NLP Trainer, with a generous sprinkling of that demystified Ancient Wisdom, so you can get yourself 'troll-proof'; and so that the fear of 'haters' no longer has to be part of your business model.

You're going to get the same deep-acting stuff that I normally share with my Masterminders and Dare To Dream Bigger Academy members, so you can build on the confidence work from Step 2 and how to be true to who you really are, and your Big Message, even if the haters and trolls throw a party in your honour.

It's time to stand in your personal power and let your light shine.

The 5 Steps To Letting Your Light Shine – Trolls Or No Trolls

This is the 5-step the process I use with my clients, and with myself, to help if trolls strike. It's really important to go through these in order - they're set out like this for a reason.

And you may find some of the concepts hit your 'buttons'. I apologise if they do, but I'm not sorry, because if those buttons are hanging around to be pressed, and this Handbook accidentally does that, then the trolls would do a much better job than I ever could. I'd rather help you to ditch those out-of-date buttons, than encourage you to pretend they're not there, until a hater trips over and lands on one of them.

Step 1: Coming Back Down To Earth

This is the bit that most of us miss out, when we're dealing with trolls. When it happens – or even if you're just imagining it happening - it's easy to get stuck in your 'story-head' and to drown in the stress and drama. Your body triggers its stress response and you get stuck in the emotions.

So it's really important to get grounded and calm if the troll strikes. Whatever you do, do NOT respond to your troll until you have done this. Otherwise you'll only make things worse! Release the stress and emotions first. You can do some belly breathing, to get grounded, and ideally go for a slow, mindful walk outside. As your feet touch the earth, imagine you're releasing the tension, stress and emotions into the ground, and that you're breathing in the solidity and strength of a mountain. There's a special 'getting grounded' meditation, over at the Readers' Club.

And remember, as Eleanor Roosevelt said: "No one can make you feel inferior, without your consent."

Step 2: It's Not Really About You

Of course, when trolls and haters strike it's easy to get knocked off balance and take it personally. But when you understand a bit more about why Trolls troll and Haters hate, it sets you free to respond from a place of personal power, rather than being eaten up by self-doubt and anger.

All criticism is borne of someone else's pain. ~ Native American saying

The unkind behaviour isn't really about you. Happy people don't attack others and make them feel bad. What might be going on in that person's life, for them to have behaved this way?

Of course, it doesn't make their behaviour acceptable. But if you stop taking it personally and realise it's a verbalising of some inner pain, instead of being about you, it might make it easier for you to reach a place of acceptance, so you can move on, and set yourself free from their venom.

It's vital to keep your perspective. If you know the 'feedback' you got doesn't really fit, then you need to find a way to let it go. Responding to the criticiser and trying to convince them that they're wrong is likely to make them dig their heels in harder.

Step 3: How To Spot The Hidden Gems

Whatever happened, there's always a way to find diamonds in the dirt. It's not about pretending you're happy that it happened, but it IS about making sure you get the Inner Gifts from the situation – in a positive and empowering way.

Whether the 'trolling' is real or it's 'just' a fear of future criticism, there are simple strategies you can apply to hoover up the diamonds from amongst the brown stuff.

My favourite way to do this is the 'woolly jumper test'. Once you have released the stress and emotions from the 'feedback', imagine that what was said is like a woolly jumper, which you can try on for size. Be totally objective and honest with yourself and ask yourself whether that jumper is a good fit. If it's not, then let it go. If it might be, ask yourself: what could I learn from this? What could I do differently in the future? Is there any 'inside work' I need to do, to make sure this isn't a problem for me in the future?

And imagine you could look back at the experience, from the vantage point of the 'you' on your 80th birthday. What would that 'you' advise?

Step 4: Cutting Ties And Letting Go

When you reach this stage, it's time to close the file – to let go and move on. You might find it helps to imagine the invisible cords linking you to the person who behaved unkindly, and a huge pair of scissors, cutting those ties and filling both ends with love. It's important to fill them with love and not with anger, because one of the ends is attached to you, and there's already more than enough anger in the world.

You might find mindful breathing helps, too - watching your in and out breath - and the following mantras help:

As you breathe in, say to yourself: "It's ok. I am here, now."

As you breathe out, say to yourself: "I let it go."

Step 5: Life After Trolls

Now you're free from the effects of Haters & Trolls, it's time to celebrate – to step up and Dare To Dream Bigger and brighter and to really let your light shine. You might want to revisit the sections in this book on limiting beliefs and check that your Inner Critic hasn't picked up any new, unsupportive "I am" statements.

And make sure you look at your 'authenticity' notes, from earlier in this section, to make sure that troll doesn't make you cover over your diamond.

And, above all, celebrate! Do a happy dance. You came through an experience that could have caused you to shut down, but instead you're using it to grow and to set yourself free to let your light shine. That's worthy of a party.

Bonus Step:

Keep a scrap book (real or virtual) of all the positive feedback and kind comments you get. If the trolls and haters get to you, go back to this with a cup of tea and enjoy reclaiming your perspective. You are doing a brilliant job and the occasional bit of negative feedback doesn't change that.

I spoke to Livia Farkas about this. She has been writing online since 1999 and has seen her fair share of trolls. She now runs urban:eve, a blog and community of over 35,000 women, and she sees putting trolls in their place as part of her responsibility to her community. But she makes sure she does it in a way that has as positive an impact as possible.

Livia is human, so when trolls or haters strike, especially if it's a personal comment, it hurts. But rather than letting that hurt turn into anger, Livia has worked on her confidence and self-acceptance, so that it doesn't hit her as hard any more.

"Hey! At least I made an effort! What have *you* done today?" is now her internal response. She knows it isn't her job to look a certain way or to say what people want to hear. She also knows that the criticism isn't really aimed at her; she is just an outlet for the other person's pain.

Sometimes she doesn't respond, but if she does, she always makes sure she gets calm and grounded first. If she does reply, she takes time to consider the long-term effect on the commenter and makes sure she is kind, but with crystal-clear boundaries.

Just because you're online, it doesn't mean you should put up with unreasonable, toxic behaviour. If your other readers see you being compassionate but firm with haters and trolls, they may be inspired to show similar courage in their own lives. You are their role model.

Livia sees her blog as being her 'online home' and that she is the 'hostess' for her community. Behaviour that would get someone kicked out of her house is equally unacceptable on her website and in her community groups. And her Tribe respects her for that.

If you let someone behave in a hateful way towards you, it risks closing down all discussions in your community, because your other members will no longer feel safe. With practice, and confidence, you can turn negative comments into a chance for everyone to learn and grow, showing leadership to your Tribe.

Above all, don't change who you are to try to please the trolls. There's no pleasing them. That's not your job. Let it go and get back to being who you really are.

If you'd like to join in the discussion about how to handle haters and trolls, or if you'd like the video course version of these five steps, there's a whole section on this over in the Readers' Club.

Please Learn To Accept Compliments

So many of us struggle with this. But if you're going to learn how to handle haters and trolls, it's only fair to also learn how to handle compliments, too. Having done the work so far in this Handbook, hopefully it will be getting easier for you by now.

Part of your credibility journey is learning to accept positive feedback, rather than feeling awkward and embarrassed and dismissing them. If someone tells you they love your work - or they're keen to read your book or do your course - then if you reject that compliment, it causes them pain. It's as though you are dismissing their experience of your work; as though you want to deny them the chance to benefit from what you have created.

I'm not suggesting you need to do an ego trip about this, but it's important to learn to accept compliments, graciously, and to actually let them sink in. They're brilliant antidotes for times when your Inner Critic drives you crazy.

As with negative feedback, it's important to try the compliment on for size - does it fit? Does it resonate with you? Can you accept that it is the opinion or the experience of the compliment-giver? After all, what right have we got to say that it's not?

Imposter Syndrome and lack of self-worth - doubting whether we're good enough - are the usual causes of this.

How often have we said things like, "Oh, thank you, but really it's not *that* good and now it's done I can see loads of ways I could have improved it"? How does that make the compliment-giver feel?

You don't have to gush gratitude. If you feel uncomfortable, you could try something like, "I'm really glad you feel that way. It's important to me and thank you for making the effort to tell me." That way you're not agreeing or disagreeing, but you're honouring the experience of the other person; they will feel heard; and you can mull over whether or not that compliment-woolly-jumper fits, in your own time.

The more you can appreciate yourself, the easier you'll find it to accept compliments, and the less often your Inner Critic will beat you up - it will do wonders for your self-esteem.

So I've got an exercise for you, right now, that might be a comfort zone stretch.

Exercise: Learning To Accept Compliments

Rather than waiting for compliments to show up, so you can practise your self-esteem-building, how about building it into your daily routine? If your self-worth is dependent on the feedback and opinions of others, then that's a fragile and potentially painful place to live. Instead, if you build it yourself, from the inside out, step by step, day by day, then you'll feel more confident, you'll have more credibility, and you're much more likely to take inspired action to get your message out there.

Here's how:

- Go and stand in front of a mirror.
- Make eye contact with yourself. Relax!
- Smile.
- Notice how lovely your smile looks.
- Now imagine you can take all of your attention to your heart, moving your thoughts from your head to your heart area. If you could say something kind to yourself, right now, as you look into your eyes in the mirror, what might you say?
- And if you could say thank you to yourself for something about you, what might that be?
- And if you could tell yourself something that you think is really good about being 'you', what might that be?
- Say those things to the 'you' in the mirror, either in your head, or out loud.
- If self-judging thoughts come up, just let them drift on through, and pick another kind one.
- If any emotions come up, just breathe through them and let them pass on by. Let them go.

If you do this each morning and evening, as you brush your teeth, you might be amazed by the difference it makes. There's a discussion thread in the forum at the Readers' Club for this - I'd love to hear how you get on with it.

To give you an idea for how others have handled Imposter Syndrome and Fear Of Haters, there are extra interviews waiting for you, in the Readers' Club. And here is some invaluable advice from the interview I did with Juliet McKenna, Co-Founder of the EU VAT Action Campaign.

Juliet McKenna is a Science Fiction and Fantasy author, who has sold over 1 million copies of her books. She was also the Co-Founder of the EU VAT Action Campaign. A State-School pupil who made it to Oxford, learning how to handle Imposter Syndrome was an essential skill. She studied Classics and credits her college's 'tutorial system' with training her to have the courage of her convictions. Each week she would have to write an essay analysis on a topic chosen by her tutor; a topic in which he or she may have been a world expert. Then Juliet had to present it, in front of her peers, for 'review'. She quickly learned to back up her point of view with 'evidence' and to present 'analysis', rather than just 'reporting' or 'opinion'.

You might think that, with that training, handling book reviews would be easy. But it wasn't. Juliet, like any author, found that critical reviews hurt. She needed to find a way to handle these reviews, which allowed her to learn from them, but didn't knock her confidence. Juliet has some invaluable advice to share with you. Here are some of her strategies:

- Don't accept the review as fact, analyse it, to decide whether their review is worth listening to.
- The review is their *opinion*, not hard fact.
- Sometimes they're not reviewing what you wrote; they are comparing it to the book they would prefer you to have written. It says more about their life experience than about your book.
- Read the review once to decide whether it's worth your time. Is there anything you could learn from it, in terms of what you wanted to convey?
- Don't take it personally. It is an honest review of why the book didn't work for *them*; that doesn't mean it is a 'bad' book.

Above all, Juliet encourages you to stick to what you want to create and to be confident. Compare yourself against whether you achieved your aims, not whether you pleased your reviewers.

Creating Your Credibility Action Plan

We're talking credibility here, not visibility, though there is major overlap. We'll be covering visibility in detail in the next step on Connection. But visibility is much easier to amplify, when you're credible - if you are already seen as an expert.

So in this section we're just looking at your credibility action plan, though it may also be a large part of your visibility action plan.

Remember:

Expertise + Passion + Authenticity = Credibility

Very few people have an action plan for becoming credible, yet there are many different ways to do it. It's different for every person and it can be fun. So here are some simple questions you can ask yourself, to create your credibility action plan. There's a worksheet for these questions in the Readers' Club.

Exercise: Credibility Action Plan

First, start by revisiting your work from step 1 - Clarity - to remind yourself who you're serving, and what your Big Vision and your Big Message are.

Expertise:
- What kinds of qualifications might those I am here to help expect? How does my background fit with those?
- Which trade associations or accountability bodies might they expect me to be part of? How could I double-check this?
- What experience might they expect me to have? How can I make it easy for them to see that I have it?
- How might they find me? Where are they looking for answers?
- How do they make decisions, in the context of my Big Vision? Who do they ask for help?
- Which kinds of testimonials might they want to see?
- How important are reviews to them, in their decision-making?
- How can I establish myself as a trusted voice, wherever they are hanging out?
- How might they hear about me? How can I make that more likely?

Continues...

- What would I want them to hear about me? How can I amplify that message?

Use these answers to make sure you've got the required qualification expertise, and also to work out where you might want to be getting interviewed, doing speaking gigs, networking or doing guest posts, if you're into blogging.

Passion:
- How much does my Big Why inspire me?
- How could I ditch from my 'to do' list the things that drag me down?
- What help and support could I get, to allow me to spend more time in my Zone of Genius, so that I feel inspired, more of the time?
- Are there any things in my life that are buckets of cold water on my passion for my Big Vision? What could I do about them?
- How can I top up my batteries, so that I have enough energy to feel inspired by and passionate about my Big Vision?
- How can I notice the progress I'm making? (This is a big part of maintaining your passion - it quickly disappears, if you're feeling demoralised and you feel that you're achieving nothing).

Use these answers to create an action plan to give you the time, energy and focus to love what you're doing, so that your passion shines through, without effort.

Authenticity – review your answers from the start of this step:
- What does 'authenticity' mean to me?
- What does it mean to people who I want to hear my message?
- Reviewing the authenticity section of this book, which actions could I take to clear out my blocks, to allow myself to be more authentic? Which block will I start with?

Use these answers to look at which inner blocks you might need to release and also which practical actions you could take, so that you feel more comfortable being 'you', day by day.

We've got a discussion thread for this, over at the readers' forum.

Bonus Exercise: if you're running your own business, then your website is often the first place that people find you and it's vital for your credibility, whether for clients or journalists or potential business partners. There's a bonus article and a worksheet over at the Readers' Club: "How To Make Sure Your Website Is Building Your Credibility, Not Trashing It". It takes you through the five vital elements you need, and how to avoid the surprisingly common mistakes that make your dream customers run a mile.

As I said earlier, please pick one block at a time; clear it, integrate it and then move on to the next action. Being single-minded and focussing in this way brings you much faster results than trying to ditch twenty old habits at once.

And remember to celebrate your successes. Each time you release an old block, you set yourself free to make an even bigger difference in the world.

So are you ready to move on to Taking Inspired Action?

Take Inspired Action

Connection

The more deeply you can connect, the bigger difference you will make.

Connection comes in three forms, all of which are essential, if you want to deliver on your Big Vision:

The first one is connection with yourself.

This is connection with your intuition, your Inner Knowing, connection by being grounded and connection with your Self.

The second kind of connection is with your Dream Audience.

This allows you to magnetise and inspire them. Confident, happy people, who are comfortable in their own skin, resonate more easily with us. Lay these foundations and connect with yourself, ideally daily, and you'll find connecting with your Dream Audience becomes easier.

The third type of connection is with your Dream Team.

You might be a solopreneur, a freelancer, self-employed, running a micro business or you might be in somebody else's business, but the fact is that you still need to work with people. We can't do it all on our own. I see so many people trying to, though; struggling with overwhelm and secretly terrified of getting new business. So your Dream Team is your support network, whether that's people you hire, your loved-ones at home, supportive friends, a Mastermind group for accountability, or even joint future business partners.

A Little Word About Introverts And Extroverts

I can't talk to you about 'connection' without handling this one. Some of us might call ourselves introverts. Some would say extroverts. Some of us are a bit of both. And I'm talking the Carl Jung school of introversion and extroversion, which is about where you get your energy from, rather than whether someone is shy around strangers or confident. So you can have a shy extrovert and a confident introvert. And there's no judgement here, though, as Susan Cain beautifully explores in her book "Quiet", our Western society and corporate world is built around the needs of extroverts.

Although I love video work, and I enjoy being on stage, I run a really strong introvert pattern. How can I tell? I recharge my batteries through quiet time at home. If I've had a busy, people-filled day and somebody says, "hey, let's go out to a bar," then it's my idea of dental work without anaesthetic. I need to go home and have that nourishing, battery-recharging time. For other people, the idea of going home for quiet time at the end of the day is a nightmare. They refresh their energy levels by going out and being with others.

This is a hugely simplified explanation of these two characteristics, but playing to your strengths when connecting with others is essential. If you want to find out more, I have a 90-minute masterclass for you, in which I interviewed Elena Herdieckerhof, who is an expert on this. In it, she takes you through exactly how to spot which your preference is and guides you through how to make the most of the positive qualities of introversion, if that's your pattern. In addition, we go into depth on how to handle being a Highly Sensitive Person (HSP) in a full-on, sensory world. I also strongly recommend reading Susan Cain's wonderful book 'Quiet', which could be transformational for you, if you're feeling lost in an entrepreneurial world full of extroverts. Details of both of these are in the Readers' Club. They will inspire and empower you to connect fully with others, whilst honouring your introvert needs.

What Stops Us From Connecting?

Sometimes it's fear of rejection. Sometimes it's because we're running an introvert pattern; which a huge number of entrepreneurs are. Sometimes we don't have the energy. We don't have the passion. Sometimes it's self-worth. Or it might be another of our hidden blocks, such as Imposter Syndrome.

When you are clear about your Big Message, your Big Vision, and who you are; when you've built up your confidence; when you've established your credibility and *then* you connect, you can almost whisper and people will still hear you, and it will resonate with them.

When you've got those foundations and you reach out to people to say, "look, here's a win/win - we could work together," you will be amazed at how often they say yes. If you approach them and you don't have clarity, you're not really confident, and you don't have credibility yet, their PA won't even send the email through.

That is why connection waits until this point of the Handbook. The more of our excuses we have ditched before we connect, the more effective that connection will be.

The Power Of Expectations

When we're looking at connecting, it's vital that we first understand the power of our expectations, to colour our experience of others. We discussed in Step 2 that our beliefs act as filters in our brain, governing what we notice from the many stimuli that bombard us, moment-to-moment. One of the ways our brain does that is through our expectations.

You see what you expect to see.

It's easy to dismiss that which we don't want to see or which contradicts our beliefs or assumptions.

A friend was telling me about her teenage son, who had been struggling at school. They had meetings with the teacher, because the teacher seemed to be 'on a downer' with the son, telling him off for under-performing and even threatening that he would have to leave the school, if his grades didn't pick up, despite knowing there had been some family stress at home. So my friend decided to make sure that her son would do well in his maths exam and spent a week of evenings, coaching him and helping him to really understand that year's key topics. She saw her son thrive during those sessions, quickly picking up the key concepts and building his confidence.

Her son flew through the exam and came home excited. When the teacher gave out the marks the next week, the teenager had got over 80%, which was a really high score and a wonderful achievement. But instead of praising him, the teacher accused him of cheating and somehow copying someone else's answers - in front of the class.

The teacher had expected him to do badly, so when he did well, she was unable to accept evidence that contradicted her expectations, so she found the only other explanation that fitted with her beliefs. The boy felt devastated and humiliated, instead of being able to feel proud of his achievement.

How we see someone affects how *they* perform. If we expect them to do badly or not be good enough, and they trust us or see us as being in a position of authority, they will tend to fulfil our expectations. If you connect with your Dream Audience whilst fearing rejection, somehow they'll pick up on that, you'll make mistakes you wouldn't otherwise make, and it's likely to become a self-fulfilling prophecy.

In the NLP world, one of the principles that people find the hardest to 'try on for size' is that you can't change others; you can only change yourself. When someone is driving us crazy, we want *them* to change. Why should we change?! When a colleague is struggling, we want *them* to improve. Why should *we* do anything different?! When someone nags us, we want *them* to stop. Why should we change what we're doing?!

The meditation world teaches us that, to feel inner peace and happiness, we need to accept the outside world, and to stop projecting our pain and stories onto our experience of it. But what if someone really 'is an idiot' or is bugging you beyond any reasonable limits?

Your actions towards them will be a clear mirror of your thoughts about them. Even if you think you're hiding the inner commentary you're running about how stupid or annoying or whatever else they are, they will sense it. And your thoughts about them are based on what you believe about them. Your beliefs filter out the bits that contradict your assumptions and expectations. So even if, say, Richard does a great presentation, if you believe he always does bad ones, then those belief filters mean you'll only spot – and remember - the mistakes.

When we criticise someone, even silently, it's about us, not them. Remember the Native American saying from the 'How To Handle Haters' section? "All criticism is borne of someone else's pain."

If we criticise others, it's a projection of our internal pain - not who they really are. If we expect someone to do something wrong or badly, that's down to our internal thought processes and fears, not them. We see what we choose to see. Yes, sometimes people make mistakes, but few people are ever as bad or annoying or clumsy or stupid as we tell ourselves they are.

So your expectations of how someone will behave affects your ability to connect with them. Your beliefs about who they are and what they are good or bad at will impact what you see of them. It acts like a box, restricting the relationship you can have.

Similarly, if you expect them to, say, dislike you, that's what you're likely to co-create, because you will subconsciously shift your thoughts and actions to move you towards that expectation.

The more you can clear out your own limiting beliefs, fears, excuses or worries, the less you will need to project them onto others.

Deepak Chopra created a wonderful exercise called "The Mirror" (link in the Readers' Club). In it, he gets you to focus on someone who is driving you crazy, and to list what bugs you. You then list what you like about them (that can be a toughie). And the conclusion of the exercise is a method that helps you to see that everything that bugs you about that person is simply one of your triggers being pressed; that we possess both the qualities we admire in others, and those qualities we reject in them – these behaviours press our 'buttons'. Once you can see yourself in others, it's easier to connect with them. It can be quite a challenging exercise, but I have used it many times with myself and my clients and it has produced miraculous results. When you deal with your inner blocks and clear out your expectations, it's amazing how often that other person seems to 'totally change' and suddenly be 'much less annoying'. You can't change others, only yourself. But in changing yourself, you allow that relationship - that connection - to change and grow.

When you see someone through the eyes of love, and consciously choose to notice only the positives about them, you will see them blossom. By changing your expectations, your self-talk and your actions towards them, they will seem to change before your very eyes.

Want To Take This To The Next Level?

In most circumstances, we would never intentionally cause someone else pain though unkind behaviour, through constantly criticising them and telling them why they're not good enough, or through believing that they're an idiot, would we?

But that's what most of us do to ourselves, most of the time, every day. We let our Inner Critic run wild, which makes it really hard to connect with who we really are, our Big Why and our Big Vision. And the harder we make it to be authentic. That's why 'connection' comes after 'confidence' and 'credibility;. And it's why we'll be starting this section with connecting with ourselves.

Your Inner Wisdom – Vignaanamayakosha

I Know, therefore I am.

The more self-awareness you can develop, the more openly and truthfully you can connect with others, and the bigger difference you'll be able to make in the world. And that means you need to connect with yourself, first.

Come back here, now! Most of us don't live 'here'. We live in the past, fretting about things that happened, or we worry in the future, about what may come to pass. But we don't live right here, right now. And to make the challenge greater, most of us don't even live in our bodies; we're living in our heads. And they're not usually even our 'happy heads'; they're our 'stress-heads'. So we're stuck in our heads, telling ourselves stressful stories about the past or the future, when the only power of choice we have is here, in this moment, in our bodies.

That's why I want you to focus on connecting with yourself, before you work on connecting with others.

What Is 'Connecting With Yourself?' And Why Bother?

This is where we go back to the Koshas, with the fourth kosha or layer of experience: the Wisdom Body – Vignaanamayakosha. 'Gnaan' loosely translates as 'wisdom'.

This layer is about Knowledge with a capital 'K' – that inner wisdom or deep knowing, rather than pub quiz facts. It's also about your self-awareness and your connection to all other living beings. It's where your most brilliant ideas come from – the ones that trigger that physical excitement in your belly. They don't come from the 'thinking mind'; they come from your Intuition.

When my students and clients learn to connect with themselves, each day, they report that they feel:

- Less stressed
- Happier
- Calmer
- Less emotionally volatile
- More at peace

- More 'connected'
- Open-hearted
- More open to having fun
- Able to take life less seriously
- More able to concentrate
- Better able to manage their thoughts - especially letting go of the negative ones
- Healthier
- More tolerant of the people who used to bug them
- Able to get more done, in less time
- More grounded
- More able to notice the good things in life
- More grateful for what they have
- It's easier to connect with their intuition and inner wisdom
- More 'present' in their relationships
- Connected with their inspiration
- Like the Universe has 'got their back'

Surely all of that is worth, say, ten minutes a day of your time? Remember the woman my friend met on the metro, who magnetised him to her, just because of how comfortable she felt in her own skin? Taking time out to reconnect with the 'real' you, for a few minutes each day, can move you towards that. And can you imagine what that would do when it comes to magnetising your dream customers and your Dream Audience for your Big Message?

How Can You Connect With Yourself?

It's important to get grounded and back in your body. The bonus MP3 on the mountain posture from page 125 helps you to do this. When you get grounded, back in this present moment, you'll feel a sense of relief and calm. If you do this regularly, you'll start to feel more at peace and life won't stress you as much.

Another option is silent sitting, where you close your eyes and observe your physical experience of life. You can do mindful breathing, where you close your eyes and let your focus rest on your breath. Or you can do my personal favourite – meditation. It only takes a few minutes a day, as my students can testify. And you don't have to turn your legs into a pretzel or go and live in a cave, to be able to do it.

To give you a taster of how good it can feel, there's a bonus meditation MP3 waiting for you, over at the Readers' Club. It takes you through a simple breath-awareness process to get grounded and to feel calm, especially when you're feeling stressed or overwhelmed. And if the idea of meditating resonates for you, there is also information about my book, the 28 Day Meditation Challenge, and the online video course version of that programme.

But if meditation or spending ten minutes a day doesn't appeal, then mindfulness could be a better option. There may be local classes that could help you. There are many simple techniques you can easily use at home - or anywhere else.

I've got a bonus article for you on what the difference is between meditation and mindfulness, over at the Readers' Club. One of the reasons my students love mindfulness is because you can do it as part of your everyday life, rather than needing to take time out to do it.

And if you'd like some inspiration, I have a 52 Mindful Moments podcast for you, based on my book *52 Mindful Moments.* It gives you practical, engineer-approved mindfulness techniques that help you to reconnect with your inner still point and feel less stressed, in under sixty seconds. You can see I'm trying to bypass all of your excuses, can't you?!

There's also a bonus video masterclass for you in the Readers' Club on *5 Reasons Why Your Customers Wish You Were Meditating*, which is all about how regularly reconnecting with yourself, through tools such as meditation, can grow your business in ways you might not expect. And it only takes a few minutes a day - time we would happily use up to surf Facebook or answer an impromptu phone call.

Other ways to connect with yourself include mindful movement, such as Tai Chi or Qi Gong or mindful walking in nature. Or maybe for you it's running or swimming or yoga or something else that brings you back into your body, in this moment, in 'the zone'. There will be a way that you'll love, and doing it regularly is life-changing.

What's Your Biggest Business Asset?

When you connect with your 'self' regularly, you start to get access to your biggest business asset - your intuition or inner wisdom.

In his book *Platform,* Michael Hyatt describes intuition as 'the map to buried treasure' and he advises us to listen to this 'inner voice'.

We usually make our major life and business choices using only a tiny fraction of our brain - the conscious thinking mind. But the wisdom that lies beneath the surface is infinite.

Have you ever had the experience of somehow 'knowing' what the right choice was? Have you ever had an 'inkling' about the solution to a problem? Ever been in the shower and had that inner 'lightbulb' come on? Have you ever walked into an empty room and somehow known that the people in there had just had a row? Ever thought of someone you haven't seen for ages, just before they unexpectedly phoned or messaged you?

All of these are examples of your intuition. When you know how to consciously connect with your inner wisdom, it can help you with everything from which route to take to avoid heavy traffic, through to which product or service might be more successful, through to which foods will boost your energy levels, for your specific body chemistry.

What's The Difference Between Instinct, Intuition & Good Old-Fashioned Common Sense?

We were chatting in a Facebook group recently about the difference between instinct, intuition and good old-fashioned common sense. And despite having been an NLP Trainer for over a decade now, it never ceases to amaze me how a simple word can create such different meanings in everyone's heads and the level of emotions that it can evoke for people. It all came up because I had been part of an International Summit where I was interviewed about how I use 'instinct' for my business – and I realised, when preparing for this, that I don't actually use my instinct, I use my intuition.

It got me thinking about how we used instinct or intuition on the EU VAT Action campaign. The breakthroughs we achieved have been described by those 'in the know' as 'impossible' and 'unprecedented' – and we have had feedback that the way we approached the campaign has been unique. But we didn't do fancy strategy work or play games or second-guess people's motivations, all of which would have been typical in the business world, especially with my NLP and Engineering background. Instead, intuition has played a key role in the campaign's success.

For me (and I'm not saying I'm right!), 'instinct' is something primal that comes from the animal part of my brain. It's that sense you get, for example, when you meet someone, that tells you whether or not you can trust them – instantly. And it might get over-ruled by later logic and data, but it is a subconscious message to your thinking mind – especially when you are in danger. The primal, animal part of your brain is specially designed to keep you safe from those scary sabre toothed tigers we met earlier, so it is brilliant at snap decision making, here in the present moment, where thinking and rationalising could lead to life's 'Permanent Exit Door'.

After all, when you're sprinting from a life-limiting carnivore, you don't want to be fussing about next week's 'to do' list. So the primal part of your brain is designed to handle immediate, short-term decision-making. And, for me, that's my 'instincts'.

But if you're in business, short-term decision-making is unlikely to create long-term growth strategies; it leads to near-permanent chaos and fire-fighting. Instead, I prefer to rely on my 'intuition'.

For me, intuition is something that feels like deeper wisdom and insight. It comes from outside of my 'thinking' brain. It's something I just 'know' – and it always brings with it a wave of clarity, Truth and, often, relief. It comes up when you get a sense of what is really needed in a situation. Intuition is something that just 'is', rather than something you 'figured out'.

Throughout the EU VAT campaign – often defying what my Inner Engineer's rational common sense was recommending – and even what international lobbying and campaign experts were recommending. Intuition brought results that rational logic might never have achieved. There's a story in the Readers' Club about how Intuition got us to break all the usual rules for the keynote speech at did at the European Parliament, and why that was a pivotal decision.

By reconnecting with your Inner Wisdom, you can access a hidden depth of understanding about which actions are needed – and when.

I have lost count of the number of times when the campaign did the exact opposite of what rational common sense would recommend – and thereby achieved breakthroughs. And we were hugely blessed to be supported by thousands of businesses who were ok with going with what might not have seemed immediately logical, but which somehow we all knew 'felt' right.

Just imagine being able to apply this to your Big Vision.

True breakthroughs happen when you shift to your intuition – that level of 'being' that the Ancients named the Vignaanamaya Kosha – the 'wisdom body' where you connect with the aspects of your Being that the thinking mind cannot understand. It transforms the way you approach your business – and life, in general.

That might sound a bit 'woo-woo', but we've all had the experience of it. It's the times when you wake up in the middle of the night and suddenly know the solution to a knotty problem. It's when you're in the shower and suddenly see the next step you need to take to leap to the outcome you were dreaming of. It's when you somehow just 'know' who you need to phone – and when – only to find out that the person was about to call you, too.

Exercise: Learning To Trust Your Intuition

People often struggle with learning how to trust their intuition – and how to spot the 'truth' from the 'wishful thinking'. So if you want to start this journey – or strengthen your confidence – I suggest you keep an 'intuition journal'. There's a worksheet for this in the Readers' Club, or you can pick a notebook to carry with you.

On the right hand side of the page, write down the date, time, and what your intuition is telling you to do – or information it is giving you about a situation. We're not talking about predicting the future (though some like to do that). We're looking at when you 'know' which actions to take or get 'insights' into someone's motivations, for example.

What were you doing at the time that the insight popped up? Give it a mark out of ten on how confident you are, with 10 being totally sure and 1 being really not at all sure.

Keep this going, whenever your intuition pops up, over time.

Then, as events unfold that you had intuitive insights about, go back and write on the left hand side of the page what actually happened. Over time, you'll start to see patterns. There might be certain circumstances that make your intuition more reliable. You might find that most things over, say, a 7 out of 10 can be trusted.

People often struggle with figuring out what is their intuition and what is just their mind's story or projection. I have had students who worried that their intuitive choices might upset the status quo and cause other people to react negatively. And it can feel hard to trust something that wasn't derived from data, if you're not used to working that way. As an engineer, I totally get that! And, over the years, I have developed strategies to allow me to learn when to trust my intuition and when to take it with a bucket of salt.

I have also learned how to communicate my intuitive 'hunches' in ways that allow others to feel safe, taking that leap of faith with me.

In the EU VAT Action Campaign, for example, I was invited to give an expert speech at the European Parliament, in front of the key decision-makers and lobbyists, who held the power to get the legislation changed. The night before, I still felt clueless about how to communicate such a complex problem in a way that was simple to understand, with enough passion to inspire super-busy people to take action to help.

At 11pm that night, I sat down and asked my intuition what it would recommend. "Tell them a story," it said. My thinking mind ranted back about how crazy an idea that was and how it would get our campaign laughed out of the Parliament building, letting down hundreds of thousands of micro businesses. But, sitting on the Eurostar the next day with my fellow campaigner, Juliet McKenna, we agreed it might work.

And it did. I got to take the decision-makers in that room through the experience of having a micro business that they loved, and then discovering that a new rule could inadvertently close it down. The story-journey achieved what no 'formal' presentation could have managed: it got their emotional buy-in. They accepted the severity of the problem and agreed to help to fix it. It was such a potent technique that I was asked to do it again it in my presentations to MEPs the next day, and later heard it being repeated, in the Parliamentary debating chamber. That intuitive risk paid off.

Can you imagine how being able to trust your intuition, at this level, might help you with the difference you want to make in the world?

Intuition doesn't have to be 'woo-woo' and it might even become your biggest business asset; I know it is mine. I love teaching people how to connect with their inner wisdom, and I'd love to help you on the next stage of your journey with this, too.

If you want to discover how to do this for yourself, there's a deep-dive a video training for you in the Readers' Club.

Connecting With Your Dream Audience

Walk a mile in their shoes.

Let's start this section by reviewing who your audience is. If you're running a business, it is likely to be your customers and clients, though sometimes it will be your support team and maybe your business partners. If you're employed in someone else's business, it might be your end user customers, or your colleagues, or your bosses. If you're running a campaign, it might be the people you're looking to help or the Body you're looking to influence. Hopefully you'll have clarity on this, from the work we did in Step 1. But if not, take a moment now to revisit that section.

We're going to start by looking at rapport - your most potent connecting tool, and how vital it is to be able to see the world through your audience's eyes, rather than your own. Then we'll look at how to make sure you're inspiring your audience, and not accidentally nagging them. Then we'll move on to strategies to help you magnetise more of the audience you would love - and to compassionately turn away those who would drive you crazy.

Your Most Potent Connecting Tool

One of the first lessons they teach you, when you're studying NLP, is about building rapport. Without rapport, NLP won't work. Rapport can be defined as 'seeing the world from the other person's point of view, without judgement' - and it can be surprisingly hard to do. So you're taught practical exercises to help you to deepen rapport and you clear out your inner blocks, to release the need to judge others. It takes time, but when you can do it, it makes an astonishing difference for a therapeutic intervention - when you need to help someone to change their life. And 'breaking' rapport is also a vital skill - especially if a client is feeling secretly quite comfortable, being stuck where they're stuck - or you need to end an overlong phone call…

In the business world - or your career or campaign - we rarely think about rapport. If we're lucky, we get to do something we enjoy, which our audience also enjoys. But we rarely step back to 'walk a mile in their moccasins', as the Native American Indians describe it. It's about deeply connecting with your audience, so you can feel their experience of life, from their perspective, and anticipate what is causing them pain - and intuitively know how to fix it.

What Happens When We Miss That Step Out?

- We accidentally create the products and services that *we* would want, rather than the ones that our audience *needs*
- We find it hard to sell our brilliant products or services, or the change we're creating, because our audience doesn't understand it
- We struggle to motivate our audience to action - to inspire them to have courage
- We risk resenting our audience, because they're not taking that action (e.g. paying us)
- We feel we have to shout, to make our message heard

The other aspect of rapport in the NLP world is 'pacing and leading'. Rather than standing on the greener side of the grass, over the scary-looking, chasm-linking bridge, shouting about how lovely your grass is and expecting people to take the risk of crossing over to your side, you stand with them, on their side of the bridge, with the summer-browned grass, and inspire them to have the courage to cross the chasm with you. To be able to do this, you need to have walked that mile in your audience's moccasins and to have connected with their 'pain points' - what's keeping them up at night - the problems they feel so passionately about that it will motivate them to take action. It connects them with that inner leverage that we talked about in Step 2 that means the pain of changing becomes less than the pain of staying the same.

You connect with your audience at such a deep level, speaking their language and resonating with them as a guide, so you can help them to overcome their fears and move towards the future that they secretly want. The more deeply you build rapport - and the more you 'pace and lead' - the less you'll resort to 'shouting' to get your message heard.

When you meet someone in their experience of the world, speaking in a way they can easily understand, and you offer them a vision of how things could be - and how easily they could fix the problems that have been losing them sleep - you will magnetise your audience to you.

If you're stuck on how to do this and would like more inspiration, I've got a bonus video masterclass for you in the Readers' Club. It brings you gems from my market research years and in it I share 21 free ways you can figure out what your customer really wants, so they feel like you're mind-reading them (in a good way!). Back in my corporate days, we would have spent many thousands on these research techniques. But with the right strategies and by using social media, all of these are now yours, for nothing more than a bit of time and effort. And I even tell you how to spot which requests contain golden gems, and which might lead you astray.

How To Stand In Your Audience's Shoes

I've got an NLP exercise I'd love to share with you called Perceptual Positions. This is about standing in somebody else's shoes and seeing the world through their eyes without judgment. You can run it with external customers, if you're in a business, or with your colleagues and internal customers or audience - or even your family!.

Exercise: Perceptual Positions

Start by imagining (or pretending) you can step into your dream customer's shoes and experience life from their point of view. It helps to stand up for this, rather than staying sitting in your favourite chair, because then you're too anchored into being 'you' to be able to fully experience being 'them'.

The bonus audio in the Readers' Club really helps for this process.

- Imagine you're holding your body the way they would be holding their body. Imagine you're breathing the way they would be breathing. Adjust your posture, and notice the kind of thoughts that they're thinking when it comes to the solution that you offer.
- Allow some answers to bubble up here, without judgment, without filtering. What are the kinds of thoughts they're thinking? What are the kinds of problems that they've got?
- What would you need to be doing and sharing and giving to become a non-negotiable part of that person's experience of life? How could you help them in ways that have nothing to do with selling?
- How could you inspire them?

... Continues

- What interests them that's kind of a lead in to the service or widget or product or experience that you offer? What kind of things would they love you to be talking about?
- Standing in those customers' shoes, what would get them excited to open their inbox and find you in there? What would make them think, "To-do list out the window - I'm reading this right now"?
- How could you make a positive difference in their lives. How could you become somebody who feels like a trusted friend or expert?

What did you notice? What have you learned? Any lightbulbs? Questions? There's a discussion thread for this over at the Readers' Club forum.

When you have the privilege of becoming a non-negotiable part of your audience's life, you don't need to sell; you don't need to nag. You're inspiring them. When they want to buy, they'll remember who you are and they will come to you first.

And it's about being authentically you, living and breathing your Big Vision. You need to feel happy (at least happy-ish!) in your own skin, to be able to inspire others to feel happy in theirs. And that's when you really get to connect.

Moving From Woah... To Wow!

A Lesson From Japanese Manufacturing

Back in my engineering days, I was incredibly lucky to get to study with Masaaki Imai, a pioneer in Kaizen techniques (Japanese continuous improvement methods, for manufacturing processes and organisations). He taught me about a concept called 'surprise and delight' - how to truly 'wow' your Dream Audience or customers. The basic idea is that you don't just give your customers what they are asking for, but you give them more. Not just 'any old more', but more of what they were already wishing for.

We're not talking quantity here. We're talking functionality. You over deliver in a way they weren't expected which delights them. They'll rave about it and tell their friends.

It's easy to imagine in the car industry. Back in those days small features like the 'remote tailgate release' (a button inside the car that allowed you to open the boot) or, later, iPod connectivity were 'surprise and delight' features. But the graph for what surprises and delights moves over time. Today's delight-features create tomorrow's expected-features and become next year's non-negotiable features. So it forces you to keep innovating and creating.

The problem came when costs got too high and someone in an office somewhere decided to save a few pennies by, for example, downgrading the iPod connector so that the iPod contents no longer displayed on the car screen. Repeat customers, and those who had been told about the feature by existing customers, would get annoyed when a feature that had delighted them went missing, and that's not a great way to build a long-term relationship.

But when you get it right, you build loyalty and word of mouth at an exponential rate. When you surprise and delight someone, they talk about it - to everyone.

And it doesn't have to be about product features, it could be elements of your service or your aftercare or your door-to-door customer experience. If this kind of thing resonates for you, then Sarah Petty and Erin Verbeck's book "Worth Every Penny" (see Readers' Club) has some great examples of how people have applied these ideas to service businesses. And we've got a special discussion thread for this in the Readers' Club forum, for more inspiration.

But the reason I'm telling you this, when we're talking about Connection, rather than Creativity, is because it's one of the little-known secrets to connecting with your audience.

Shhh! Not many people realise this one...

Your audience doesn't really care what you do. They care about how you make them **feel***.*

My time as Head of Market Research and my subsequent decade in mentoring passionate World-Changers has confirmed this. We buy on emotion and post-rationalise - justify - it with logic. Your beautiful sales pages or brochures that are full of features and facts are less enticing than the emotions you trigger as someone reads through them. They're not even that bothered about the 'benefits' of the features. They care about *why* they should care and how they will *feel*, when they have experienced whatever it is that you offer.

People don't buy the shampoo because of its chemistry. They buy it because of how it will make them feel - and the kind of person they will be - when they have the kind of hair that the product promises.

That's why we started the process in this book with the 'why', not the 'what' (see Step 5), which is where most businesses would normally start. When you're totally hooked up with your Big Why and your passion shines through, that will be contagious and will inspire your audience - as long as you're in front of the right audience - more on that in a bit.

When you put building a relationship with them at the centre of your efforts, the profits will come. When you put the profits at the centre of your efforts, you'll find it harder to get repeat business, because your customers won't have connected with you, emotionally, so they won't feel loyalty. You'll end up bribing them into loyalty, with discounts and sales.

Exercise: Surprise And Delight

There's a worksheet for this, over at the Readers' Club and a discussion thread, to share inspiration.

- What actions could you take to deepen your relationship with your audience - as a group and individually?
- Do you ever get to 'surprise and delight' them?
- What might surprise and delight them to the extent that it gets them talking? How might that fit with your business model?
- How do you make them *feel*?
- How does your Big Why line up with theirs? What is motivating them and driving their behaviour?
- Are there any areas where you are *not* surprising and delighting your audience? Which of these might benefit from a review?

Make sure any of your decisions on this keep in mind your brand's positioning (don't deliver Harrods quality if your pricing is closer to Aldi), keep your costs in mind, and remember to factor in your time to fulfil any promises. And if you're stuck for inspiration, here are some quick ways to come up with ideas:

- Review the most common questions you're asked by your audience
- What advice do you find yourself giving, over and over?
- What do you get told people *wish* your product or service could do?
- Which complaints could you fix?

- What do people enjoy most about working with you? How could you give them an experience of this, between-times?
- Look outside of your industry: what are others doing to delight their customers, which you could 'translate' to your field?

We're talking about this over in the Readers' Club forum, if you'd like more inspiration or would like to share ideas of your own.

There's A Caveat To All Of This

Please, please, please make sure you're aiming to surprise and delight the *right* audience. If you have to change who you are to connect with and inspire an audience, then they're the wrong audience for you. Lisa Sasevich shares a beautiful quote from her father on this - one that has inspired her choices for years:

"Don't change your act, change your audience."

In case you have been risking falling into this trap, there's a bonus article in the Readers' Club, from Step 3, on why it's so important not to let other people's expectations change who you are.

How To Magnetise Your Dream Audience?

It's important to focus on attracting more of the audience you would love, and to compassionately turn away those who would drive you crazy:

- Be authentically, awesomely you
- Live and breathe your brand. Don't water it down - especially if a non-ideal customer reacts negatively
- Don't be 'beige' (unless that's your brand colour). No one gets truly excited by 'neutrals'
- Stand for something: be totally clear about your Big Message; accepting that there will be people that it turns off
- Don't be scared to say 'no' - see Step 5
- Build a movement - a revolution - not a business
- Set your intention to inspire them, rather than accidentally nagging.

Some of my favourite role models on this are Lisa Lister, Gary Vaynerchuk and Derek Halpern (more on why in the Readers' Club – it's well worth checking this out).

Once you know how to connect deeply with your customers, *that* is when it's time to get visible. And we have done the 'connecting' bit first, so that your 'visibility' work will be much more effective. After all, there's not much point in being seen everywhere, if your message turns your customers off, is there?

It's Time To Be Seen – How To Get Visible

I thought long and hard about visibility, as I was writing this book for you. Should it go under 'connection'? Or should it be under 'credibility'? Logically, you could argue that being visible is a vital part of credibility, and to a certain extent it is. However, having worked with so many people on this over the years, visibility without credibility is both difficult and dangerous.

If you try to get visible whilst you're still running a major dose of Imposter Syndrome, while you're secretly terrified of trolls, or while you're trying to appeal to everyone, or aren't sure what your customers are looking for, it isn't going to work. You will risk self-sabotage or exhausting yourself. If any of these apply to you, please go back and review the techniques in the Clarity and Confidence steps, to see if any of those techniques might help.

There are plenty of the strategies in this visibility section that you can apply now, even while you deal with any hidden blocks, so I suggest you pick what resonates for you here and just do it, but with a super-keen eye on whether you're letting self-sabotage get in your way.

Also, you don't want to raise your profile if people don't think you know what you're talking about. That's why we did 'credibility' first. And now you have shown you are a credible expert in your field (or at least have an action plan for it), it's time for your Dream Audience to start seeing you *everywhere*.

If you concentrate on growing your audience before you have established yourself as the go-to expert in your field (or at least someone who knows what they're doing), then they will see you more as a friend and a peer, than as an advisor, and you're likely to find a tricky combo of the following happening:

- They'll try to 'pick your brain' for free, because you're 'one of them'
- They won't value the advice you give, but will pay someone else for poorer-quality advice
- You'll get chucked out of social media groups by antsy admins, for being a know-it-all
- You'll press people's 'ego buttons', as you give spot-on advice that they don't want to take from you, because they don't see you as an authority or someone they should listen to
- It's hard to step up to become a paid part of their lives, when they see you as 'one of the Tribe'
- Leadership is either awarded, earned or battled-for. So if you try to move from 'peer' to 'leader', you're likely to face resistance - and I have even witnessed cases of social media mutiny
- Your former peers are more likely to quibble your prices, once you do start charging them

I'm not suggesting you wait until you're the biggest expert out there before taking any action towards visibility; all of these 7 C Steps can be worked on in parallel. But you need to make sure that *you* are convinced of your expertise and the value you add, before you dive in deeply with your connecting strategy. And the more credibility you have built up, the more quickly your connecting and visibility will happen.

There's another side to it, too. It's easier to get visible when you're credible, when your Expertise, Passion and Authenticity (remember the Credibility Equation in Step 3?) shine through each and every interaction, and when your intention is lined up with your Big Vision. And your visibility makes you more credible. It's a virtuous circle.

So let's start with an essential visibility exercise, which is built on work we did in Step 1: getting clarity over your Dream Audience, revising some of those questions (the answers may have changed) and adding in others; this will form the basis for your Visibility Action Plan, later in this Step.

Your answers in this exercise will help you to formulate an action plan to get you connecting with your Dream Audience, as you work on your visibility. There's a worksheet and an audio for you on this in the Readers' Club. Keep theses answers handy. We're going to refer back to it at the end of this section when you create your Visibility Action Plan, shortly.

Exercise: Where Do You Need To Get Visible?

Go back to the Step 1 (Clarity) and remind yourself who you really want to work with. Has that changed at all?

- Now take some inspiration from your market research ideas. What is causing those people pain? What keeps them up at night? What stresses them, that they might not even tell their closest friends?
- How do they express those problems? What kinds of words and phrases do they use?
- How do they want to feel instead?
- How, specifically, does your solution take them on that journey?
- Where are they hanging out?
- Where are they currently looking for advice?
- Where are they *not* looking?
- What advice are they getting? How does that compare with what you would recommend?
- What would they need to see, read, or hear from you, to believe you could help them? What might they need to experience?
- Where would they need to see, read, or hear that?
- How could you inspire them to take the first step towards committing to solving their pain point?
- What could you talk about that would get their attention?
- Who does your Dream Audience already know, like and trust? Where do they go to for advice, when they're stuck? Who is already serving them? And don't just think about your niche: you can be more general - where do they go to for advice on other areas of their life?
- Looking at your answers, brainstorm a list of places you need to be writing articles, publishing videos, getting interviewed, sharing images, or whatever else your Dream Audience (and you!) would love.
- Which contacts do you have, who could help open the doors for you for those places? If you don't have the contacts yet, how might you build them?
- What might stop you from doing all of this - dump all of your excuses here! e.g. "I can't go visible, because…"
- Which sections of this Handbook might help you with those blocks, fears or excuses? Get it in your diary to work through the solutions. Make that commitment. I don't want your hidden silent saboteurs getting in the way of your audience loving your Big Message!

How To Make It Easy For Them To Find You

The key to growing your audience is making it easy for them to find you. We're talking 'quality', not 'quantity' here. 'Quantity' will suck up too much of your energy and risk filling your inbox with people who aren't a good fit for working with you.

It's ok to have boundaries; in fact, it's essential.

To step up to the next level in your Big Vision, you want to make sure you are spending as much of your time as possible with people who are a great fit for working with you or being inspired by your message. Those who are only an 'ok' fit - or even a 'bad' fit - will have an uncanny ability to swallow up your time, for zero gratitude or reward.

Let's park the numbers game for a bit here. Social media followers can be bought. Aiming for high numbers is a vanity game.

Personally, I'd rather connect with a group of 1,000 highly-engaged people who resonate with the way I work, than 100,000, who rarely read my messages. It takes energy to connect with people, and I choose to spend mine consciously. And, also, please stop comparing yourself with total strangers on the internet. So what if so-and-so has half a million Instagram followers and you only have 300? That's them. You're you. Focus on doing what you do best, and doing it well, and never, ever, ever let 'comparisonitis' derail your dreams. Start from where you're 'at', right here, right now, and move forwards. Wherever someone else is 'at' in their journey is in no way relevant to *your* Big Message.

When you're looking at making it easy for people to find you, you actually want to make it easy for the *right* people to find you. That's why we've just reviewed the 'who are you serving' exercise. Some of the benefits of this approach include:

- It's easy to grow your credibility, because your Dream Audience will start seeing you 'everywhere' that they are hanging out
- It's easy to figure out which opportunities to accept, and which to say 'no' to, which saves you time, money and energy
- You'll see much better results for less effort
- You'll find 'hot spots' where you get higher levels of engagement and excitement - and those are great places to focus your efforts
- You won't exhaust yourself or empty your bank account, by aiming for world domination on a shoestring, solopreneur budget

- You don't dilute your credibility, because being seen in all the wrong places risks counting against you. Those who would love to work with you might assume you're not really the right person for them, because they don't see themselves as belonging to the 'tribe' of people who would read that magazine or website.

That last point is an important one. About ten years ago, I accidentally (yes, I know there's no such thing as an 'accident' in these things!) got stuck writing a column I didn't really want to write, for a magazine that was only a loose fit with my Dream Audience, unpaid, which attracted nothing other than phone calls asking me if I wanted to advertise elsewhere. Why did I do it? Because I was desperate for exposure. Had I had clarity and confidence and had I done that last exercise, I would have turned it down. And I would have used that offer as leverage to gain credibility and get a column in a magazine that my customers *did* read. Ironically, I was set free from this by the magazine closing down after six months (*not* due to my column, I'm sure!), but it could have been a costly, long-term, low-return energy drain.

And while we're on the subject, "free for exposure" - should you? Or shouldn't you? This is another book I have sitting in draft form on my office shelf, and it might get published one day! But in the meantime, there's a bonus article waiting for you in the Readers' Club, complete with a list of must-ask questions, to use *before* you make that decision.

How To Choose Your Visibility Strategy?

Each of us is different, and I strongly suggest you play to your strengths in your visibility strategy, but also try new things on for size, before rejecting them.

For example, you might hate the idea of being on video, but it's such a powerful way of connecting with people that you might consider getting some training, before you dismiss the idea. I offer a free 7-day course on how to get comfortable on camera, If that might help you, you can find details in the Readers' Club.

Whichever method you choose, the most important thing is that you need to be yourself, comfortable, authentic and passionate about your message.

Let's take a quick tour through some visibility options. Remember: your decisions need to be based on what your customers want and need, rather than what's cool or trendy at the moment. Don't spend hundreds of hours on a particular platform, unless you know your customers will be looking for you there. Don't write long-winded articles, if your customers are more motivated by 3-minute videos. Don't invest in creating a podcast, if your audience never listens to them.

*Stand in your dream customer's shoes and get visible where **they** want to find you.*

Top Visibility Tips:

* Hang out where *your audience* hangs out, not your peers. This is such a common mistake, especially in social media business groups, which can often become a low-hit-rate pitch-frenzy.
* Become a hugely useful advisor, whilst still having clear boundaries on what is paid vs. what is paid-for.
* It's ok to ask for the sale (in fact, it's essential), but beware breaching group rules or cultural norms of where you're hanging out.
* Build rapport first

We have all had experiences of new members joining a group, be it online or 'real world' and pitching, almost before they have said 'hello'. I interviewed Jenn Philpott about this. She is the Founder of Born Ready and the inventor of Flaparaps – a unique cloth nappy solution that is inspiring a generation of parents in baby-led potty training.

Jenn recently entered a UK competition for a chance to pitch Sir Richard Branson with her business idea (more on this and Jenn's inspirational strategies in Step 6 – Commitment). To get through each round of the competition, Jenn had to collect a certain number of votes from the public, each day.

One of the strategies she used for this was asking Mums in suitable Facebook groups. She had great success with inspiring people who were total strangers to vote for her. Here are her secrets for success on connecting with your Dream Audience in this way:

Make sure your Dream Audience really is in the group – which means you need total clarity on who you are serving.

Introduce yourself – don't just 'sneak in' quietly. Then take time to get to know the group, the vibe, the members, and for them to get to know you – focus on building rapport and being authentic.

Become an active helper, answering their questions and connecting. You have to earn their trust and respect.

If you want to pitch or ask for help, do so (if the rules allow – or ask the group admin first), but be honest about it. Don't disguise a pitch as a 'helpful post' or 'quick question' or 'could you help me' or 'who else would like to XYZ?'– all of which are epidemics in social media groups, especially if there's a no-pitch rule. You're there to connect, not manipulate.

Know how the platform works. For example, Jenn described Facebook as 'nobbling links' in groups, meaning very few people saw them in their newsfeed, so she had to get creative, to find ways to make sure her requests for help didn't disappear.

Don't be attached to the results. People will sniff it out if you have an agenda.

Where's The Best Place To Go Visible?

I brainstormed with my Dare To Dream Bigger Tribe some of their favourite and most successful ways they have found to show up in front of their Dream Audience. And below is the list we came up with.

There's also a bonus interview on this with Erik Slater, a Digital Platform Consultant, in the Readers' Club. In it, we discuss 'content marketing' and how it has changed over the years, and the single most important factor you need to consider, before you throw your eggs into your favourite 'platform' basket. And we take a tour through the easily-avoidable mistakes that people are making, when they choose *where* to get visible.

Your Blog Or Website

This is your online business card - your portfolio - a chance for people to experience your work, before they commit. It might be the just the standard business website sections, like an online brochure, or it might have an integral blog with articles, images or videos. The choice is yours.

And to get the most out of it, and to make sure you avoid the most common mistakes, make sure you check out the advice on Credibility in Step 3.

An Email Newsletter

Now you know their pain points, how they express them, and how you solve them, how could you become an essential part of their inbox reading? What could you share that would make them look forward to hearing from you?

How often would they want to hear from you? Why bother with a newsletter, when social media is where most people are spending their time? Simple: you don't *own* your social media followers. A platform can shut your account down or change its rules in a heartbeat, effectively closing your business.

When people sell a business, aside from the stock, equipment and buildings, the most valuable asset is the customer base and goodwill. If you don't have contact details for potential customers, then you're risking losing your most valuable asset, if your favourite online platform changes its rules.

To prove this point for you, I've got a bonus article in the Readers' Club on how Facebook's strop about my name could have closed down my business, in under sixty seconds, had I not had my email subscriber list as a backup. And there's a second bonus article, inspired by Nathan Barry, founder of Convert Kit, on whether or not the traditional weekly newsletter is dead...

Bonus tip: please make it really easy for people to figure out how to join your email list. Yes, 'opt-in bribes' can help (more in the Readers' Club), but what matters most is giving people a way to stay in touch, until they're ready to work with you. It amazes me how many sites either make this hard to find or don't offer it at all.

And there are also resources in the Readers' Club on how to figure out what to send in your newsletters, how to repurpose your most popular online content, how to keep people engaging with you, so they actually open your messages, and how to make sure that your newsletter doesn't become a time-sucking energy-drain that you dread, instead being a way of connecting with and inspiring your readers.

Remember: as you change and grow and your Dream Audience shifts, you might need to change what you're talking about in your newsletters – and even compassionately clear out your subscriber list. It is quality and engagement that count, not subscriber numbers.

Guest Blogging

This is where you write articles for other people's websites - usually unpaid. It might be a small business website or it could be an international business like the Huffington Post. If you choose to go this route, make sure that the website you're writing for is somewhere that your Dream Audience actually hangs out. It takes a lot of effort and you need to make sure it will genuinely help your visibility.

Some sites are ok with you reusing articles you have already published elsewhere; others require original content. Make sure you are clear on their editorial requirements, before you approach them.

Website Interviews

Many websites look for people to interview, to create interesting content for their readers. This can be an excellent way to grow your audience, because the fact you are being interviewed positions you as an expert, giving you an instant credibility-boost. Again, make sure your Dream Audience is actually hanging out at the site that's interviewing you. Otherwise you risk getting lots of non-ideal client enquiries.

Social Media

There are so many options here - from Facebook to Twitter to LinkedIn to Google+ to Pinterest to Periscope to Snapchat to Instagram - and the list grows on, with new platforms being launched every week. Indeed, by the time you read this book, that list might seem out of date.

So instead of advising you on the minutiae of how to get visible on each of these platforms (Uncle Google can help you perfectly well with that), I want to give you three golden rules for social media visibility:

1. Don't run after the next shiny thing.

Just because a platform is new and exciting, it doesn't mean you have to be there. By all means have a play, but remember that you're running a business, not a hobby, and you need to see a return on your investment.

2. Hang out where your Dream Audience is looking for solutions.

Don't make them hunt for you. Figure out where they're hanging out, and where they're looking for help, and show up there. It's different for each business. And it changes over time. For example, my most popular articles get shared 100 times more often via Facebook than they do via LinkedIn or Google+. But my tweets bring me way more interaction than my Facebook page.

3. You are a limited resource.

If you still want time for your life, your loved-ones and occasionally sleeping, you'll need to 'spend' your social media time wisely.

Videos

If you love doing videos, then go for it! It is one of the most powerful ways to connect with your Dream Audience, short of sitting in a room with them. And if you're not comfortable on video yet - or you want inspiration on how to avoid rookie mistakes (that are incredibly common) and how to feel more confident, my free 7-day course on this is waiting for you in the members' area.

Podcast

Amy Porterfield and Lewis Howes both credit a large portion of their current success to their hugely popular podcasts. If you look more deeply, you'll also see it's down to massive investments in Facebook advertising, but their podcasts are the central hub of their content marketing efforts.

Another person who has had success with her podcast, Fearless Birth, is Alexia Leachman. In little over a year she has grown to a multi-thousand following and built a thriving business, through her dedication to a weekly podcast that informs, inspires and entertains her Dream Audience. I've got an interview with Alexia in the Readers' Club. In it she shares what she has learned on her podcasting journey and insider secrets to help you to shortcut your learning curve, so you can deeply connect with your listeners, using your podcast to crank up your visibility.

Pat Flynn has an incredibly detailed and helpful training course on how to set up your podcast – which he shares as his gift – and you can find details of this, too, in the Readers' Club.

If your Dream Audience loves podcasts, consider launching one - but only if you're going to be committed to keeping it up - and you enjoy it. Make sure its tone is in line with what they would expect from you. Be yourself. Create your own style. Use it as a chance to show your authenticity, and to have fun.

Online Summits

These are where a group of experts get together and are either interviewed or present on their topic of expertise, via a webinar or audio broadcast over the internet. They can attract thousands of viewers. I have taken part in a wide range of these - and even ran one myself earlier this year, which is looking like it will become an annual event.

Some of them have brought me gorgeous, highly-motivated clients and hundreds of new email subscribers. With others it was radio-silence - or even a reduction in my email list (I'll explain why, in a mo!).

What makes the difference?

Firstly, the higher the number of presenters, the more thinly people are spread, the less likely they are to listen to your session and the less likely they are to sign up for whatever your bonus, product or opt-in is. And after the event, they suddenly find themselves on possibly 30 new mailing lists, with an overflowing inbox, without realising that was what they were signing up for.

That's a fast way to get virtual skips full of spam complaints, because they feel irritated at suddenly getting so many emails (many of which will be promotional) and they hit the 'spam' button in frustration, even if you weren't spamming. That gets you into trouble with your email service.

Secondly, it's better to say 'no' than to do a summit that's not a great fit with your brand or Big Vision. Many people running summits are doing so purely to grow their mailing list, via your efforts. You will often be 'required' to send out numerous 'solo emails' about the event to your subscribers, which means extra emails to your readers, outside of your usual schedule. It might have taken you years to build your email list, but when your readers sign up, they end up on the organiser's mailing list. If your readers love that stuff, it will reflect well on you. If they don't, they're likely to leave you, so your list will shrink.

I've got a guide on how to pick the right online summits to magnetise your Dream Audience - and the most common mistakes to avoid - over at the Readers' Club.

Live Events

These can be great fun and are a brilliant way to connect with people. Again, make sure your Dream Audience will be in the seats and check out my guide on 'free for exposure?' before you commit (it's in the Readers' Club). It's also essential to know, before you decide to take part, whether you can 'sell from the stage' and how the event will be promoted – how the organiser will fill the seats. It's important to make sure you know what is expected of you (for example, how much promotion you might be required to do) and to get all of this in writing.

If you're going to do a live event, it's essential to make sure it is professionally organised, because you want people to have a really positive experience, while they're watching you.

Local and National Press And Magazines

You might think that, in these online days, print newspaper and magazine visibility is less of a priority. However, when someone sees you in print - in a physical newspaper or magazine - your credibility rating sky rockets, much faster than it would with most online coverage, just as printed books still carry more clout than eBooks.

With the savage cuts most print publications have seen in journalist numbers, they are hungrier than ever to get help with features that will appeal to their readers. So if you pick a publication that is a good fit with your Dream Audience, you've got a strong chance of getting coverage. You can connect with the editors and journalists who write for the publication and get to know them - get to understand what they might be looking for.

And if you want to send them a pitch or a press release, do the exercise, earlier in this section, on standing in your customer's shoes, so you can figure out what will fascinate the editor or journalist - and what's in it for *them*, rather than writing it from your own point of view.

Advertising

This is still an effective option and is often essential in social media platforms such as Facebook, where organically reaching your page followers is nigh-on impossible.

Top tip: if you're going to go for paid advertising, test out small campaigns first, to see what works, and then scale up. And it's essential to be able to measure the response you're getting to each advert, so you can check you're getting a good return on your investment.

Other Ideas?

What has worked for you with visibility? There's a special discussion thread in the Readers' Club forum where we're sharing ideas and inspiration on this.

Avoid The #1 Mistake

This is something that Ken Evoy drummed into me, back when I was launching my first ever website, in 2002.

Whenever you are connecting with your audience and getting visible, for each point of interaction, make sure you have a 'Most Wanted Response' or a 'Call To Action'.

Don't just assume that your reader will spot your newsletter signup in the header or footer or sidebar, for example. Specifically tell them to sign up and give them a reason why. Content upgrades are a brilliant way to do this, and there's a bonus for you on those, in the Readers' Club.

If you're doing an article, make sure there are links woven into it, to guide people through to the next logical stage in their journey. If you want them to share it on social media, tell them that. They might be so caught up in what they have just read that they forget it's an option. We've all been there!

If you're doing a video, make sure you tell them to subscribe to your YouTube channel - and even tell them how. It's not obvious.

Once you have built up rapport and connected with your audience, they will be more open to taking whatever the next step is - as long as you remember to tell them.

And it's essential to think about the 'what's next' for your audience, before you create that visibility content. Make it a natural progression, a flow, so that they feel safe to take the next step with you on their journey.

The Importance Of Reputation Management

When you go visible, and connect with a wider audience, there will be 'feedback'. We already covered how to handle haters and trolls, in Step 3 on Credibility, and we looked at how to learn to accept compliments, in that same section. But reputation management is about more than that. It's about proactively acting to show the best of who you are, wherever you are visible, and handling any negativity professionally, before it spirals.

We have all seen social media posts about crazily-bad customer service replies from big brands. A frustrated customer can share the business's response and get it going viral. That's bad press on steroids.

Sean Burrows has an excellent, short video with advice on how to manage your reputation, proactively, by preventing issues. You can find it in the Readers' Club. He explains that 'bad reviews' come from your promise being out of synch with what you deliver. And he advises you to take care of your customers, to the point of 'loyalty', not just 'satisfaction'.

Over the years, I have seen how it is also essential to make sure you are only working with your Dream Audience, compassionately turning away those who wouldn't enjoy your style or what you create. If your product or service is matches up with what your audience is looking for, then all should be fine. Reputation issues come up when you under-deliver (and don't handle it well) or when the 'wrong' person tries to get what *they want* from a product or service that wasn't designed for them.

There is another vital part of reputation management and your visibility strategy: assume you are *always* on the record. Everything you post on the internet will be there, in some form, forever.

Every whinge, bitch and moan will be there. Every uplifting quote, inspirational article and world-changing video will be there, too.

When we post on the internet, it's like taking out a front page advert in an international newspaper. If you wouldn't want what you're posting to be seen there, don't post it.

This doesn't just apply to social media; it's even more important when you're giving interviews.

During the 2016 UK Conservative Party leadership election, for example, one of the candidates discovered the hard way that you're *always* on the record. Andrea Leadsom was interviewed by a journalist and she made some comments at the start of the interview, which she later said she thought were off the record, disparaging her rival, Theresa May, for not having had children, and strongly hinting that she was therefore a less suitable candidate for Prime Minister.

Unfortunately, the journalist published these comments. Leadsom's subsequent objections in the media made matters worse, because her defence of having thought she was 'off the record' with a journalist lost her credibility and trust, as a potential Prime Minister. She ended up having to withdraw from the Leadership Election and lost the chance to become Prime Minister, partly as a result.

When you're doing 'visibility', always assume that whatever you say or do could be seen or read or listened to by everyone, and do your best to behave with dignity, integrity and compassion - and whatever your core values are. Whatever you do, don't give an interview when you're feeling angry! Do some of the calming techniques we've covered, first.

The Three Biggest Myths About Visibility

I spoke to Sandra Pilarczyk, a Visibility Mentor, on this one. And here's what she said (check out Sandra's interview in the Readers' Club):

Myth #1: I've got to 'change' to be 'visible'

When Sandra entered the world of online entrepreneurship, she quickly discovered the power of connecting with clients through video. Others made it look so easy, so she did what she thought she had to do: she copied them. She didn't feel she could be her 'geeky, introverted self' on video. But she found she didn't get any engagement on her videos, no likes on her posts, no views on her YouTube channel - let alone sales.

Then she discovered a 'secret': it's best to be your authentic self. That can feel scary, because you're making yourself vulnerable. But once you do it, you start to attract your Tribe, and they will want to buy from you.

Myth #2: It has to be perfect

So many people are hiding, because they think it has to be 'perfect'. "I haven't got the right equipment!" "I don't have a great background for my videos!" "I haven't washed my hair!"

Just because the 'gurus' have near-perfect hair, makeup, lighting and studios, you don't need any of that when you first start off or when you're in the middle of establishing yourself as an expert, because the most important thing is to communicate your Big Message. That's all.

Of course it needs to be professional. However being clear on your message, delivering excellent value and seeking long-lasting relationships with your Dream Audience is much more important than 'perfection'.

Myth #3: If I join a lot of Facebook Groups I will get lots of business

Sandra sees so many of entrepreneurs joining lots of Facebook Groups, commenting on the thread of the day and posting their offers under the promo posts. And guess what? It rarely leads to sales.

She reiterates what Jenn Philpott said earlier: it's about building relationships. Just like with in-person networking, it takes time and effort. It's not as simple as just posting links and random comments.

Treat your online relationship-building just as you would meeting somebody in-person. And if they like you, they might join your Facebook Group or join your email list. Once they feel they know you, if they need your offering, they will buy from you.

Your Visibility Action Plan

It's time to turn all of this from 'nice ideas' into a Visibility Action Plan. Wherever you are on your visibility journey – whether you're just starting out or you're an old-hand, stepping up to the next level – if you don't have goals and a plan to crank up your visibility, it won't happen.

Visibility is a long-term, on-going strategy, but with enough clarity and focus, you can make good progress in the next 90 days. I suggest you pick just one or two visibility options and follow through with them until you have cracked it, rather than trying to spin ten plates at once.

Exercise: Your 90-Day Visibility Action Plan

Go back through your answers to the questions in our last exercise. Reviewing them, in the context of what you have learned or decided in this section, use the follow questions to prioritise your visibility goals:

- Where do I want to be seen? (Pick one or two targets at first, then build on your success with these).
- Are there any contacts I need? Journalists? PR experts? Do I know anyone who could introduce me?
- Do I have the 'media' section I need on my website? (See the Readers' Club for essential elements for this)
- Do I have decent-quality photos that people can use for an article?
- What's my 'hook'? What's in it for the person I'm asking to help me get my message out there?
- What's my 'Call To Action' or 'Most Wanted Response' for that visibility project?
- How will I measure the effect of that visibility project?
- Where do I want my visibility to 'be' in 3 months' time?
- To support that, what actions do I need to take by 2 months' time?
- And in the next 30 days?
- In the next 2 weeks?
- This week?
- In the next 24 hours?
- Which of my hidden blocks might get in the way?
- What actions will I take to release those blocks and make sure I don't accidentally self-sabotage my visibility efforts?

Connecting With Your Dream Team

No man is an island. No one is self-sufficient;
everyone relies on others. ~ John Donne

Why You Need A Dream Team, No Matter How Small Or Big You Are

Ask any successful person about their journey to success and they will tell you that there came a point where they couldn't do it on their own any more.

Letting go of trying to do it all yourself is what makes the difference between being a freelancer, or a self-employed person, or someone running a hobby-come-biz and actually running a functioning business. And it's true outside of the business world, too. Every leader who ever inspired you had a Dream Team around them. Every successful musician had a Dream Team of parents who probably ferried them to music lessons (and paid for them) and teachers and agents and publicists and concert organisers and beyond.

If you have ever worked in the corporate world, you'll remember that the business you were in was made up of teams where - hopefully - those inside the team were specialists in what they did. You didn't have the sales guy doing product development, as well as the venue booking and the stationery ordering and IT maintenance.

So why is it, then, that when we step out to become our own CEO, we try to do it all ourselves?

You are trying to get clear on your business goals, define a target market, figure out how to reach that market, do the graphic design, create the promotional materials or website, get the PR coverage, do the networking, set up the sales systems and shipping systems, handle the email and phone enquiries, give the interviews, make the tea - and create the product. All on your own. Feeling like you need a lie down yet?

If we're really honest, how many of those jobs are we great at? And how many aspects of our work could someone else do better?

It's no wonder most entrepreneurs feel they don't have time for their loved-ones - or themselves.

I interviewed a group of entrepreneurs about this, and here are the most common reasons they gave for why they try to do it all themselves:

- It's hard to find someone I can trust
- I don't plan far enough ahead to be able to schedule someone else's workload
- I'm scared I won't earn enough to pay them
- I haven't got the time or headspace to manage someone
- I'm a control freak perfectionist and the thought of letting go and trusting terrifies me
- I have no idea how to find someone I could really trust to do a great job
- How would I trust them to bill me for the right hours?
- It's quicker to do it myself, than to train up and brief someone else
- I'm too spontaneous and it would drive an employee crazy
- I'd have to work even harder, to create enough work for them to do
- I find it hard to predict what support I might need and when

---

Exercise: What Are Your Dream Team Blocks?

Do you have any blocks of your own? How can you spot them? Complete this sentence with at least 5-7 answers:

"I can't / don't want to hire support, because…"

We'll come back to your answers at the end of this section.

Back in my engineering days, I saw plenty of research and best practice on how to simplify processes and improve production quality. Some of it came from the early work of Henry Ford, with his famous 'time and motion' studies. Much of the more recent research came from Japan with their Lean Manufacturing and Kaizen.

What they all agreed on was that you need specialists in specialist roles. If you try to give too many differing tasks to one person, then quality suffers and stress levels rise. The Japanese also emphasised the importance of empowering people at all levels of the organisation, by trusting them to carry out the most complex or important tasks they were capable of. For example, you don't use up CEO-level time by getting him or her to do their own travel booking. You delegate, so that people play to their core strengths. This is a close approximation to what Gay Hendricks recommends in his Zone of Genius studies (see Step 1). The more time you spend doing what you're great at, the more productive and inspired you will be, and the bigger difference you will be able to make in the world.

And for every task that drives you crazy, there will be someone out there who would love it.

So why do we find it so hard to build a Dream Team to support us on our journey towards our Big Vision?

The Vital Mindset Shift That Makes Inspired Action Easy

Or... why most people get stuck at the burnout-inducing, hobby-business stage.

When you start your business, unless it's a shop, or it's a really big dream and you have funding, it's likely to be mostly about you doing all the doing.

At the risk of rotten tomatoes, that's not really a business; it's a freelancing job. If you're doing everything, and you're getting paid by the hour, you're *earning* money, not *making* it. An employee *earns* money. A business-owner *makes* it. There's nothing wrong with hanging out in the freelancer space. It's a great place to be. But if you want to grow a legacy that is bigger than 'you', and if you ever want to take time off, but still get paid, then you need to make different decisions.

And if your business suddenly grows, you risk joining the ranks of those wishing they had more hours in the day and considering sacrificing sleep, to get everything done.

The thing is: you do have more hours in the day.

No, I'm not suggesting that being an entrepreneur comes with time-warping superpowers or Hermione Granger's time-turner. I wish it did. But if your business is going to grow, to break through to the next level, to make a bigger difference in the world, then at some point you're going to need help.

No one changes the world on their own.

Fear of overwhelm is one of the biggest triggers for self-sabotage behaviour, as you're growing your Big Vision. We are secretly terrified that we're creating a time-munching monster that isn't scalable and risks fast-tracking us to burnout. It is one of the biggest barriers to business growth. That's why we started this book with Step 0: clearing out to make space for breakthroughs. You don't want to amplify chaos.

Just imagine what would happen if you got an unexpected bit of publicity, tomorrow, and suddenly had ten times your usual levels of enquiries and sales. What would happen? Does the thought fill you with excitement? Or does your body instantly tense up and your mind race to panic? If it's the latter, then you'll be subconsciously self-sabotaging your business, to make sure that doesn't happen.

And what if you want to take a holiday? Does your business grind to a halt? Or can it run for a while, without you? If it grinds to a halt, then you need to get yourself support, to make it sustainable. What would happen if you were to get 'flu and need two weeks off? Or if you got offered a have-to-say-yes-to-it speaking gig that meant you had to travel to the other side of the world for a week?

If you want your business to grow, you have to feed it what it needs. And if *you are* your business, then you must prioritise looking after yourself, otherwise there won't *be* any business in the future.

The number of hours in a day will always limit what you can achieve in your business - and whether you still have time for your loved-ones - unless you get the support that your business needs.

When you're drowning in your 'to do' list, I promise you that most of it is nothing to do with your Inner Genius. If you have followed through the steps in this book, you'll have clarity about what you want, what your dream customers want, and how you solve their burning problems. You'll have cleared out the blocks to success, you'll have built up your confidence and credibility, you'll be well-connected and you'll be letting your creativity flow. Your business is going to grow.

Why on earth would you kill that off by trying to do it all yourself? But we do.

Who Needs To Be In Your Dream Team?

Your Dream Team might be employees, it might be contractors or suppliers, who work with you occasionally, it might be your loved-ones, it might be getting a cleaner or someone to help with extra childcare, it might be potential business partners or Joint Venture partners, it might be your friends, it might be an accountability Mastermind. Whatever support you need, it is out there, waiting for you, but you need to let it in.

A fellow coach posted on social media recently that she was considering getting up before dawn, to get everything done, cutting out at least one hour of sleep per day, so she can grow her business. We all know that feeling of having too much to do and not enough hours in the day.

But this is one of the fastest ways to shrink your business. If you start sacrificing sleep (unless you are already Rip Van Winkle), then you risk feeling exhausted, not being able to think straight or not making good decisions, and you will risk under-delivering and making mistakes, because you're too tired to concentrate.

What you need in these circumstances is support - to work out *why* you feel you need to do so much, and then give the tasks that don't 100% need to be done by you to someone else. It's not just about productivity – getting more done in less time; it's about getting the *right* things done.

Most of us are getting time management back-to-front.

It's not about doing more, though a productivity-sticky-plaster can help. It's about being focussed, and choosing to spend your time wisely, on actions that move you towards your Big Vision, whilst getting the support team you need in place - ideally before you need it.

You don't grow your business by running yourself into the ground, to get more done. You grow your business by expanding your team. And the more your business grows, the more vital it is that you spend as much time as possible in your Inner Genius, doing what you do best, rather than being a jack-of-all-trades.

Yes, it can feel scary to ask people for help - either because you're worried about managing them, scared of trusting, or concerned about having to pay them. But the alternative is burnout and not getting to make the difference you're dreaming of.

Let's take an example from the manufacturing world. Back in my engineering days, I specialised in diesel engine manufacture. And some of the machines that made key components were worth millions. They were vital business assets. If they broke down, then stopping the production line cost $2,000 per minute.

If you wanted to make more widgets and you had a widget-making machine that was irreplaceable, would you work it harder? Would you reduce the frequency of scheduled maintenance? Would you crank up the speed of production to the extent where it risked being damaged and breaking down? Or would you look at whether you needed a second widget-machine? Would you look at how you could change the process so that the widget-machine only did the vital bits and the other stuff was done by other machines, to increase capacity?

So why do we think we can grow our businesses by working even harder, sacrificing doing the things we love, and wearing ourselves out?

Exhaustion and overwhelm are two of the biggest killers of inspired action. You aren't meant to be doing this on your own. The help you need is out there. But you need to give yourself permission to accept it.

Want to find out what might be getting in the way for you on this? Are you running Superhero Syndrome? There's a bonus article with a deep-dive worksheet waiting for you in the Readers' Club.

How Do You Decide Who To Hire?

Only hire people whose skills you admire, with whom you find it easy to communicate.

Thinking you can get your Dream Team on the cheap is a false economy. The most successful entrepreneurs I have ever met all hire people they admire. They figure out the bits that they, themselves, do best, where they truly add value, and they 'hire out' the rest. When you value your time, and the difference that you make, delegating becomes easier.

When you think about the time and effort and expense of hiring, training and managing someone, whether in your office or remotely, the few pounds an hour you save by getting someone inexperienced, are more than spent again. That doesn't mean avoiding trainees. But your experienced core support team needs to be in place, first.

I was at an event recently and I met a woman who runs a copywriting consultancy business. She is a freelancer who is starting to look at commissioning out work, so she can escape from the 'pay per hour' gerbil wheel, and turn her career into a sustainable business. She was beginning to get in more work than she could deliver, despite raising her prices to try to slow down the flow of work, which was great news. I asked her what kind of person she might be looking for, in case I knew someone suitable or could help her find someone through my network.

Bearing in mind that the work this lady was doing was high-end, high-quality bespoke work, and she quoted for each project individually, so she got to set her own prices, her reply was, "As cheap as possible. I'm happy to train them up."

When I asked her for a figure, she really meant cheap. And the plan to 'train up' her copywriter, in order to save money, came on top of her complaints that she was drowning in overwhelm and barely remembered what her kids looked like. In order to save money, she was prepared to risk:

- Her reputation as an outstanding copywriter, by selling *her* 'standards' but getting someone without those skills to complete the work
- The stress of having to train the person up, even though she was already really busy
- Having to redo much of the person's work, to bring it up to standard, and certainly having to check it closely
- Having to do the client meetings herself, because she couldn't let a trainee represent her brand for such high-end services
- Putting right any mistakes or trainee-level work that might accidentally reach the customer
- Losing customers who might feel unhappy about paying for a top-end pro and getting an intern delivering the work

And I double-checked: she wasn't planning to commission out the admin and email work - this was the actual fee-earning copywriting she was talking about.

When you fill your team with people who are at the start of their learning curve, you need to spend more time teaching, giving feedback, supervising and training them. And you have to expect that mistakes will be made. If you have the time and energy for that, that's brilliant - it's a wonderful gift to give to the future.

When you hire people who are so good at what they do that you admire them, you can brief them and then 'let go and trust'. You know they'll do a great job. You know they'll keep their promises. And they may even (shock, horror!) do it better than you could have done. (Anyone else's inner Control Freak objecting?!)

When you have people in your team who you really trust, it allows you to stop spinning the extra plates. You can use that energy to feed the stuff you do best. Hiring the cheapest person is a false economy. Your Dream Team is the key to growing a business you love, which makes a positive difference in the world, that doesn't leave you on your knees with burnout. You'll find the journey so much easier – and more fun – if you hire people you trust, respect and even admire, who are better at their role than you are, than if you try to economise and hire newbies who you'll have to chase up the whole time.

One of the common objections I hear when I talk about doing what you do best, sticking with your Inner Genius, and delegating the rest to your Dream Team - is that if we all did what we loved, who would do the stuff we hate? In the past, whenever I added a new member to my Dream Team, I used to find myself dealing with 'guilt' of giving someone else work I don't want to do any more. But if I hired the right person, then I was giving them work that they *love*, which gets them excited, which they excel at. Had I kept doing it myself (badly and with a major case of overwhelm), then they wouldn't get to do it – and they wouldn't get to grow their career or business.

I interviewed Lorraine Dallmeier, CEO of Formula Botanica, for this Handbook (more from Lorraine in Step 6). She said that one of the things that made it easy for her to focus on doing what she does best – quietening her inner control freak and allowing others to take on tasks she no longer had time to do – was seeing how her delegating allowed them to grow *their* business.

For example, she worked with a part time videographer when she upgraded all her online training materials. As a result of that project, he has been able to expand his client base and is now doing what he loves full time.

So if you need a reframe, how about instead of delegating to help yourself, you choose to delegate to help others?

Are You Beating The "I'm Not Supported" Drum?

When you're working as hard as you can, juggling too many balls, it's easy to feel unsupported. So, before we look at what support you need, let's spend a few moments handling those 'Nobody is helping me!' feelings, first. If you try to attract your Dream Team, while you're feeling resentful and angry, you're likely to attract the wrong kind of people.

The major reason why most of us feel unsupported is because we haven't asked for help yet. We expect those around us to mind-read what we need and give us that support, without being asked. And when they don't, we secretly seethe.

Feeling 'unsupported' can also come from not wanting to ask for help- from feeling like we have to do it all ourselves. It's like a Badge Of Honour. So here are some simple things you can do, right now, to turn those support-stories around, **before** we do the next exercise.

You get what you think about.

Remember that Reticular Activating System in your brain, from Steps 1 and 2? If you are focussing on what is wrong – and how little support you feel you have – then your brain takes that as an instruction to point out even more examples, to back up your point of view.

How can you turn this one round? By shifting your focus to gratitude. It's not about denial or white-washing. It's not about rejecting your feelings of not being supported. It's about allowing those feelings to get back their sense of perspective, by spotting the ways that you *are* supported. They will be context-dependent: you might not feel supported, say, at home, but you will be well-supported in other areas of your life.

Exercise: Are You More Supported Than You Realise?

It's easy to get stuck feeling unsupported. If that happens, this exercise provides a valuable reframe and can shift the way you think about 'support'. Let me know how you get on with it, over at the Readers' Club forum.

- Think of one way that you *are* supported right now.
- It might be something as random as the person who served you coffee on your way to an offsite meeting last week, or the person in the supermarket who rang your items through the till.
- Be specific in your gratitude – picture the person's face, if you know them – and *feel* your 'thank you'. Imagine saying it to them.

If feeling unsupported is a core theme for you, you might benefit from writing this down, even daily, for a while, until you shift that pattern with the new evidence of being supported.

When we step off of the complaining train, it is amazing to realise all of the ways that we *are* supported.

When you recruit your Dream Team from *that* energy, you'll magnetise people to you who are excited about your Big Vision, who will truly support you. And, if you're stuck with asking for help, remember the power of 'because' in the photocopier queue? When you tell people *why* you need help, you might be surprised how often they say yes.

Let's Get Your Dream Team Sorted

It's time to get your Big Girl / Boy Pants on and ask for the help you need. If you have blocks on this ("I can't ask for help, because…") then take those blocks back to Step 2 of this Handbook and deal with them. I know you can. You know you can. And make sure you pay attention to that pesky Secondary Gain – your Big Message is too important to let that get in the way of the difference you're here to make.

Exercise: How To Figure Out What Support You Need

- How do you decide what to delegate?
- What are you spending your time on, in a typical week?
- Now go through and mark the things you love and the things you hate doing. The stuff in the middle we'll handle later.
- Start with figuring out what you would be employed to do, if someone else were running your business. In other words, where would someone objective and not living in your head see you adding greatest value to the business?
- Does that line up with the stuff you love?
- Of the stuff you hate, does it really have to be done by you?
- If you could wave a magic wand, which tasks would you give away?
- What's stopping you from delegating? Not sure? "I can't / don't want to delegate, because…"
- If you could easily create any Dream Team you can imagine, what help would you want, and why?
- How might you fund this?
- How could you find the time?
- Which role would make the biggest difference?
- What's the worst that could happen, if you allowed yourself to be supported by a Dream Team?
- What's the best that might happen?
- Action challenge: what could you delegate by the end of this week?
- Which action are you going to take today, to feel more supported?

Let me know via the forum discussion thread in the Readers' Club.

So, once you start getting your Dream Team around you, how on earth do you manage them? Especially if they're spread across the world? I've got some excellent advice for you, from Penny Pullan:

Overcoming Your Dream Team Obstacles

Penny Pullan is the author of Virtual Leadership, and she consults and teaches internationally how to manage change, and how to lead virtual teams.

In her interview (more from Penny in the Readers' Club) she explained how the landscape of teams has changed, and that most entrepreneurs are now managing not just employees, but contractors, suppliers, freelancers and ad hoc team members, across the globe. This requires a different approach to traditional leadership and management skills.

Her own virtual leadership journey began when she ran her first virtual summit, but the conference call company she was using under-delivered on the promised sound quality for the recordings. Penny needed to urgently fix the sound issues, but she knew that sound editing wasn't her forte, and she didn't have the time to learn how to do it, mid-summit. Necessity forced her to delegate. So she had to hire a sound engineer, and let go and trust. He was in New Zealand, working during Penny's nights, and he was able to take the sound recordings and turn them into something of appropriate quality, overnight, after each summit. It taught her that this was easier than she had thought it might be, and she wanted more of it!

Penny has seen that virtual leadership is about the 'inside work' for everyone in the team, not just the 'leader'; everyone needs to step up to be the best they can be, to do their best work, so that everyone trusts each other.

There are two types of virtual team: the 'star' team model, where the leader is the central node and checks up on everyone's progress, and the 'spaghetti team' model, where everyone is connected with each other. In a virtual world, there needs to be a massive amount of trust, and you have to consciously work to build the relationships that would happen by default, in a physical-world office. A weak link in the team can affect everyone else's work. That's why the 'inside work' is so important for everyone in the team. And that is why it is so important to hire people you respect and trust.

She acknowledges that it can feel hard to let go of things that you are used to doing, but Penny finds that delegating is often the only way to make sure things actually happen. Often it's better to have it not quite as perfect, but to get it done.

Penny has found that entrepreneurs may feel scared of hiring their Dream Team, because they fear delegating, or they are used to doing it themselves and aren't convinced that others will do it as well as them, or they are worried about bringing in enough money to pay their team.

But without your team, you limit how much of an impact your business can have. So you have to do the 'inside work' to get past those blocks and fears – and to have the business plan that means you know you'll have funds to pay people.

Penny recommends one simple strategy for making sure things run well: agree the ground rules up front. Have those 'potentially awkward conversation' about what needs to happen if there are problems, before you start working together. Then everyone knows where they stand and your team members are more likely to tell you, before problems arise.

The human side is vital, yet easily forgotten. Yes, your team members need the skills, but you need to make sure you're not missing out on building relationships, just because you connect through a computer screen. Engage and inspire your Dream Team with your Big Vision. It makes them more likely that they will do their best work and also prioritise your work, if they're feeling stressed.

Narrative is more engaging and memorable, so share your story with them. Help them to understand **why** you are doing what you are doing together, and the difference you want to make. Involve them and connect more deeply with them, so they feel trusted and empowered.

Connecting With Your Mastermind Team

There's nothing so potent as a team of trusted friends who help you avoid life's mistakes and who inspire you to grow your dreams to the next level.

It is said that you become the sum of the 5 people you spend the most time with. The same goes for your business.

If you're spending your days hanging out in social media groups with people who are at your level of business - or even behind you on the learning curve, it's easy to stay stuck playing small. Yes, you can inspire and empower others on their journey, but if you want to really grow, you need to step up to the next level and hang out with people who already have that t-shirt.

Remember we talked about the way beliefs act as filters in your brain? The communities and groups we choose to belong to set those filters for what we see as 'normal' and 'possible' and even 'acceptable'. If you're spending lots of time as a peer (rather than mentor) with people who are struggling, who find it hard to get customers, and who complain about the ones they have, then that is what you are programming your unconscious mind to accept as being normal in your business.

If you hang out, instead, with people who have a clear vision, who don't indulge in complaining, who know how to connect with others outside of the group, who step up and take inspired action, then they will inspire you to do the same. At a subconscious level you will be modelling the thought processes, attitudes, self-belief and other 'inside work' traits that make them successful. And their Daring To Dream Bigger will kick your butt to do the same.

So many online groups are full of people who are feeling stuck, complaining, stressed, overwhelmed, lacking clarity and feeling scared. That's a potent, negative vibe to hang around in and it reduces the chances of you turning your dreams into reality.

But if you can find yourself a group of people who are positive, problem-solvers, upbeat, action-takers, difference-makers, then that's a very different energy to immerse yourself in. And one of the best ways to find that is through a Mastermind group.

Intentionally hanging out with a group of people who have chosen to support each other, to grow each other's businesses, works wonders at an idea-bouncing and accountability level. One of the things about running your own business is that it can be lonely. Those 'water-cooler moments' from your corporate days have gone. And your public social media profile might not be the best place to get the answers you're looking for and to let off steam, if you're feeling frustrated.

One of the other huge benefits of a Mastermind is that it can introduce you to potential Joint Venture partners or high-profile affiliates, who can help you to get your voice heard by a wider audience. When you build your network to include the key influencers in your industry, you will get to make a bigger difference in the world. If you're interested in this, Daniel Priestley's book *Key Person Of Influence* is an excellent how-to guide (see Readers' Club).

I've also got a bonus video and article for you in there on why your Dream Customers WISH you were part of a Mastermind - and how you can find one that you'll love. It covers the vital CEO-skill of 'asking for directions' and why so many of us find it so hard. If you'd like to join one of my Mastermind retreats or programmes (of course, others are available!), you'll find details there, too.

If the idea of joining a Mastermind resonates with you, here's some invaluable advice from one of the best experts I know on the topic:

William Buist is a Business Consultant, Speaker, Author, and founder of the exclusive xTEN Club. He is passionate about helping businesses to grow and avoid costly mistakes and he is a highly-respected Mastermind Facilitator, having helped thousands of small businesses and entrepreneurs, through his career.

I spoke to him in depth about the pros and cons of being part of a Mastermind, how to find one you'll love, how to avoid the most common mistakes, and how to step up to the next level, when you have outgrown your current Tribe. His full interview is in the Readers' Club. But here are some insights I want you to know, right now.

William has seen Masterminds transform someone's business success, even in the very first session. He prefers face-to-face Masterminds, because you are more focused and people's intentions are less likely to be misunderstood than in a social media discussion thread. The 'real world' connection builds a level of trust and openness that builds a commitment to grow each other's' businesses.

He has found that the idea-bouncing within a Mastermind can take a 'good' idea and turn it into something 'brilliant' – as long as the original idea owner is willing to give it a go. The smallest comments or insightful questions can create breakthroughs. It's essential that all members are adding value and that the process is based on open questions that invite exploration of ideas, rather than simplistic advice, telling someone what to do.

William has found that you don't need to be in a Mastermind with people who are in a similar industry to you; indeed, it often works better if you're not, because great ideas from one industry can inspire cross-pollination in another and lead to leaps in performance. For example, if you have a social media Mastermind group that is full of coaches, then you risk being an echo chamber for each other, complaining about the same kinds of problem clients, getting stuck on the same types of problems, trying to fix them with the same old tools. Meeting face-to-face, with a clear focus on positive and constructive feedback, with a mix of industries, leads to successful Masterminding.

He suggests you find a group that needs the strengths you bring, which has members who already have the strengths you need. By having members who are at different stages of their journey in different industries, you are likely to all 'pull each other up' and to grow, than if you're with your peers. Focus on what you can offer, rather than what you want, if you want to approach an existing Mastermind.

If you want to set up your own, or find one you'll love, or even leave the Mastermind you're currently in, then I suggest you listen to William's full interview in the Readers' Club, first.

How To Handle People You Secretly Want To Strangle...

We can't talk about 'connecting' without dealing with this one... Have you ever had a customer or colleague you secretly wanted to strangle? They're the kind of people who, whenever you open your inbox on your customer service email and you see there's one in there from them, your heart sinks.

But if someone has a 'go' at you, it's not really about you; it's about them (unless it's your inner Drama Queen embellishing the story...) It tells you about how they see themselves and how they talk to themselves. And what you're on the receiving end of is all of the mind-stories they've been telling themselves for days or even weeks - or years. You suddenly get it like a bolt out of the blue with all of that angst, all of that anger, all of that projected stress and dissatisfaction, and you've got to deal with it.

I want to share with you some practical ways that you can handle this, so you can keep your energy clean, so you don't have to take on their 'anger-monkeys', and five different things that you can do, beliefs you can try on, to help you handle that kind of person more effectively, making sure you've got crystal clear, but compassionate boundaries.

1. Deal with your 'stuff'.

No one can push your buttons if the buttons are no longer there. Often the people who are driving us crazy are offering us the chance to release an old block that was keeping us stuck. They act as mirrors to us of the characteristics we're potentially avoiding dealing with. If you look beyond their behaviour, to understand what – specifically – is bugging you about it, you'll find hidden gems.

If you then look at which elements of your personal 'baggage' you could release, within you, so that their behaviour no longer produces an emotional response, you set yourself free – forever. Of course, it doesn't suddenly make their behaviour acceptable, but it means you won't be letting them live, rent-free, in your headspace.

The happier and more grounded you are in yourself, the less likely it is that other people's crazy behaviour will blow you off-track. If you're high as a kite, absolutely exhausted, and if your adrenals are on full-alert, you're going to be using the fight or flight part of your nervous system. You're going to be working from the reptilian part of the brain that doesn't think about long-term consequences. You're more likely to lash out and make things worse.

And you risk projecting your brain's filters and assumptions onto the situation, not realising that the issue might be with your *interpretation* of the situation and that you're filling in gaps that aren't really there.

One of the best ways to keep your cool and easily be able to deal with difficult people is to reconnect with your Self - your Inner Peace - each day. Remember the techniques we covered on meditation, mindfulness and mindful movement earlier in this section? Even a few minutes a day can make a huge difference.

2. Don't dive into the drama

So many people these days are up for a fight. They're stressed. They're fed up. They're harassed. And it's so much easier to attack someone else than it is to look in the mirror and deal with your own pain. It's your job to be the grown-up.

Your job is to be calm, to understand that, at some level, they're experiencing pain and anger; that it's not really about you. If you stick to the facts, stripping out the emotions and the drama, and respond from your grounded inner stillness, then you stop the dance. The fire will quickly go from their behaviour if you stop feeding it with your stress-reactions. You can't change them, but you can change how you respond.

3. Stick to the facts

You've got their rant in your face, and it's hit all your buttons, whether you're imagining being back in front of the headmaster's office at school or being told off by your parents or reliving all those years of self-talk of, "I'm not good enough". It hits every button you've got, and people in that space don't realise how painful it is to be so aggressively communicated with. They're not thinking about that. They're coming from their inner pain.

There's a critical difference between responding and reacting. If you 'react' then you're meeting emotion with emotion, without considering your options. When you 'respond', you have taken time to figure out which role you want to play in their Stage Production.

Before you respond, ask yourself what is real in this and what is projection. What are the actual facts? Specifically, what is the problem and what is the solution that I can offer to help this person? Bear in mind some people don't *want* to be helped. They just needed to vent their spleen, to create a sense of relief or release, and you were in the way.

4. Crystal clear boundaries

The first three steps focus on 'accepting' the behaviour, so that you don't have to get stressed by it. But there's a difference between 'acceptance' and 'acceptable'. There's no law stating that you have to put up with behaviour that feels toxic.

If trying to help somebody compassionately, dealing with the facts, not the drama and the emotions, but it isn't working, then it is ok to say no. It is ok to have crystal clear boundaries. In fact, it's essential. If you struggle with this, I've got extra resources for you in the Readers' Club.

5. Show compassion, then move on

Remember we talked about the Native American saying: "all criticism is borne of someone else's pain"? Happy people don't criticise like that. Happy people don't tell you that you're stupid, that you're an idiot. They don't send out rage and pain.

That difficult person's behaviour isn't really about you; it's about them. That helps you get to a place of compassion. Once you're there, responding to the facts of the situation, rather than the emotions and the drama, can diffuse things quickly.

Once you have shown that compassion, move on. You don't have to keep dancing their dance. Use the techniques we have covered in this Handbook to reclaim your personal power. And if that person dumped a tonne of brown stuff on your head, imagine you can stand under a beautiful light-filled waterfall, washing it all away. Get out those imaginary scissors and cut the invisible ties, filling both ends with love. Take from the situation only what you needed to learn, so you can grow and feel free to be who you really are. The rest never belonged to you, anyway.

If energy-vampires are your thing - you know, the kind of people who love hanging around with you, but leave you feeling drained - then there's a bonus video for you in the Readers' Club, with my personal strategies for how to handle this.

Connection is a long-term strategy and I hope this section has inspired you with ideas and practical steps that will pay dividends for you. And wherever you're up to with this, now is the perfect time to explore Step 5: Creativity. It's time to take massive, inspired action.

Creativity

Nothing happens unless you take massive, inspired action. Get off your butt now!

Creativity is where your inspired actions hang out. You will *never* change the world just by reading books and taking courses. You need to turn that passion into action.

The reason we have left creativity until Step 5 is because, when you come to take action, if you have laid your foundations with clarity on your Big Vision, if you're feeling confident, if you've worked on your credibility, and you've connected with your audience, then you'll intuitively sense what they really want. Your inspired actions will be different. And they will have a bigger impact.

If you're not really clear about what you're doing, or why, who you're doing it for, or what makes you different, and you're only part-confident, if you haven't yet got that credibility and trust running, and you haven't started to connect with your Dream Audience, and you *then* create, you're going to have to work much harder to get your message out there. Can you see how we've been building up the layers, based on super-strong foundations?

Once you take inspired action, you'll get much better results, for less effort. You are less likely to suffer from distraction, because if you're feeling excited and passionate, your thinking will be clear and focused. Those cute cat videos will only get ten minutes a day, not hours.

You no longer need to procrastinate and you won't let irrelevant stuff get in the way. It's easier to spot when to say 'no' and when to say 'yes', so you won't feel overwhelmed as easily. And the actions you choose will be lined up with your Inner Genius, so you'll enjoy the journey more, feel more inspired, and delight your audience – a virtuous circle.

'Inspired Action': What It Is - And Isn't

Creativity Is All About Taking 'Inspired Action'

Creativity doesn't have to be about painting like Van Gogh or composing like Beethoven. It's about connecting with the creative aspect of your Inner Genius so you can take actions that create breakthroughs towards your dreams. That's why we covered Vignaanamayakosha (your Inner Wisdom) in Step 4.

What is 'inspired action? It's the kind of action that gets you excited - that sparks your passion for your Big Vision. It might give you goosebumps or skin tingles. At some deep level it will 'feel' right. I know, as a business woman and an engineer, that taking action that 'feels' right isn't always what's approved of, but your gut tends to make better business decisions than your thinking mind's Inner Critic. I tend to go with the gut and double-check with the data.

Inspired action creates leaps and breakthroughs and might take you in surprising directions, but it's what your Heart and Soul (and Dream Audience) wish you were doing. It pops up when you're doing what you do best - living what you love.

Inspired action is not the mundane 'to do' list-filling distractions that mean we're usually too exhausted and overwhelmed to even remember we once had a dream. Yes, much of that stuff needs to be done, but it needs to squeeze into much smaller sections of your schedule - or get delegated to someone else who will love it.

I had many examples of inspired action, as I was writing this Handbook. I would suddenly stumble across someone's name multiple times in a few days, and then take the hint that they were somehow 'lined up' for me to interview. And when I took inspired action on that hunch, it would work out brilliantly.

I made a decision to print the book in hardback, instead of paperback, because I wanted it to *feel* lovely in your hands. I wanted it to be a book to keep and to come back to, as your Big Vision grows. Within 2 hours, I had 'stumbled' upon the ideal company for the print run, who have been hugely helpful in this process.

Each time I felt lost or confused or needed support, someone would 'appear', like the Fancy Dress Shop Owner in Mr Benn[10].

---

[10] 1970s British children's cartoon – details in the Readers' Club, if you want a treat!

In this section, I'm going to guide you through how to figure out which inspired actions you need to be taking, how to maximise your creativity, how to get the headspace you need, how to avoid the fastest way to kill your creativity, the most common traps that catch out far too many of us, and how 'little & often' will get you to your Big Vision faster than 'blitz & burn'.

Why 'Manifesting' And 'Law Of Attraction' Fall Over

Writing Down Your Goals Is Not Enough

Remember that Urban Myth of the research from Harvard (see Step 2) where they were supposed to have tracked the 3% of graduates who had had written goals and found that, decades years later, they now earned more than the other 97% put together? That's often cited as justification for writing down your goals.

But the 'writing down' is not why people succeed.

Writing down their goals meant they had a clear vision about what they wanted to achieve, create or become. But then they cleared out their blocks and took inspired action.

The writing down of the goals didn't get the results. The block-clearing and inspired-action-taking did.

This is where most people fall over with 'manifesting' or the 'Law Of Attraction'. They dream their big dreams, they create their vision boards, they diligently do their journaling, and then they wonder why what they wanted never shows up. Sometimes it's because they didn't clear out the hidden blocks that meant they didn't believe, deep down, that they could line up with their Big Vision. But usually it's down to a lack of inspired action.

It's all very good to sit on your comfy sofa or behind your desk, silently reciting mantras like, "My Abundance is coming to me," or "I believe my dreams will come true," but you need to get off your backside and take real-world action, to turn your dreams into reality. It's not 'any old action'. This isn't about 'busyness' (more on that in Step 6).

Inspired action is the kind of thing that makes you feel excited inside; perhaps a little scared. It produces a physical and emotional response, when you think about it, and deep down you know it could lead to something exciting. It's an action that aligns with your Big Vision and your Inner Genius. It might be sitting just outside your comfort zone. And it's never boring! When you carry it through, it's like something turbocharges the results.

Clarity + Inspired Action = Breakthroughs

For example, Heather Bestel, who I interviewed earlier in this Handbook, is a published author, who also runs live events and online courses. One summer she was asked to do a series of workshops, which she was more-than-qualified to do. However, she didn't feel excited about it. It was well within her comfort zone, but things kept 'not working out'. She kept holding back on taking action, as though she knew she wasn't 'meant' to be doing them, and yet she didn't feel ready to say 'no'.

Then, out of the blue, she got asked to create a series of CDs with meditations for children. This project got her excited and feeling alive, and it was a huge success, launching the next phase of her Big Vision. But had she been on the planned workshop tour, she wouldn't have had time and would have had to turn it down.

How To 'Find' Your Inspired Actions?

Over the years, I have concluded that you can't 'find' inspired actions - they find you. But here are five ways to make it easier to line up with them, so it becomes part of your natural way of living.

The first is to slow down.

If you're already at overwhelm and burnout, then when the inspired action pops into your mind, you'll most likely dismiss it, and justify that with a raft of excuses. You need to create time and space for your inspired actions - and that is why we started this book with Step Zero - Clear Out And Declutter. You need to allow yourself the space to grow.

The second is to be aligned with who you really are, and with your Big Vision, each and every day.

If you're stuck spending 99% of your time doing things that aren't reflecting your Inner Genius and aren't moving you towards your Big Vision, then you risk being stuck on the complaining train, feeling stressed and exhausted. It's as though your inspired actions can't 'see you'; so you won't line up with each other. You're also giving your unconscious mind clear signals that you're *way* too busy to bother with anything that might inspire you - you'd much rather drown in the dross.

The third is gratitude.

There is nothing like saying 'thank you' for what you have in your life already, to bring more of it to you. Leaving the engineer-approved woo-woo to one side, gratitude can reprogram your brain to get off the 'complaining train', so you think thoughts that make you feel happier. And when you're feeling happy and grateful, it's easier to feel inspired.

You are also changing the physiology in your brain. The neural pathways that are normally wired to spot what is wrong (we spent decades training them to do that) get rewired to spend more time finding what is going right. This means your body chemistry will line up with the hormones that make you feel happier and healthier, and it becomes a virtuous circle. Yes, we can sometimes connect with inspired action in times of extreme danger and stress, but it's much more common when you're feeling relaxed, happy and in-flow. I have deep-dive resources for you in the Readers' Club, if you're interested in playing with gratitude and experiencing how it can transform your life in just a few days - without 'pretending' or 'white-washing'.

The fourth is to quieten your mind.

A chattering mind is like having a radio station running at full volume in the background, and then expecting to be able to hear the whisper of wisdom. You don't have to quieten your mind completely. In fact, in nearly a decade of teaching meditation and mindfulness, I have found very few people who can. But it is hugely helpful to be able to calm your chattering mind. And if that's an issue for you, I have a bonus 'quieten those thoughts' meditation for you in the Readers' Club.

Learning to meditate for ten minutes each morning is one of the most effective ways to calm your mind, feel less stressed, and connect with your inner wisdom - with inspiration. And if the ten-minute meditation resonates with you, the Readers' Club also has suggestions for how to make meditation and mindfulness part of your daily life, no matter how busy you are.

The fifth is to connect with your Intuition.

If you can connect with your Intuition on a regular basis, your inspired actions will beat a path to your door. Your Intuition - your inner wisdom - is the voice that guides you from wherever you are right now, to the heart of your Big Vision, and beyond. Over the past few years, with the Intuition Breakthrough Blueprint, I have been able to guide over a thousand people, just like you, to be able to connect with their Intuition, much more reliably. Whether you have previously resisted the woo-woo-feel of 'intuition', or whether you're an old hand looking to dive in more deeply, the process I teach for this gets you measurable results, in under a week. And if you'd like to try it on for size, there's a free taster waiting for you, over in the Readers' Club

With the EU VAT Action Campaign, we were so busy that we often spent every waking hour on the campaign, even though we were volunteers. It was hard to find time to plan or to work on strategies. But, looking back, much of that 'busyness' didn't produce very big results. We could always tell when we were taking an action that was going to create a breakthrough, because it would feel very different to the usual 'pushing'. It came from a sense of intuitive knowing, rather than rational thinking. In fact, it was often the opposite of what rational thinking would suggest - and what most people would advise. We could feel the anticipation and excitement and it would magnetise the support we needed. Suddenly things would flow and fall into place and we knew we had broken through the next barrier.

'Inspired action' got us doing crazy things like organising a Twitter storm, to get the attention of the media and the key decision-makers. Thousands worked together to get 20,000 tweets out there with the #EUVAT hashtag, which ended up trending at #3 position, worldwide.

'Doing' creates exhaustion and overwhelm. Inspired action creates energy, excitement and breakthroughs. Which of the two would you rather choose, to grow your Big Vision?

How Do You Connect With 'Inspired Action' If You're Feeling Stuck?

Stop! Take time out. Move your body. Dance to your favourite music. Get some endorphins flowing.

If you and I were on a retreat together, there are some fabulous yoga sequences I could teach you, that line you up with your inspiration, and which only take a few minutes to do at home. Some of them you can even do in an office! And going on a retreat is one of the most powerful ways I know to reset 'busyness' into 'inspired action' and creativity-driven breakthroughs. That's why my Masterminders join me on retreats, several times a year. It's why I love to take myself away on retreats. It's amazing what you can achieve in a few days of deep-dive, away from your 'to do' list and usual commitments, sharing the space with others who also want to make a bigger difference in the world.

If taking time out isn't an option for you just at the moment, then the quickest way to get unstuck is to do something, right now, that excites and inspires you. It doesn't matter if it's nothing to do with your Big Vision, it's about getting into the groove of feeling inspired, rather than bored. Then let go and trust.

And you might find that inspiration strikes in the strangest ways, in unexpected places.

As I was writing the section in this book on 'connection', I was on retreat in my favourite hotel in Turkey. I *thought* I knew what I was going to write, but my Inner Wisdom knew better. Each time I got out my laptop, someone different would 'appear' and teach me even deeper lessons about connection. I don't mean these people showed up with mini-blackboards, teaching me about connection; I learned by being fully present with them, and seeing that each of them held a message for me, which reshaped what I was about to write. I could have got irritated at those distractions, but my Intuition told me that these were messengers who needed my full attention. It was a mind-blowing morning. I felt so grateful to them.

Then, just as I had my laptop out for the final time, a song came on the Turkish radio and the first four lines from it inspired another section of this book. They summed up perfectly what I wanted to convey.

Your inspired action messages can come to you in any way, at any time, from any source. All you need to do is clear your mind and reduce your stress levels enough, so that you're open to spotting those messages.

Sama Vritti: How To Clear Your Mind

Here's the third breathing technique I promised you. It's called 'Sama Vritti' and it is known in English as 'equal ratio breathing'. It helps you to clear your mind, so you can focus more easily; it rebalances your nervous system, so you can drop the stress-response and feel more creative.

It's simple to do. Though a quick caveat: if you have breathing issues or glaucoma or high blood pressure, please don't do the 'pause' bits in this technique – just breathe in and out. For everyone else, please do this at your own pace. There's an audio to guide you through it, in the Readers' Club.

Exercise: Sama Vritti

There's an audio to guide you through this technique, in the Readers' Club.

Start by thinking of a problem you're feeling stuck on, or an idea where you need more creativity. Notice how it feels in your body, your thoughts, and your emotions.

Now gently closing your eyes, take three, deep sighing breaths, in through your nose and out with an 'ahhh' sound, allowing yourself to let go of tension and come back 'into' your body.

Allow your breathing to settle in your belly area, if that's comfortable for you, spending a few moments just observing it, experiencing it.

On your next breath, use the equal-breathing:
- Breathe in through your nose for a count of two.
- Lightly pause for a count of two.
- Breathe out through your nose for a count of two.
- Lightly rest for two.

Repeat this a few times, to get the rhythm. Make sure the counting rhythm feels comfortable for you.

If it feels ok for you, gradually extend the 'count' to be 3 and then 4. Continue for at least a minute.

Now return to breathing normally. Open your eyes and notice how you feel. What has shifted? How do your thoughts feel? How do you feel about the problem you were thinking about, at the start of this technique? What actions might you take?

Let me know, via the Readers' Club forum thread.

What's The Quickest Way To Kill Your Creativity?

There are many ways to put a swift halt to your creative spark; low self-esteem, exhaustion, overwhelm, your Inner Critic and interruptions are just a few of them. But none of these is a patch on the biggest and quickest way to kill your creativity. In fact, this one will most likely stop your creativity before that racehorse even gets out of the stable.

Exercise: Are You Killing Your Creativity?

Let's play for a moment: think about something creative that's on your 'to do' list - something that might fall under the 'inspired action' label - and notice what your thoughts and posture do when you say to yourself the phrase:

"I *have to* do XYZ."

"I *should* do XYZ."

Really allow yourself to sink into this experience. Breathe as you would be breathing. Allow your body to move. Let your thoughts have a moment to do whatever they please.

And what did you notice?

What happened to your posture? To your breathing? To your thoughts? And how are you feeling?

Do you feel open and expansive and inspired? Or perhaps contracted, and somehow smaller, and constricted?

When I work in Mastermind Intensives or on workshops with people on this, the most visible and near-instant change in their shoulders. They slouch, as though they are giving Atlas a quick break from carrying the weight of the Heavens. Their jaw clenches. Their breathing moves from the belly to the upper chest, or even the throat. And their face tenses up, with worry-lines appearing between the brows.

And those thoughts turn into stress-stories of obligations and commitments and all the reasons why they're not [*insert-preferred-self-insult-here*] enough.

When you're feeling this way, are you feeling creative?

No. Didn't think so. So what's going on?

You're suffering from 'shoulditis'. We have mentioned it before, in Step 4, but it's so important, that I want to talk about it again, in the context of taking inspired action and being creative.

And it's a modern epidemic.

Now, before I spill the beans any more on this, I want you to shake that off, otherwise you'll be too busy with your 'have-to stories' to listen to me. So give your body a shake and give yourself a great big smile. I don't care if you're on the train. Just do your best not to get arrested.

I have lost count of how many thousands of people I have met who were running this as a major life pattern.

And you can spot it with the words you use to talk to yourself. If you're running a case of shoulditis, you'll be saying things like,

"I have to…"

"I ought to…"

"I must…"

"I should…"

Most of us do this without thinking. But did you notice the shift it created in you?

Obligation is one of the quickest ways to thwart your creative inspiration. While we sometimes put ourselves under time pressure and still create near-genius work, that's about urgency, rather than obligation. It kicks your backside into the 'zone'.

When you think back over the last few years, how were you feeling when you created your best work? I'm guessing you were feeling inspired and free, rather than stuck and 'forced' to do it?

Inspiration rarely strikes when you're feeling trapped by obligation.

So what's the alternative? How can you reconnect with your creative spark, and stop shoulditis from getting in the way?

This simple shift can have a profound effect on all areas of your life - in an instant. In fact, master this one and your life will never be the same again - in a good way!

I want to share with you Marion's story, or how I ended up teaching yoga at 33,000 feet.

I was on my way to lead a business breakthrough retreat in Turkey, when I met Marion, on the flight. The first two words she said to me were, "I should…" I can't actually remember what came next, because those first two words grabbed my attention. Gentle-mannered, friendly and unassuming, when 60-something Marion uttered these words, she visibly shrank.

My automatic response came out - a warm smile and, "but there's no such thing as 'should' - it's ok!" She didn't even register it.

I bumped into her again later, in the queue for the loos. Her next sentence to me also included the words, "I should." And the same was in the fifth or sixth sentence. At that point, I let her jump the loo-queue (how very English), so I could come up with some ideas. While she was doing whatever she needed to do, I did some simple yoga stretches and postures to get the blood flowing in my calves again. The last time I flew, by the time we landed they were scarily rock-solid and stayed that way for a few days, and yoga stretches are a great way to prevent that.

When Marion came out of the toilets, she saw me doing a balance posture called 'The Dancer' (Natarajasana - for the purists).

Marion paused to watch and then made a throwaway comment:

"Oh, I could never do that. I'm rubbish at balancing. I *should* be able to do it, but I just can't. In fact, I'm thinking of giving up yoga."

My heart sank. I'm a yoga teacher. And I know how revitalising and empowering yoga could be to a woman of Marion's age, with her Inner Critic patterns. Mentoring auto-pilot kicked in. Marion had used the scary combo: "I *should* be able to do this, but I can't do it well enough, so I'll give up."

Big red warning light.

We have all done it, haven't we? We've judged ourselves so badly that we ended up quitting - even if it was something we really wanted to do. Our Inner Critic won over our desire to change or learn or grow or do something we loved. And our fear of not being 'good enough' or not fitting in and being as good as others can stop us from even trying.

I could see the fear in Marion's eyes, and I ended up running an impromptu yoga masterclass on balancing. I taught her, some of the cabin crew, and a few others who didn't think we were overly-crazy, how to love yoga balance postures, even if you secretly fear you're rubbish at them. There are some simple adjustments you can use to make them much easier, and to get massively better at them, even on a plane, as long as you're prepared to let go of your inner perfectionist and allow yourself to visualise the postures.

But the real thing here was Marion's use of 'should'. Who on earth said that she 'should' be able to balance? Who on earth said that she should give up yoga if she couldn't? How did she end up believing that she wasn't good enough to be a yoga student?

But we all do it, don't we?

This is where 'should' moves into dangerous territory. It moves from obligation to self-judgement.

The fact is that no one told Marion that she 'should' be able to balance, effortlessly, with her heel tucked into her groin, doing the perfect 'tree' posture. That was all a projection that Marion subconsciously created, and then judged herself against.

And that's the other, more sinister, side of 'shoulditis'.

I'm not a genius yoga teacher, but I do know a lot about psychology, and I my instincts told me I had a few short minutes to give Marion evidence - mid-flight - that she *could* balance; that she *is* good enough, so that she wouldn't have to give up the yoga she loves.

By the end of our short session, Marion had learned the techniques she needed to feel confident balancing - even at 33,000 feet, in mild turbulence. And the beam on her face is something I will never forget. She had made that transition. "I can't, but I should be able to..." became, "I can... And I choose to... So I will... In my own way."

I felt so excited. I'm quite sure she has no idea and just thinks of me as the 'crazy yoga lady on the plane'. But there was so much more to her transformation than yoga. Marion had an experience of how "I should" can be turned into something totally empowering.

And that's the answer to unleashing your creativity, when you're feeling stuck in shoulditis.

"I choose to... my own way!"

Whenever shoulditis pops up to say an ugly 'hello', your antidote lies in one simple word: choose. "I choose to..."

Exercise: Setting Yourself Free From Shoulditis

Try it on for size. Imagine that same creative endeavour you thought about in the last exercise this section, but instead of saying, "I have to...", say "I choose to".

Notice how different your body feels. Notice how different your breathing feels. Notice how your thoughts feel.

How might your life - and business - shift, if instead of saying, "I have to..." you played with "I choose to...", instead?

Let me know via the Readers' Club forum thread on this.

The Two Most Common Traps

When you're looking at getting creative and taking inspired action, there are two incredibly common traps that I see derail people every day - and I don't want you to fall into them.

Back in Step 1, I talked about how we can create anything that we can imagine, as long as we give ourselves permission. Well, these three traps are classic permission-removers, and being aware of them makes it much easier to spot them, before they get in the way of your creativity and inspired action.

1. If At First You Don't Succeed....

As we discussed in Step 3, in the UK we have a saying, which is often used with children, when they are learning new skills:

"If at first you don't succeed, try, try, try again."

The meaning behind it is that you need to pick yourself up and start again, if you get knocked down. But as adults, this translates into crazy behaviour. Einstein is rumoured to have said that insanity is trying the same thing, over and over, whilst expecting different results, which is what so many of us accidentally do.

Practice doesn't make perfect, unless you're getting quality feedback.

If you go to the Tube (metro) in London, you'll often see this with tourists. Locals have a special 'Oyster card' ticket that they hold against a reader, to enter and exit the Tube lines, which charges them for their journey. Infrequent travellers have tickets that need to be fed into a slot that reads the magnetic stripe on the ticket. If you're new to the city, this isn't obvious. I have lost count of the number of times I have seen tourists hold their paper ticket to the Oyster card reader, as they watched the person in front do with their wallet containing their Oyster card. The barrier won't open. The tourist looks confused. So they try again. And again. And again. Until someone helps them.

We all have aspects of our lives where we do this. We stay stuck in our gerbil wheel, taking the same old actions, but somehow expecting to reach a different destination.

So if we 'try, try, try again', then it's vital that our 'trying' is flexible.

It's essential that we look at what didn't work and we learn from it - and then change our 'trying'. When you're taking the actions needed to move you towards your Big Vision, the more of your old habits you can release, the more quickly you'll get there. The more flexible you can be with your behaviour, the faster you will get results.

And there comes a point where you need to stop 'trying'. If you feel like you're pushing and forcing and everything is hard work, then it's a sign that the door is currently closed. Either the timing isn't right, or the door isn't the one you need. If you keep 'trying', then you won't notice the nearby door that's wide open.

You'll get the best and fastest progress towards your dreams when you get in flow and allow yourself to create with the energy of 'allowing', rather than 'pushing'. Does that make sense? When you're in flow, you'll feel a sense of excitement or anticipation; your body will be relaxed, rather than tense; and inspiration becomes your new best friend.

When you 'try, try, try again' from a place of flow and flexibility, life will fall into place.

2. The Curse Of Comparison

We talked about the Green-Eyed Monster back in Step 2, but I want to bring the topic up again, because it so often gets in the way of our creativity. I have seen this happen countless times:

You have a great idea, so you go out to see what else there is out there, in a similar vein, and by the time you've spent an hour surfing the internet, you're feeling so demoralised, you give up.

Or...

You're ticking along happily, when a 'competitor' posts something great and gets huge interaction from their Tribe. Within seconds your self-esteem is in a pit deeper than an ocean trench and you start telling yourself stories about how you'll never be that good.

Comparing yourself to random strangers on the internet is more likely to demoralise you, than to inspire you.

Most of us end up doing this by accident. Maybe we're bench marking what other offerings are out there. Perhaps our searches end up influencing the ads we see on other sites or in our social media feed. And suddenly someone's glitzy sales page with gorgeous-looking bonuses knocks you off-track. Self-doubt kicks in.

How can you handle this? Start by shaking off those emotions – stand up and shake your body. It works! Then, get grounded and go back to your Big Why, Big Vision and Big Message. Above all, remember:

You have a unique voice that your Dream Audience is craving to hear.

Going back through the Credibility strategies from Step 3 will help to mean your Dream Audience notices you, whoever else is around. You can let go and trust that your message will be heard.

I've got a bonus article for you in the Readers' Club that takes you through some highly-effective strategies for carrying out your market research, without falling prey to the curse of comparison. And make sure you revisit the strategies in Step 2.

Forget The 80/20 Rule – Why The 1% Rule Needs To Become Your New Best Friend

Or how 'little & often' will get you to your Big Vision faster than 'blitz & burn'.

Have you ever heard people talking about how they went from zero to six figures in just 90 days? And offering to sell you the 'formula' they used, so that you can do the same? Here's a money-saving tip for you: it rarely works. If you've been running your business for a while and you're not hitting those levels, it can leave you feeling like a failure. But, you aren't.

Overnight success is a myth. It's normally the product of years of dedication, inspired action and generous dollop of good luck.

It's time for you to meet the 1% rule. Yes, the Pareto Principal of 80/20 is really important, and you hear experts talking about things like 80% of your customers might only bring you 20% of the revenue and the value, so you really want to put your focus in there. And, as a rule of thumb, 80% of your results will come from 20% of your efforts. It's not an exact science, but the Pareto Rule does work, most of the time.

But when time is tight and we're busy working *in* our business, and sometimes we're too busy to work *on* it, then this is where the 1% rule comes in.

Back in my engineering days, I studied Japanese lean manufacturing quality techniques.

After the Second World War, the Japanese were able to rebuild their manufacturing industry and create the most incredible leaps in quality, but it wasn't through radical change. It was through continuous improvement; techniques like Kaizen, looking at incremental changes that built up quickly over time to make a big difference, and the whole team was empowered to help on those changes.

Take the idea, for example, of climbing a mountain. Instead of having to leap or run up it, Kaizen focuses on each step instead. What this does for your team, for you, and your customers, is that suddenly that action, that leap feels possible; manageable; less scary. And if you were to imagine making 1% progress towards your Big Vision, every few days, it's easier to come up with ideas for inspired action.

Can you imagine if I set you a challenge of, say, increasing the size of your email subscriber list by 1% this week? That would feel much more achievable than if I said, "I want to have a 50% increase by the end of the year." It's less likely to bring up the old fears, blocks, and self-imposed glass ceilings and self-sabotage patterns.

Improving any of your business metrics by, say, 1% every few days, will mount up and the compound effect is powerful. It's so much easier than looking for doubling or quadrupling, yet it creates the same output. You'll create the breakthroughs, but with much less stress and resistance. And it frees your mind to get more creative. That inspired action is no longer dismissed by your thinking brain as being terrifying or impossible.

Take the first step in faith. You don't have to see the whole staircase, just take the first step. ~ Martin Luther King Jr.

Of course, it's important to have the big stuff in your strategy too, but lots of small, easy changes and improvements can bring you faster results. The bottom line is that growing your Big Vision doesn't have to be back-breakingly hard. It can even be fun, and fun is essential, if you want to get creative. As soon as you stop focusing on having to create the breakthroughs and the leaps, and instead you look at the 1% rule, it's a great way to get you unstuck.

We've got a special discussion thread for this, over at the forum for the Readers' Club, where there are also details of my 30-day programme to help you get back on track with working 'on' your business, not just 'in' it. All of the actions in that programme take under five minutes, but have the potential to turn things around for you, so there are no more excuses!

Exercise: Applying The 1% Rule

There's a worksheet for this, over at the Readers' Club. We're going to look at how you could apply the 1% rule to growing your business, and how it feels when you break down big objectives into smaller chunks.

- Which metrics do you currently measure in your business? How much do they grow by?
- What actions have you been taking, to grow them?
- Knowing what you now know, do those metrics move you towards your Big Vision?
- Pick a metric that does. What actions could you take today to grow any of your Big Vision metrics by, say, 1% in the next week?

Maybe it's the number of website visitors. Maybe it's the number of people signing up for a particular opt-in that you have. Maybe it's the number of customers. Maybe it could be spending 1% more time in your Zone of Genius? What could you do in the next week to increase that by 1%? If you brainstorm a list, you'll come up with plenty of ideas.

- Now, go back through that list and look at the amount of effort versus the return and pick the low hanging fruit, because they taste just as good as the ones that you need the ladder for.

There's nothing wrong with picking the low hanging fruit. It doesn't mean that you're a failure. It doesn't mean you're copping out. It means you're going with the flow, making the most of the simple strategies, and saving your high-effort energy for the few extra-juicy actions that will really make a difference.

- Which of those actions could you most easily implement, and how much difference might that make over the next three months?
- Is there anything that might be keeping you stuck? Which of the techniques from this Handbook could you use to get 'unstuck'?
- What support do you need?
- How might the 1% rule help you to grow your business?

How does that feel, now? Has the change in perspective set you free to feel more creative? More inspired?

How To Figure Out Which Actions Will Get Results

I want to share with you a process that I normally use one-to-one or with my Masterminders. It's another version of the 'time travel' technique we used earlier, but this time you're starting at the end and working backwards, to figure out the key steps you need to take.

There's an audio to guide you through this, in the Readers' Club, which takes it to a different level. You'll want to be somewhere that you can walk in a straight line, for this to work. And if your thinking mind objects to your time-travelling, give it the job of being your note-taker. This process really works, as long as you allow it to.

Exercise: Creativity Action Plan

Start with the next major step towards your Big Vision and Big Message. Imagine a line on your floor, representing time. Start at a point which is 'now' and walk in a line to a point **just beyond** when you have achieved your next goal.

- Close your eyes and take a moment to fully experience how it feels, how you are holding your body, which thoughts you are thinking.
- Open your eyes, turn round and look back towards the 'now' point, where you started. Imagine there is an invisible line, linking that future point with the present.
- Take one step back along the line, towards the 'now' point. How far back in time does this 'feel'? Which actions have you been taking? Which blocks did you need to clear? What will you need to have done, to have reached this point? Jot down notes!
- Repeat with each step, back along your invisible line, towards the 'now', noticing the key goals and actions.
- Once you get back to the present moment, turn round to look back towards the future.
- How different does it feel, now, knowing that you have your actions lined up, ready to achieve your goal – and even to go beyond it. What have you learned from this exercise?
- And which is going to be your next action, in the next 24 hours?

Want accountability? Share your 'next 24 hours' action in the forum!

Are You Aiming High Enough? How Not To Fall Short Of Your Dreams

A long time ago, I heard a story.

Many years past, there was a young man, who was standing by a riverbank, trying to throw stones to the other side. But no matter how hard he tried, they kept falling short. A wise old man approached him and offered to help.

"What would *he* know?" wondered the young man, as the wise old man picked up a stone and prepared to throw it.

The young man was convinced his older companion had zero chance of hitting the other side. There was no way he could possibly be strong enough to throw it as hard as the young man had been throwing. He chuckled to himself, as he waited for the splash.

It never came.

The wise old man's stone landed, audibly, on the opposite bank.

"But you barely even tried!" said the young man, "You put almost no effort in! How did you do it?"

"Where were you aiming for?" asked the wise old man.

"The opposite bank!" came the reply.

"That's the difference. Your stone fell short because you weren't aiming far enough. Me, I aimed for that tree over there," he said, pointing well beyond the bank, "that's how I knew I would make it to the easier goal."

And that's why it's so important for you to connect with the feeling for *after* you have created what you want to create. That way you programme your unconscious mind to experience it as being true; to experience having completed your next goal. It reduces resistance. It softens old blocks and beliefs. It opens you up to the possibility – and even probability – of success. You're much less like to land short of your dreams, once you have experienced life after achieving them.

So make sure you pay attention to where you're aiming that stone.

Now it's time to move on to Step 6, which is the vital fuel that your inspired actions need, if you want to make a bigger difference in the world.

Commitment

*"I can" changes nothing;
it's "I will" and "I have done" that change the world.*

Commitment is what makes the difference between a nice idea and actually making a difference in the world. And it's the bit that so many of us find hardest, once the initial excitement of a spark of inspiration wears off. It's all very well clearing out your blocks and dreaming up things to do, but if you're not truly committed to your dreams, they're not going to happen - the first tiny obstacle risks derailing them.

What Are The Symptoms Of Not Being Committed?

- feeling overwhelmed by tiny jobs on your list
- struggling to find the time to make progress on your goals
- watching every webinar you can find and signing up for every free (or paid) training, rather than taking action
- feeling bored and frustrated
- starting lots of exciting ideas, but not finishing them

If you're experiencing any of these, then there's a chance you're not fully committed. How does this happen? We can lack commitment for many reasons, but there are three main causes:

- that you haven't really bought in to your Big Why - perhaps it's someone else's idea for you, or it comes from a place of 'shoulditis', or it's not quite big enough?
- you've got a hidden block that's causing you to self-sabotage, by prioritising other actions first

When you're really committed to your Big Vision and making your difference, it takes priority - sometimes too much priority - but it never drops off your 'to do' list.

Why do you need commitment? Because that inspired action isn't going to take itself! Going back to what we discussed about 'manifesting' and 'law of attraction' in the Creativity section, this is another place where these fall over. People put out their intention about what they want to attract into their lives - once. Then they wait. They might take one or two inspired actions, while they're still feeling excited in the first few days, but then it peters out. And they wonder why, three months later, they're still sitting there with no sign of what they wanted to create in their lives.

I'd like to start this section by talking about an addiction that so many of us run, which is a classic sign of not being truly committed to your Big Vision.

How To Escape From 'Shiny Object Syndrome'

This one is familiar for most of us: we have a brilliant idea. We put all our energy into it. We push, push, push, push, do, do, do, do, do. And, before you know it, we've crashed and burned - or lost interest.

Very few passionate entrepreneurs are completer-finishers. We tend to be passionate about creating ideas, but implementing them quickly bores us, which means we often don't get things finished and launched, so we struggle to grow our business or make that difference in the world.

There's another side to this too. I was talking with a large group of female entrepreneurs about how they spot themselves self-sabotaging their success. Between us, we came up with many answers, but one of the most common themes was that we chase the next shiny, exciting project.

You're halfway through something and you suddenly have a brilliant brainwave for something completely unrelated, so you shift direction and work on that instead. If we're really honest, that distraction is exciting, but it rarely grows your business. If we don't finish things, then we can't sell them. You can't sell a half finished product or a half finished widget or course. People can't benefit from something that's not 'out there' and ready for them.

There are some common strategies to motivate ourselves to stick with it and finish things. For example, maybe pre-selling a course will force you to knuckle down and get it done, providing you with the leverage you need. But it's hard work!

Although chasing the next shiny thing can be fun, it can leave you exhausted, because it uses up your energy and time. You might be creating ten times as many things as you need to. Whereas, creating one, doing it really well, letting it grow, marketing it, and then creating the next one is what will grow your business and allow you to make a bigger difference.

Can you imagine if you were employed, and you behaved the way half of us do as entrepreneurs? We'd have been fired within weeks. Now, most of us go into being entrepreneurs because we're absolutely in love with that feeling of freedom and choice. But, the CEO mindset is what turns that hobby into a business and that business into a legacy.

We need to cultivate that CEO mindset. We need to be totally committed to the Big Vision we're creating, and have enough self-discipline, so that Shiny Object Syndrome doesn't distract us, as though we had shareholders holding us accountable. We need to find ways or support teams to make sure things actually get done and out there, before we chase the next exciting project. If you're not a natural completer-finisher, hire one! If you need a regular kick up the backside, to keep you committed, then hire an accountability coach or join a Mastermind (there are suggestions for these in the Readers' Club).

If you're constantly chasing the next shiny thing, then you're going to feel demoralised because you're putting so much of your life force, your passion, your effort, and your energy into something and it doesn't bring you any return.

There's only so much creativity your customers can handle.

There's another problem that most of us don't think about. I had this one a few years ago. I went through a super creative phase but, after about six months, one of my biggest clients quietly and politely said, "I just can't keep up with you. I can't keep up with the speed at which you're creating stuff. I want to do all of it, but I'm feeling utterly overwhelmed." Another told me he was completely confused; he didn't know which course he was meant to be on. He didn't know which free thing I was offering. There was too much being created too fast.

It reminded me of a story that my meditation mentor, Chris Barrington, co-founder of Dru Yoga, used to tell back in the days when I was training to become a meditation teacher. He was talking about the world of meditation and how, when you sit down to meditate, it's like striking a match. He was encouraging us to sit and meditate for longer than we previously had. He described it as being like lighting a fire. You strike the match; you hold the match under the tinder, and you have to hold the match there until the flame has caught, otherwise the match goes out and there's no fire lit. Until they are fully alight, they cannot light the logs and the fire will die out. It takes that initial commitment to holding the flame of the match still, to be able to light the fire.

It's the same with our businesses. If we're constantly running from one exciting project to the next, it's like we're constantly lighting matches, then throwing them away, never allowing the fire to catch.

My Favourite Business-Growing Sanskrit Word

This brings me on to my favourite Sanskrit word: abhyasa. Apologies to all Sanskrit scholars out there, but I like to translate it as "keeping going when you're not in the mood". It means using your passion to take the actions that your Big Vision needs you to take, not necessarily the ones that look easy.

If there are things that you hate doing, then you need to get your dream team around you to do those things for you, if you know you're not going to do them yourself. Abhyasa, - keeping going even when you're not in the mood - is about creating the daily routine, the rhythm, the step-by-step actions that will grow your business faster, more effectively, and more easily than the old crash-and-burn model.

Abhyasa is what gets you results.

I teach abhyasa when I'm teaching meditation and also when I'm helping people to change habits. If you're struggling with commitment, then it's time to go back and revisit how excited you are by your Big Vision. When you know your Big Why, and it is big enough, it will keep you going. It fuels your abhyasa.

Jenn Philpott, Founder of Born Ready, whom we met in Step 4, gave me a brilliant example of abhyasa. As mentioned, she had entered a competition for the chance to pitch her Flaparap nappy to Sir Richard Branson. The competition required her to collect a certain number of votes from the public, via a website, to get through to the next round. The thing was that the number of votes required kept going up and, of course, people could only vote once. So Jenn had to get creative.

She was driven by her Big Why for the competition –she wanted to be able to have conversations about her Flaparap nappies and baby-led potty training with a wider audience. She realised that mentioning Sir Richard Branson's competition gave her a great opening. So she took her campaign for votes onto public transport, asking complete strangers to vote for her – even sitting with them as she guided them through the voting app on their phone.

To make it easier, and less threatening for the potential voters, she carried a toy zebra that was wearing one of her brightly-coloured nappies, as a conversation-starter. She chose people who weren't looking busy, who looked like 'the kind of person who might vote for me' – not just Mums with babies. And Jenn told them, up front, what she wanted them to do, so they didn't feel nervous that they might be asked to buy something.

Jenn's insights into how people might react meant she was able to prepare conversation flows for every eventuality. She was highly creative with this. She had to pluck up courage every time, but her Big Why kept her going. Each knockback, even a polite one, affected her confidence a little, but she kept herself going – good old abhyasa – by celebrating the fact that each vote moved her closer to that day's goal.

Jenn also says that one of the reasons she got so far through the competition was because she hadn't initially realised how many daily votes she would need, by the end. The number kept going up gradually, so her goal was broken down into chunks that she felt were potentially achievable – a critical factor for her motivation.

Although Jenn didn't win the competition, she had some fantastic conversations with people and got to experience connecting with a much wider audience for her Flaparaps and baby-led potty training courses.

For me, Jenn is an inspirational example of how you can show abhyasa, even if it feels scary, doing whatever it takes to get your message out there, standing in your audience's shoes, making it easy for them to connect with you.

Whatever it is you're resisting doing, that's most likely to be the next step that will create the biggest difference for your Big Vision. Put it in your diary. Set yourself an alarm. Then you don't even need to remember to do it. That's how you create the habit. And just do it!

These actions are rarely as scary as we make them out to be. Once we strip them of the drama and the emotions, they're usually quite straightforward. Getting them done feels great - and it's how you create change. It's that consistent action and that dedication to keeping going when you're not quite in the mood that will get you the results when you've built it on those firm foundations. There's a bonus article for you on this, in the Readers' Club, about practical ways to turn that mountain back into a molehill.

There's also an excellent video there from Daniel Priestley, in which he explains why your environment (your peer group or Tribe) is so important to your commitment and avoiding procrastination. He recommends surrounding yourself with peers (e.g. in a Mastermind) whose own actions and expectations 'normalise' the level of success you're looking to achieve. They will bring you the 'how-to' and the contacts that you need, as you will for them. And he recommends working with your Mastermind, to break 'big deadlines' down into smaller accountability deadlines, each week, so you're no longer tempted to put everything off until the final few days before your final deadline. You don't want to let your Mastermind peers down on your weekly promises, so it helps you to stay committed, long-term. It provides you with leverage for your abhyasa.

But there's one widely-believed myth that gets in the way of abhyasa. Shall we ditch it?

The Myth Of "I'm Too Busy"

How often have you heard yourself lamenting, "I'm too busy...!" or "I don't have time, to...!"? For most of us it's a daily occurrence. But is it really true?

The problem with this statement is that it is self-fulfilling. It starts with 'I am', which means it hits us right deep at the identity level, bypassing the usual rational filters. And it triggers all the auto-pilot responses in your brain and your body to support the unconscious instruction of 'be too busy'. Your endocrine system will fire off its favourite stress hormones, and you'll find your heart rate changes, your breathing shifts to your upper chest, and your adrenals kick in.

This feeds thoughts and self-talk stories about being too busy, and it boots you into your sympathetic nervous system - the fight / flight / freeze mechanism that is meant to defend you from life-threatening predators, not your 'to do' list.

Once you're hanging around in 'fight or flight', the primal part of your brain kicks in. It's the bit responsible for short-term decision-making, because any wasted thinking time ups the chances of ending up as something else's lunch. Strategic thinking and analysis of consequences fly out of the caveman's not-yet-invented window. The likelihood of getting to the bottom of your 'to do' list when this is running is sub-zero.

And all of that was triggered by an 'I'm too busy...' story.

When you run this pattern regularly, it leads to chronic stress and even adrenal fatigue. You'll find it harder to concentrate, nearly impossible to connect with inspiration and you really will be too busy, because everything will take so much longer.

You might genuinely be too busy, but then you need to either learn to delegate or start partying with the word 'no'. (Remember the time management resources in the Readers' Club. But from what I have seen over the years, "I'm too busy" isn't usually true. It usually - subconsciously - means, "I don't want to."

But being too busy is more socially acceptable than saying 'no'. Or it might mean, "I'm secretly scared to..." And that's why I encourage you to deal with your hidden blocks, excuses, fears, and limiting beliefs as soon as you notice them, so that they don't get in your way.

It's also a badge of honour - being too busy has massive secondary gain, in the form of sympathy from loved-ones and peers, or even admiration, depending on your circles, as well as providing us with an excellent excuse for turning down opportunities that could create the breakthroughs we're dreaming of. Being too busy is the perfect antidote to Imposter Syndrome - as long as you don't mind staying stuck where you're at.

Being honest with yourself about your "I'm too busy" excuses is a wonderful stress-relief. If it's because you don't want to do something (and it's not just feeling-like-a-fraud, wearing a grandfather-clock-sized disguise), then find a way to 'not do it' - ditch it or delegate it.

And if that excuse is just that you've filled your time up with things that are getting in the way of your Big Vision, then it's time to reprioritise.

We always find time for the things we decide are most important. Just sometimes we're a bit ropey on that decision-making process.

But it could be that you're addicted to 'busyness', which is a dream-killing modern epidemic. Read on to find out if you're stuck in this trap, and what you can do to set yourself free.

If You Want To Grow A Business, You Need To Let Go Of Your Addiction To 'Busyness'

There's something about being an employee that makes us spend our time more wisely. It makes us think twice before we 'lose' an hour on social media or spend half the morning on those videos we stumbled across that were 'really important' and which we 'simply had to watch'. It's easier to stay focussed and to get everything done. Perhaps it's because we know there's someone out there checking up on what we're doing and whether we're meeting our goals and deadlines. Or perhaps it's just a different mindset.

Over the years, I have seen thousands of entrepreneurs start off with all the self-discipline they had in their 'day job', but gradually fritter it away, until they wind up overwhelmed, exhausted, and never having enough time.

I have seen two main causes for this. The first is trying to do everything yourself, rather than playing to your strengths and delegating the rest. We talked about that in Step 4 on Connection; getting your Dream Team around you.

The second is subconscious addiction to 'busyness'.

'Busyness' is the stuff we distract ourselves with, so that we're too busy to work towards our Big Vision. It's a brilliant avoidance strategy and great for self-sabotage... And it's a modern addiction in our multi-tasking, multi-screening world.

When you're totally connected with your Big Vision and you've cleared out the blocks, there's no space left for busyness. Distractions tend to fall down the priority list. You just get out there and do it. You live your Dharma, your Purpose, with passion, and it excites you. You see results. But when you're running hidden fears and blocks, or you're lacking clarity, then we subconsciously fill our time up with little actions (the Germans call this 'Kleinkramm', which is a fabulously fun word to say and it beautifully dismisses those actions as being low value-add).

There's a parallel here with the world of teaching meditation:

I often talk to people about why we're so scared of silence. We drown it out with radio, music, TV and multi-screening. The idea of sitting silently (whether or not you choose to meditate) is frightening for many people. Actually slowing down and perhaps even stopping is a nightmare scenario for them, because we're addicted to being busy - to doing. The Secondary Gain is massive (see page 84).

For people running that pattern, I don't start them off with traditional meditation. It wouldn't work. Their body and mind would scream. Instead we cover ancient mindfulness techniques that can bring them back into the moment, connecting them with the essence of who they really are, even if they're busy doing stuff. There's time for silence, once the fears have melted away.

I find it's the same with entrepreneurs and passionate World-Changers. The more disconnected you are from your Big Vision, the more likely you are to fill your available time with 'doing'. And that 'doing' is likely to be lower-priority, low-return tasks.

The same thing happens if a subconscious block is running, especially one of those around confidence and Imposter Syndrome. If you haven't handled those blocks, then your mind 'helps you out' by making sure you're too busy and stressed to have time to stretch that comfort zone. It obliges you with distractions to help you to self-sabotage.

That's why this Handbook deals with getting clarity and clearing out the blocks, before you dive in to take action.

I run an online course called "Time Secrets For Busy Entrepreneurs" and when people are looking for help with finding more time, the most common question I get asked by people who are interested in the programme is:

How can I be more productive?

In other words, how can I get even more of the non-value-adding stuff done, in less time?

I taught my first time management course over 20 years ago, as a recent graduate, teaching a room full of people twice my age how to manage their time. Since then, I have thrown away most 'standard' time management techniques. I kept the best, but the way I see it, most of us are looking at time management back-to-front. Yes, there are things you can do to get more out of your time, which mostly revolve around correctly prioritising, removing distractions, learning how to concentrate (mindfulness is great for this) only handling things once, batching tasks and focussing in shorter bursts, with battery-recharging breaks. But I usually refuse to talk about 'productivity', because unless what you're doing is already the kind of thing that will lead you towards your dreams, there's no way I want to help you do more of it. Instead I talk about 'choosing how you invest your time'.

When you choose to view your time as a resource, like money (except more valuable), the choices you make will change.

It can help to schedule your most creative tasks for the times when you're feeling most clear-headed and productive - resisting the urge to waste those hours with 'to do' list minutiae. For me, first thing in the morning works best, especially if my family is still asleep. It's standard practise for them to come down for breakfast at the weekends and find me on the sofa with my fountain pen leaving a trail of smoke behind it, as it whizzes across my notepad.

It also helps to get an understanding of what's driving you, if you procrastinate or start yet another project. For me, I find that I get stuff done best when I'm on retreat or on a deadline. Both options allow me to create at what can feel like superhuman speed, for short periods of time. One is significantly less stressful than the other.

Look at what works best for your rhythm and use that as your starting point.

Time is a currency, more valuable than money, yet we rarely consider how we spend it.

If you want to grow your business, you need to let go of your addiction to busyness. If this is a big issue for you, you'll find more deep-dive resources in the Readers' Club.

Next up we're going to look at the easiest way to get committed, make massive progress, and cut the stress of your 'to do' list.

Do Your M.I.T. First

I often work with people who are either in full-time jobs, who dream of launching their own business, or who are running a business that's at the solopreneur level, where it's just them and maybe some freelance contractors, and they want to step up to the next level, with a team around them.

The challenge with these scenarios is that you're already incredibly busy working in one business, while you're effectively trying to grow another one. Time is tight for them, so being focussed, having total clarity and taking the inspired action that will really make a difference is absolutely essential.

It's easy to feel overwhelmed and wonder how you'll ever make progress towards your Big Vision. Life gets in the way; your inbox yells at you; the kids still want feeding; and there's that pesky little thing about still needing to sleep. I know how this feels - it sometimes catches me out, too. So when those stress levels are rising, I do my M.I.T. first.

I forget about emails, social media, returning calls or anything else that might steal my attention - and use up my energy - and I do my Most Important Thing first. Having broken my Big Vision down into steps, it's easier to spot the Most Important Thing each week, and even each day. I try to remember to set up my desk the day before to make it simple to start with my M.I.T. the next morning. I don't always get to leave it set up that way, but when I do, it makes a huge difference, especially for Monday mornings. Once that M.I.T. is done, anything else I achieve that day is a bonus, because I know I have made progress towards my big vision. And I often do the most 'fun' thing on my 'to do' list next, to celebrate – and as leverage! I'm quite happy to bribe myself, if needed.

One of my friends has a great strategy to help her stay in line with her M.I.T. and avoid Shiny Object Syndrome. She sets up her computer filing system, to help keep her focussed. She allows herself a maximum of three key projects, to build towards her Big Vision. If she finds herself wanting to do something that doesn't fit into her filing system, then it doesn't belong on her 'to do' list. You can capture those great ideas in a way that means you can come back to them later, but staying focussed on a few main projects will massively increase your productivity and reduce your stress levels.

There's a daily planning sheet template for you at the Readers' Club, if you'd like to play with this strategy.

Become A Completer-Finisher – Or Hire One

Once you've got your Most Important Thing at the top of your 'to do' list, it's essential to actually finish it. Unfinished projects are like throwing away time. They turn into spinning plates in a circus act - you have to feed that project with mental energy, even when you're not working on it, and it will drain your batteries. If it's not finished, then it's unlikely to be moving you towards your Big Vision. You don't get a return on your investment until the project is done.

Now most entrepreneurs and passionate world-changers are not natural completer-finishers. There are, of course, exceptions to this rule, but most of us prefer Shiny Object Syndrome, to wrapping up projects. Though nothing beats the satisfaction of ticking an item off your 'to do' list - do you ever add things to it, when they're done, just so you can tick? I do…

So if you're not motivated by getting the final i dotted and t crossed, what can you do?

Hire someone who is. Be the CEO that you are.

Play to your strengths. If attention to detail and completing projects isn't your forte, find someone who loves this and does it better than you, and bring them into your team. You'll be amazed by the difference it makes. And if you're resisting adding to your Dream Team, it might help you to go and deep-dive on that section of Step 4: Connection.

We heard from Lorraine Dallmeier, CEO of international skincare school Formula Botanica, earlier in this Handbook. One of the things that inspires me about Lorraine is her CEO-mindset. She is a living, breathing example of how great ideas aren't enough. If you want to transition from freelancer to business owner, to creating a legacy, then you need to step into your CEO-shoes, showing massive commitment to your dreams.

Lorraine has put her love and dedication into her business, growing it from a few small training courses to become an internationally-accredited training school, with students in 95 countries.

She did this through having total clarity on her Big Vision and breaking that down into annual and then monthly goals. She has built her Dream Team around her, and actively involves them in the planning and idea-generating process, so that they feel inspired and empowered. She has a policy of hiring people who are 'better at stuff than me', which allows her inner perfectionist to let go and trust.

Lorraine doesn't let her fears get in the way. If she needs to step outside of a comfort zone to, say, ask a Big Name in her industry to support a project, she takes courage from the fact that others have done it before her, so it must be possible. Then she presents a win-win idea, having stood in the shoes of the person or business she is approaching, and they are usually thrilled to say yes.

Her motivation isn't about what she can get out of her business for herself; talking to Lorraine makes it clear that she wants to leave a legacy and that her priority is empowering people to learn to love organic skincare and then to set up their own business. She offers them all the tools and qualifications that they need. And her business has created a community for them, where they hang out and support each other. Lorraine says she loves hearing about her students meeting up, in the 'real world', as a result of meeting in her Formula Botanica student group. And this year's Formula Botanica conference in London has students flying in from as far afield as Australia.

Without clarity and commitment, having cleared out the blocks, there is no way that Lorraine and her team would have created what they have achieved. Lorraine's CEO-mindset is one of the keys to her success.

How To Crank Up Your Commitment

We talked earlier in this Handbook about the power of making a decision - a choice - when it comes to releasing blocks (See Step 2). Well, this is just as effective when it comes to being committed to taking action on your Big Vision. If you make a daily commitment to making progress, then you'll be there in no time.

All it takes is a decision: my Big Vision is more important than my other tasks and I will prioritise it.

Inspiration gives you the idea;
Motivation gets you started;
But it's rhythm and routine that create results.

For the majority of us, it is enough to keep our big vision in the back of our mind as we start each new task and ask ourselves "is this really going to make a difference?" If it's not, we need to ask ourselves "is it really my job? Does it really need doing?" Sometimes the word 'should' gets in the way of our big vision more than we'd like to admit.

I find it helps to set an intention, before I get out of bed in the morning, to consciously choose the theme for my day and I use it to motivate myself - sometimes with incentives! It might be something like:

- Today I will edit chapter four, before I get my coffee.
- Today I will talk to three people about finding support on X aspect of project Y.
- Today I will set aside time to connect with my intuition to find ideas for how to solve problem Z.

And, before I get out of bed, I imagine myself going to bed that evening, having done this. It's like I 'line up' with the version of me who has already achieved this.

When you want to achieve something, but part of you is coming up with all the reasons why it might be hard or you might not have enough time, rather than beating it up, give it the experience of how good it feels, to get it done.

By travelling through time - in your imagination - to the point in time where that intention has been delivered, and fully experiencing how it physically feels, what it looks like, what it sounds like and even which thoughts you're thinking and which emotions you're feeling, you're creating new neural pathways in your brain. Remember that your body can't tell the difference between reality (whatever that is) and imagining, which is why it fires off your stress responses when you retell yourself the story about difficult events? Well, in this process, we use it positively.

You can crank up your commitment to an action by programming yourself to believe it is possible - after all, what you can imagine, you can create. And you are creating the neural pathways that will support this, so your unconscious mind can beaver away behind the scenes on the 'how'.

If you do this regularly (engineer-approved woo-woo alert!), you'll find that synchronicities line up for you and things more often fall into place. It can feel like a magic wand. The key is to connect with the full sensory experience of having completed your intention, and of knowing which actions you need to take. Then resistance melts away.

The other way you can use this is to sense any blocks that might get in the way, so you can pre-empt them. You do this by really tuning in to the experience of getting it done and noticing whether there are any areas of tension in your body, as you imagine it. Ask that tension: "what is it that you want me to know or be aware of?" and let the answer bubble up, without analysis or judgement. Then ask yourself, "for this answer, which block, fear, worry, excuse or limiting belief do I need to handle, to allow it to get go and enjoy the ride?" That might then become your M.I.T. (Most Important Thing) for the day.

I'd love to hear how you get on, playing with this. And there's a special discussion thread for you, over in the Readers' Club.

'No'? It's The Fastest Way To Create Your Big Vision

So many of us are overwhelmed and have no time to be committed because we're being pulled in too many directions. We say 'yes' to everything, either because we're hoping it might move us in the right direction, or because we have deep-down issues about upsetting people by saying 'no'.

The word 'yes' can be brilliant, if your Heart and intuition are telling you that the 'yes' action will move you towards your Big Vision - if it feels like an inspired action. But if it doesn't, then you need to play with saying 'no'.

Saying 'no' to things that don't line up with your Big Vision is one of the best ways to prove your commitment to it. It frees up your time to focus on inspired action and it helps you to get the maximum return on the time you have.

Saying 'no' because you're secretly running Imposter Syndrome or other hidden blocks isn't great - and revisiting Step 2 on Confidence or step 3 on Credibility will really help.

It's useful to ask yourself:

"What is my motivation for saying 'yes' / 'no'? How is that helping me? What is it doing for me?"

This will help you to uncover whether the intention is positive -

keeping your schedule clear for inspired action - or fear-based - protecting you from having to deal with a hidden block.

Your mission is too important to let guilt and obligation and 'shoulditis' get in the way. You *are* free to choose how you spend your time.

I ran the Dare To Dream Bigger online summit earlier this year and one of our presenters was unable to take part, at the very last minute. So I approached someone I really admire, to ask if she could help. She said no, but the way she did it was gorgeous and left us both feeling great. She simply explained how the audience for the project was an 'ok' fit for her dream client audience, but that that wasn't enough for her, and she only accepted projects that were a 'great' fit. But if I ran anything that was a great fit with her audience (she described them beautifully) and her Zone Of Genius, she would love to hear about it.

When you say 'no' from a place of fear and worry and guilt, it spreads that energy. When you say 'no' from a place of love and clarity and positive intentions, it spreads more of that and people are much less likely to take offence. But even if they do, as long as you acted with integrity and dignity, that's their issue, not yours. You are not responsible for how people feel if your dreams mean you have to say 'no'.

So you can increase your commitment to your Big Vision by saying 'no' to things that don't support it or fit into your Zone of Genius. Once you get over the initial fears and blocks to saying 'no' more often, it's liberating. If you could get your Dream Team around you so that you could aim to spend, say, 80% of your time in your Zone of Genius, delegating the stuff that isn't your Magic, you will be amazed at how much more you can achieve, how your overwhelm disappears, and your results exponentially increase. You'll get to make a much bigger difference in the world.

Given that the word 'no' is one of the fastest ways to create your Big Vision, I now want to share with you one of the most dangerous words you can use, which will fizzle away your commitment faster than flushing a toilet.

The Most Dangerous Commitment-Trashing Word

Three letters can trash your commitment, at the speed of thought. And most of us use this word every day.

When you use it, you're giving your unconscious mind to treat your commitment as being optional - a nice-to-have, a 'maybe'. Yet we don't realise this is what we're doing - and then we wonder why we don't get results. We explored in Step 2 the power of our self-talk over our actions and progress towards our Big Vision. Well, this one little word is the quickest way to derail your positive intentions.

Exercise: Are You 'Trying' Too Hard?

I invite you to try on these two sentences for size. Say them to yourself and feel the reaction in your body, and your thoughts.

"I will get that project finished by the end of the day."

Then
"I will try to get that project finished by the end of the day."

What difference did you notice?

Adding in the word 'try' gives us subconscious permission to 'not' do the statement we're making. It tells your mind that it's ok if it doesn't happen. You are letting yourself off the hook, before you even get started. You're telling yourself that you're not really serious about it and it's ok if it doesn't happen.

Back in my corporate days, I was already an NLP Master Practitioner and I knew all about 'try', so I used to have a radar for it with my team. Sure enough, at our short daily meetings where we shared our core objectives for that day, every time one of us added 'try' to 'I will', it was near-guaranteed that the action wouldn't get completed.

The certainty and commitment that comes with "I will" is a powerful motivator and it lines you up with getting that done. Adding in a 'try' dilutes this and casts doubts in your mind, creating uncertainty about whether it's achievable.

Try not. Do. Or do not. There is no try. ~ Yoda

How about spotting when you use this word in your self-talk or your promises to others. If you notice it, you could pause and ask yourself, "What do I really mean with this?" If you mean you're not sure, or don't really want to do something, say that. But if you want to crank up your commitment, start by ditching that one little word. It's one of the easiest things you can do to fast track your progress towards your Big Vision.

Just Because The Door Looks Closed...

So often, we give up, just before we get the results we were dreaming of. And that's heart-breaking. We have tried so hard, but those doors just seem to be closed, so we walk away.

One of my favourite things to do when I'm on retreat in my favourite hotel in Turkey is to finish the day at the 'Roman Baths'. It's an incredible room with floor-to-ceiling marble and little alcoves with marble sinks and no plugholes. You sit in your alcove, on a gently-heated marble bench, fill your sink with hot water from the high-volume taps, take the silver dish and slowly - deliciously - pour the water over yourself. If you want a scrub, you can use the soap and loofah mitts. For me, the sensation of the hot water relaxing tense muscles is blissful. It is the most deeply relaxing thing I have ever experienced - and that is saying something, with the arsenal of relaxation techniques I have as a meditation and yoga teacher. Then you go to lie on a huge area of heated marble in the middle of the room. It's about 3 metres wide. At first it can feel uncomfortable, after all, it's marble, not a mattress. But as your body lets go of tension and worries, that uncompromising warmth eases muscles as deftly as the best masseur.

I always feel wonderful after I have been to the Roman Baths.

But here's the thing: hardly anyone who visits the hotel makes it to them. People hear about them, and get excited at the idea, but they never quite make it. Sometimes it's because self-care isn't a priority for them - and that's fine. But usually it is because the door is closed. It has to be, to keep the warmth in the room, but that doesn't mean it won't open.

I have lost count of how many people have told me about the soft cushions and fountain in the room before the Roman Baths, but said that didn't seem very exciting, so they left. It never occurred to any of them that the real treasure lay just beyond that closed door. Even though the 'Roman Baths' they are seeing don't look like the brochure photo and there's no sign of bathing, it never occurs to them that this is just a stage on the journey. They never even walk to the other side of the room, to see if the door is locked or not. They took a step towards a dreamy experience, but when they didn't instantly find it, they turned away and gave up.

And I don't blame them. We're trained to respect closed doors, both physically and mentally. And if you don't immediately find what you're expecting to find, then all sorts of auto-pilots kick in, to help you handle the situation.

But when you inspire someone to walk that little bit further and try that next door, they are blown away by what lies beyond. And once they have found it, they will always know how to get there. And they will want to.

Once you have been in those Roman Baths, you will never forget the experience. That deep physical, mental and energetic relaxation and letting go stays with me for months, between visits.

Just because the door looks closed, it doesn't mean it won't open, if you give it a nudge.

When we're moving towards our Big Vision, it's easy to assume that all doors should open instantly for us, that the signs should be bright neon, with our name on them, and that it should all be easy. But sometimes you have to walk up to that door and try the handle, rather than assuming it's locked. It's as though your inner wisdom wants to give you a little test, so you can show you really mean it.

And yes, sometimes the door is closed. Perhaps it's not the ideal door for you right now; perhaps the timing isn't right; perhaps it might take you off-course, away from your Big Vision.

But sometimes that door is just patiently waiting for you to say 'yes'.

I'm wondering: is there a door which you have been assuming was closed, but which might open for you, with the lightest touch? Which action could you take, in the next hour, to find out for yourself?

How Committed Are You?

I was told a story about a man who went to a classical guitar recital and the musician was extraordinary. The way he could make the guitar sing blew the audience away. One man in the audience was so excited and felt so grateful that he went up to the musician at the end to thank him.

"I *wish* I could play the guitar like you!" he said.

"Really?" asked the musician.

"Yes, I do!, replied the man.

"Then show me your fingers."

Confused, the man obliged by showing the musician his fingers. The musician held up his own hands for the man to see. "No you don't," he said. The man looked at the callouses on the musician's fingers and the total absence of them on his own.

The musician's commitment to his dreams showed in his fingers. "If you *really* wished it, your actions would show," he finished.

Exercise: How Committed Are You?

There's a worksheet for this, over at the Readers' Club, and you can share your answers, via the discussion thread in the forum.

Thinking about your Big Vision, how committed are you to it? Which of these answers best fits for you?

- I'm totally committed? If it doesn't support my big vision, it doesn't even get on my to-do list.
- I'm fairly committed? It's always there in the back of my mind.
- I think about it sometimes, but it doesn't play a big role in my daily decisions yet?
- I'm not very committed. I'm feeling stuck, confused, and overwhelmed.

If you want a deep dive on this, it's worth asking yourself:

- What percentage of my daily actions are moving me towards my big vision? You might be surprised.
- What gets in the way and derails me?
- Do I have my Dream Team around me, to support me?
- What do I need to do or think or believe differently, to crank up my commitment?

Now you've made progress on cranking up your commitment, it's time to celebrate; it's the key to turning your Inner Critic into your Biggest Cheerleader.

Celebrate

Celebrate even your smallest successes and your Inner Critic starts to turn into your Biggest Cheerleader.

Celebrating your achievements as you go along, rather than waiting for the 'ultimate success', keeps you feeling motivated, keeps your team inspired, and can even turn your Inner Critic into your biggest cheerleader.

If more of us did this, we'd feel much happier and much less stressed. We'd get so much more done, because our self-doubt wouldn't lead to procrastination and self-sabotage.

You're well on your way to getting your clarity sorted; you've worked on your confidence. You're establishing yourself as an expert and you're connecting far and wide. You're taking inspired actions that make a difference, and you're showing commitment. What's not to celebrate?

The Miracle Of Gratitude

Celebrating is a way of saying 'thank you' to your Soul, for wherever you are on your journey so far. And this is perhaps the single most important shift you could create, as a result of this Handbook.

Most of us spend our time focussing on what is 'wrong' in our lives; on the bad bits, the hard bits, the sad bits, the missing bits. Those are the stories we tell ourselves. It's an easy trap to fall into. Then you get the world of 'online spirituality' telling you that feeling sad about what's wrong or missing is 'bad' and that you 'should' feel happy, because you should 'look at all those people who would *love* to be lucky enough to have your problems'. Enter white-washing and 'spiritual bypass', stage left, and take your bow. Bring with it its close-relatives: emotional shutdown and trashing-self-esteem.

Most of us delay our happiness until our external circumstances have changed; until they have reached some arbitrary level of perfection. Early warning signs include:

"I'll feel happy, when…"
"I'll celebrate, when…"
"I'll know I'm successful, when…"

Some facts for you:

You are successful each and every time you take actions towards your dreams; each and every time you stretch a comfort zone; each and every time you make a difference in someone's life. There is no need to wait until you reach your final goal, to celebrate the progress you are making.

When our happiness is dependent on things that are outside of us, it will always be conditional; at risk; endangered.

We can't always choose our circumstances. We can't control how others behave. But we *can* always choose how to feel about it; how we respond. And that emotional choice, in that moment, might be joy or rage or confusion or frustration or bliss. The beauty of being human is that we have all of these emotions to choose from. Experiencing emotions we don't enjoy can be the catalyst for positive action and change. And remember: you can choose which thoughts to feed, and you can shift 'stuck' emotions through movement.

The quiet, underlying dissatisfaction with life that is pervading our Western culture is responsible for so much emotional, mental and physical ill-health. Trying to fill that 'emptiness' inside can trigger addictions, from online shopping (*I'll feel happy, when I have that bag!*) through to food, alcohol and even substance abuse.

If you have spent years running a strong Inner Critic pattern, then learning to celebrate your small successes, as you go along, helps to set you free from the 'I'll feel happy, when…' cycle. It encourages you to see what is going well, what you love in life, rather than just the day-to-day, drama-filled mini-disasters.

When we feel happy with what we already have, and where we already 'are', it's a very different energy to feeling dissatisfied and 'lacking', which is how so many of us can feel, most of the time. It's the difference between 'acceptance' and 'acceptable'. When we *accept* life, each day, with gratitude, we're not saying it's all ok and we never want to change anything. We're simply allowing ourselves to experience life as being what it is – pretty incredible and a gift, no matter what is going on.

But if there are things that your *discernment* tells you need to shift, or your Heart wants you to create differently, then you are in a much better position to take inspired action on them, if you're starting from a place of 'things are basically ok', rather than 'everything is broken and terrible'.

If you create a daily gratitude habit, one minute at a time, it rebalances your nervous system and it creates fresh neural pathways in your brain. It reconstructs old drama-filled stories about the past, it retrains your Inner Critic's commentary to talk to you about what is going well, rather than what is going wrong and it boosts your self-confidence. You'll find you worry less, you're more likely to achieve your goals, and your loved-ones will enjoy being around you more.

Gratitude is a way of saying 'thank you' for the life you are living, rather than waiting until everything is perfect, which it probably never will be, especially given how often we move the goal posts.

Turning Your Inner Critic Into Your Biggest Cheerleader

In Step 2, we looked at taming your Inner Critic. Well, now it's time to give it a new job. It is getting the badge of being your Biggest Cheerleader. You can use all of the techniques from Step 2's inner-critic-taming to do this, such as altering its tone of voice, its speed and its volume, and choosing which thoughts to feed. But practising gratitude and celebrating your daily successes is the fastest way to retrain it.

We're so good at beating ourselves up. We're so good at being stuck on the complaining train. Please take time out to acknowledge what you've achieved, even the tiny things because sometimes they cost us more than the big results. We're not talking pride and ego. We're just talking, "Hey, you did it! Well done!"

When you make celebrating part of your daily rhythm, you're telling your unconscious mind, "I want more of that," instead of, "yeah, ok, *that* was all great, but what about *this*?"

Celebrate each step of your journey and your Inner Critic will take the hint.

Beating yourself up hasn't exactly worked, so how about celebrating your successes, instead? When you regularly take time out to acknowledge what you've achieved, to celebrate your successes, and get excited about them, you shift that vibration subtly, but in a really profound way. And you may inspire others around you to do the same.

Make daily celebrating and gratitude part of your rhythm.

Try keeping a Gratitude Journal and, at the end of each day, write in it what you feel grateful for that day. (Here's one I prepared earlier: A Year Full Of Gratitude. Details are in the Readers' Club. But, of course, other gratitude journals are also available!) You could think of it as being your Inner Cheerleader's diary. You might want to have a specific focus, rather than writing about life, in general. For example, you might want to list what, specifically, you have achieved each day that you feel happy about. At the end of each week, look back and see what you have achieved. Acknowledge your progress.

Here is how one of my readers, Rosie Slosek, Founder of One Man Band Accounting uses her copy of A Year Full Of Gratitude:

I have a business and at the start of my business year, I use the Year Full Of Gratitude course as structure for my business goals for the year. It keeps my core goals (or KPI's if you prefer) in the frame of love and thankfulness, rather than in 'must', 'should' and fear, which creeps in easily otherwise.

Each day I write my goals in the space for 'I am grateful', for example, 'I am grateful I have grown my revenue by 30% in 2016-17'. Try it!

Fourteen years of facilitating 'inner work' has taught me that one of the things that derails us most often is not noticing the progress we have made. If, at the end of each week you make yourself a cup of tea and ask yourself, " What have I achieved this week? What am I pleased with? What's gone well? Which 'inner work' changes did I make? Which 'outer world' changes did I make?" and you jot down some notes, then you're finishing the week on a high. This retrains your Inner Critic to become your Biggest Cheerleader.

At the end of the month, and at the end of the year, take time out to look back at your weekly notes, to reflect and to celebrate what you have created. That will motivate you so much more than beating yourself up.

You Are Not Alone

See Yourself Through Someone Else's Eyes

We can be too 'close' to ourselves, and sometimes it's hard to see the beauty of who we are and what we are creating, especially if we're used to beating ourselves up. So this is another way to retrain your Inner Critic to become a cheerleader. Imagine someone who you know can see your good points, your skills, talents, and inner genius. And imagine what *they* would want to celebrate about you.

It can even help to imagine that *they* are the ones writing down what you're celebrating each day. The key, though, is for you to dive in and experience how that gratitude and celebration *feels*; enjoy it!

Celebrating Your Success Doesn't Make You Egotistical

Let's stop it with the 'false modesty', already?! Honouring what you have achieved and the difference you have made isn't self-centred or bad. It's essential for your mental and emotional health. And it will help you to make a bigger difference in the world.

If you need a butt-kick on this, then pop by the special discussion thread in the Readers' Club forum. We're ready and waiting to celebrate with you!

How could you celebrate your successes, today?

Get Your Accountability Tribe Around You

You don't have to celebrate on your own. This is where an accountability Tribe or Mastermind comes in. They will understand the effort that went into your successes, and it feels great to celebrate each other's achievements.

Masterminds are a wonderful way to be shown your successes, if you can't see them yourself. Others aren't running our mental filters, and if they know you well, they will get a feel for what is 'status quo' for you and what is a 'big deal'. A supportive Mastermind team doesn't just help you to improve your ideas and get through your blocks, they genuinely, unconditionally celebrate your breakthroughs – big or small – helping you to see yourself differently and keeping you motivated.

It's much more fun to celebrate your successes with others, than on your own. Just imagine being able to pick up the phone or ping over a quick email or social media message, to tell someone about what you're celebrating, knowing that they'll 'get' how important it is to you?

If you're interested in joining a Mastermind, there are resources for you in the Readers' Club.

Make sure you also thank your Dream Team and your customers. Celebrate what you've created with them, too, because they'll be blown away. When did a business that you worked with last thank you? We're so busy, we forget to thank those who support us, and it doesn't have to be employees. It might be that your friends on social media have given you some extra support that week. It might be your contractors. It doesn't matter.

When you get into this habit of gratitude with your business, celebrating what you've created, achieved, and the difference you've made, you will create more of it, more easily.

Exercise: How Will You Celebrate?

Before we wrap up this section, I invite you to jot down some ideas for how you could start to make 'celebrating' part of your routine. There's a worksheet and audio for this in the Reader's Club.

- What are three ways you could build 'celebrating' into your rhythm?
- How might you remind yourself to do these?
- What might get in the way? ('inside' or 'outside world' blocks!)
- What will you do about those?
- Who could you find to celebrate *with*?
- What could you celebrate, right now, before we move on to the final section? Be specific – and allow yourself to rest in that feeling.

Connecting With Your Self – Anandamayakosha

I am, therefore I am.

There's a part of you that has no self-imposed rules, no limits, no blocks, no baggage. In fact, it's the REAL you. It is your inner diamond; your infinite possibility and potential.

When you do inner work to allow you to connect with that aspect of 'you', you'll feel in flow; in the 'zone'. When you create from that space, synchronicities line up. Miracles happen.

But how do you do it?

Meditation, yoga, mindfulness, gratitude, compassion, being in nature, singing - anything that opens your heart and brings you back to this moment, with a sense of lightness, freedom, love and joy. Doing what makes your heart sing is a wonderful way to move towards that space.

Breathe. Everything else is optional.

When we impose rules and limits upon ourselves, we restrict who we can become. We lock ourselves into boxes.

Those rules and limits only serve to restrict us. In any moment we can choose to set ourselves free, to experience the true freedom, which comes from within.

You only need to look at Nelson Mandela and his 27 years in Robben Island's prison or at Ghandi's regular imprisonment, to see that where you are is independent of your state of mind.

The biggest prisons in which we live are those we construct for ourselves; those we carefully tend, like beloved gardens, in our minds. Yet they're not reality.

Each of us has more freedom than we imagine.

When you celebrate the life you are living, in each moment, and what you have already created, then you start to set yourself free from the 'rules' in your mind that were restricting you.

How might you celebrate, right now?

PULLING IT ALL TOGETHER

Creating Your 7 Cs Business Plan

A journey of a thousand miles begins with a single step. ~ Lao Tzu

Wow! Can you believe we've been through all seven steps? How do you feel? It's a wonderful achievement! And now it's time to wrap it up with your 'next steps' business plan. Whether you're just starting out or taking a step up to the next level, having a clear, stage-by-stage plan is the most important element for turning your dreams into reality.

I know I don't need to tell you that, but we're usually too busy working 'in' our business, to work 'on' it. So to celebrate you getting to page 306 of this Handbook, I invite you to grab a mug of your favourite whatever and turn off all distractions for the next hour or so. Go through the process, below, and then let me know what your 'very next step' is, over in the Readers' Club forum.

There is an audio and mini-workbook for this exercise, waiting there for you, too. We're going to go through the key decisions you have made, as you have been reading this Handbook, we're going to pre-empt any blocks that might get in your way, and we're going to jot down key notes for your next 12 months' action plan, along with how you're going to get support, and what accountability you might need.

Exercise: Your 7 Cs Business Plan

It's time to look back through your notes for the 7 Cs, to jot down some key decisions.

Step 1: Clarity
- My Big Why (wherever you're currently up to) is…

- My Big Vision is…
- My Big Message is…
- What support do I need, to get more clarity on these (if any)?

Step 2: Confidence

- The main blocks I identified are…
- Which blocks have I already worked on, as part of this Handbook?
- Which one am I going to work on next?
- How will I do that? What support will I need?

Step 3: Credibility

- What are the key next steps from my credibility action plan? How will I measure my progress?
- What are the key next steps from my visibility action plan? How will I keep myself on track?
- Do I have any credibility or visibility blocks I need to deal with? Which will I handle first? And how?

Step 4: Connection

- What would you most like to achieve, with regards to connecting with your Inner Wisdom?
- What support or resources might you need for this?
- What are your priorities for connecting with your Dream Audience?
- What support might you need?
- Who could you recruit to be part of your Dream Team?
- Which blocks might you need to release, to be able to step up to the next level, with your support around you?
- What are your options for joining a Mastermind, or diving in more deeply, if you're already part of one?

Step 5: Creativity

- Where do you want to 'be', in 12 months from now?
- Go back to your time travelling exercise and walk to the point just past 12 months from now. How does it *feel*? How might you anchor that feeling, so you can create from that sense of 'knowing', each day?
- Are you making enough money to meet your needs?
- Is your Dream Audience loving whatever it is you're offering?

- Is there anything you need to tweak, about the 12 months' time's Big Vision, to make sure things are how you want them to be?
- Looking back to the 'now', what have you created, in 12 months' time?
- Can you spot any current blocks that need to be released, to get to that point?
- Moving back to the 9 months point, which key actions have you taken? What support did you need? Which blocks did you need to release? What are you believing about yourself and your dreams, at this point?
- Ask yourself the same questions for 6 months from now.
- And again for 3 months from now.
- Six weeks from now, how are you feeling? Which initial actions have you taken? What is different in your business? And in your life?
- A month from now: what kinds of thoughts are you thinking? How does it feel? What have you achieved already? Which blocks have you begun to release?
- Two weeks from now: how are you reminding yourself to take action, to move you towards your Big Vision?
- Which actions have you taken?
- Which blocks have you released?
- What support might you need?
- 24 hours from now: what is the 'very next step' you could take, that will move you towards your next 12 months' goal?
- **Come and tell us when you have done it, in the Readers' Club!**

Step 6: Commitment
- Which of the potential commitment blocks have you been running?
- What are you going to do, to crank up your commitment?
- How might you find the time, to work on your dreams 'little and often', so that 'life' doesn't get in the way?

Step 7: Celebration
- What could you build into your routine to allow you to celebrate your daily, weekly and monthly successes?
- Which actions could you take, to retrain your Inner Critic to become your Biggest Cheerleader?

How To Keep Your Support Going

Congratulations! We're nearly there! How has the journey been so far? I'm so excited that you made it to this point – and I would love you to feel supported, for the next phase of your path, too.

Experience has taught me that this is actually the most important point for you to feel supported. While you're working through a book or course or seminar series, the support is there, with you, each step of the way. Then you launch out on your own, implementing the strategies, trying the techniques on for size, making those changes. No one is holding you accountable. No one is getting excited with you, when you 'crack it'.

So your job, right now, is to take action to make sure you have the Tribe you need, walking by your side, for the coming months and years. That might be your Dream Team. It might be your loved-ones. It might be our Dare To Dream Bigger Tribe in the Readers' Club forum and the Facebook group. It might be a formal Mastermind.

Whatever support you need, it's your job to get it. No one will mind-read it for you. And it's much easier than you might think.

Exercise: Keeping My Support Going

Let's make sure you're feeling supported, before we get to the end of this Handbook! There's a worksheet and audio for this, in the Readers' Club.

- What moral support might I need, to implement the decisions I have made from this Handbook?
- Which actions am I going to take, in the next week, as a result of this work? And do I need support or accountability with those?
- Who, from my current circle of friends, loved-ones and business colleagues, might help me through the next stage?
- If I could wave a magic wand, what would I like my accountability and moral support network to look like? How do I want it to feel?
- What could I do to find that network? When will I do that?

And Finally...

Remember those original outcomes for reading this Handbook? How did you get on with them? Have they shifted? Here's a very final exercise to celebrate the progress you have made.

Exercise: What Do You Want Next?

It's nearly party time! Let's review the journey you have taken over the past 310 pages, and honour the progress you have made.

- What has changed? Which shifts have you created?
- How do you feel?
- Are there any bits of this Handbook that you loved? That resonated with you?
- Are there any bits you want to go back to?
- Do you know anyone else it could help?
- What do you want to do / think / feel differently, as a result of working through these techniques?
- What are your next steps?
- How will you make sure those actions happen?
- And when?!
- How do you feel about your business / career / mission, right now?
- How is that different, from at the beginning of the book?
- And if you could zoom forward in time, five or ten years from now, standing in the Soul-Shoes of that 'future you', what advice might you give yourself?

If you'd like to share any of your answers or insights from these questions, there's a special discussion thread, over at the Readers' Club.

THANK YOU!

Thank you for each and every action you have taken, whilst reading this Handbook, and for each and every block you have shifted, and for every ounce of extra clarity you have discovered. I feel so proud of you.

In the words of the wonderful Bugs Bunny: "That's all folks!" Except it's not. It's just the beginning. And I can't wait to see where this journey takes you. Please stay in touch.

With love, Namaste, xx Clare

Want To Work Together?

I'd love to be able to keep walking by your side on this journey. I specialise in helping you to spot and deal with the deeply-hidden blocks that you have been playing dodgems with, for years. Then we focus on the inspired actions that will allow you to make the biggest difference possible in the world. If your Heart is calling you to work together, here are some ideas – full details are in the Readers' Club:

Just Dipping Your Toe In The Water

- Make sure you have joined the Readers' Club. Not only do you get the bonuses that accompany the Handbook, but it also gets you my weekly newsletter and our Dare To Dream Bigger Handbook forum.
- Subscribe to my podcast on iTunes – Dare To Dream Bigger.
- Take one my courses (links in the Readers' Club)
- Buy one of my other books – you'll find them in the Readers' Club or you can order them from your favourite bookstore or online retailer.

Getting Ready To Step Up

Join the Dare To Dream Bigger Academy.

The Academy is a wonderfully supportive group of like-minded, Passionate World-Changers. We do a monthly live teaching masterclass and monthly live group coaching calls. It's all online, so you can connect from anywhere in the world, and you can download the videos and audios of the live sessions, as well as transcripts, so you have all the resources you need, whenever you want them.

Membership also gets you access to my entire online course vault, which includes all of the deep-dive resources mentioned in this Handbook, and much more. It's effectively your complete Dare To Dream Bigger Entrepreneur's Toolkit.

Diving In – You Mean Business

Join A Stepping Up Mastermind

I run these several times a year, either face-to-face, in London or Sussex, or as an online group programme. You also have the option of a 3-day luxury retreat in the sun, if you prefer that. They are transformational and you get lifelong access to your Mastermind group.

Join Me On A Retreat

I run regular retreats on all aspects of 'inner work'. Some of these are business-related, some of them are for personal development, focussing more on meditation, mindfulness, yoga and NLP. I also run antenatal workshops for mums-to-be and their partners. Full details on the upcoming events are in your Readers' Club. I would love to meet you on one of these retreats.

Deep-Dive With A One-To-One Package

I offer one-to-one mentoring via Skype, but I prefer working face-to-face, if we can. It works more deeply and it's more fun!

You also have the option of joining me for a deep-dive VIP package, where we'll spend 1-3 days together, focussing on clarity, clearing out the blocks, and taking inspired actions towards the next level of your Dharma.

Bespoke Business Training

I have been running bespoke management training courses for corporate clients since 2002. They are based on NLP, but include many of the engineer-approved woo-woo methods we have discussed in this Handbook, as well as insights from my own corporate life, at Department Head level. My favourite way of working is to start with the entire layer of senior managers, so that they create their own 'inner change', and then we get to work down through their teams. This way the changes the teams make are understood and supported by their bosses.

If the way I work resonates with you, please use the contact page at www.ClareJosa.com to get in touch, with details of your project and which shifts you want it to create for your business.

Book Me To Speak

I have significant senior management-level experience of running a business, I'm a member of the Institute of Directors, and I speak internationally on all aspects of the 'inside work' needed to make a bigger difference in the world.

If you would like to talk about booking me to speak at your event, please use the contact form at www.ClareJosa.com to get in touch with my team. Please include details of the event, the audience and the energy exchange.

I'm guessing we 'know' each other pretty well by now, but just in case you want some background blurb, here I am:

Don't Know Me Yet?

I have been mentoring Passionate World-Changers since 2002. As an entrepreneur myself, the creator of over a decade of online and face-to-face training courses, and the author of 4 published books, I know about the hidden blocks that keep us stuck, dreaming big, but playing small. I have been through most of them, myself.

But as an NLP[11] Trainer and long-time business breakthrough mentor, I also know how to get past them, and have helped many thousands of people, just like you, to do exactly that. I specialise in being able to spot the smallest changes that will produce the biggest results for you, and in sharing solutions with you in a way that makes it super-easy for you to learn and apply them, no matter how busy you are - or how much your monkey mind might object.

I used to be an engineer (I have a Master's Degree in Mechanical Engineering And German), but I'm also a certified Meditation & Yoga teacher, so I love demystifying Ancient Wisdom into practical actions you can take in less time than it takes to boil a kettle. My clients call it 'engineer-approved woo-woo'. And it all comes with a bucket load of common sense and a generous dollop of humour.

I know about being busy, too. I'm a mum of 3 young boys, I run my own business and have a passion for dancing like a crazy thing to loud music in my kitchen. If I can find the time to write this book, you can find the time to go through the techniques in it - and I'll even help you with that shortly, because I know what a block it can be.

If I had a superpower (more on that in step 1), my clients would say it's bringing intuitive clarity to where confusion and chaos previously reigned, combining with inspiration and enthusiasm.

Want to work together?

www.ClareJosa.com/work-with-clare-josa/

---

11 NLP is Neurolinguistic Programming – a branch of practical, modern psychology that deals with how our thoughts create our experience of life, and how you can change your thoughts, to change your life. It's like the user manual for your brain.

Acknowledgements & Gratitude

To my R&D team for this Handbook:

Thank you for volunteering your patience, your feedback and for your generosity of time, to work through the draft of this work. You helped me to take 14 years of insights and translate them from something that worked for live training and online courses, into a stand-alone resource to inspire and transform the entrepreneurial journey of passionate world-changers, even while they're sitting on their sofa, maybe even in their PJs on a quiet Sunday morning, reading through this book.

Liz Alderson, Amanda Bayley, Bonnie Boucek, Callie Carling, Karen Campos, Iris Furer, Chris Hogan, Debs Milverton, Isobel Moore, Penny Pullan, Alan Rae, Rachel Retallick, Joy Shallcross, Rosie Slosek, Diane Stafford.

To my deep-dive interviewees:

Heartfelt thanks, both to those who had informal interviews and also to those brave Souls who agreed to share their journey with you in this Handbook. They include:

- Heather Bestel
- William Buist
- Crista Cloutier
- Lorraine Dallmeier
- Adam Dobay
- Livia Farkas
- Nancy Marmolejo
- Juliet McKenna
- Jenn Philpott
- Sandra Pilarczyk
- Penny Pullan

Their contact details are in the Readers' Club, if you feel inspired to connect and work with them.

To my support team for this manuscript:

Tina Pham, who transcribed so many hours of my masterclasses and live trainings, which gave me a huge head start on writing this book.

My book cover designers: Jo Smith and Richard Playall. Thank you for translating the ideas into something so beautiful.

The team at Clays St Ives, especially Georgina Aldridge, who showed patience in answering so many questions – and thank you for your excitement for this project.

Beatrice Sanfelice, at the wonderful Palazzo Juvalta in Teglio, Italy (http://www.palazzojuvalta.it). The magnificent space you have created was at least partially responsible for the breakthrough that transformed Step 2 of this Handbook to be what it now is. Thank you for having us to stay again. I can't wait to run a retreat with you!

My friends at my favourite hotel, the Hilton in Sarigerme, Turkey (www.hiltondalaman.com), thank you for your friendship, your curiosity and your excitement for this project. You helped keep me sane and inspired as I sat in the sunshine writing the first draft for this book. Thank you for not minding me being the crazy-lady-with-a-laptop. To Semihbey, Hasanbey, Mahmut, Nurgül, Huseyin, Nuri, Akif, and the rest of the team - heartfelt gratitude and I can't wait to see you again soon.

And finally, to my gorgeous family - Peter and our boys. Yet again you kept things running while I spent more hours than I would ever have imagined could be needed, to write and research and test and interview and edit and generally disappear off the planet, for months. Thank you. Thank you. Thank you. I couldn't have done it without you.

List Of Exercises

Step 3: Credibility

Step 4: Connection

Step 5: Creativity

Step 6: Commitment

Step 7: Celebrate

Pulling It All Together

Index of Sanskrit And Technical Terms